NO MATTER WHAT THE COST

SAMMY TIPPIT
WITH JERRY B. JENKINS

WORD PUBLISHING

Nelson Word Ltd
Milton Keynes, England

WORD AUSTRALIA
Kilsyth, Victoria, Australia

WORD COMMUNICATIONS LTD
Vancouver, B.C., Canada

STRUIK CHRISTIAN BOOKS (PTY) LTD
Maitland, South Africa

JOINT DISTRIBUTORS SINGAPORE –
ALBY COMMERCIAL ENTERPRISES PTE LTD

and

CHRISTIAN .... LTD
H..............

SALVATION BOOK CENTRE
Malaysia

To the glory of God

With appreciation to
My wife, 'Tex',
who is and always will be the love of my life;

My mother, Lavada,
who so influenced me in the foundational years;
Our children, Dave and Renee,
God's special blessings to us;

Billy Graham,
whom I have never met but who has been an example of
    integrity;
And evangelist Mike Gilchrist,
who has been a source of continual encouragement.

In memory of
David Thomas Tippit,
a great basketball player and a great dad;

And Ken Leeburg,
a great friend.

NO MATTER WHAT THE COST

Copyright © 1993 by Sammy Tippit and Jerry B. Jenkins.

First published in the USA by Thomas Nelson, Inc., Nashville, Tennessee.

First UK edition by Nelson Word Ltd., Milton Keynes, 1993.

ISBN 0-85009-618-9   (Australia ISBN 1-86258-287-4)

Scripture quotations are from the New King James Version of the Bible, copyright © 1979, 1980, 1982 Thomas Nelson, Inc., Publishers.

Reproduced, printed and bound in Great Britain for Nelson Word Ltd. by Cox & Wyman Ltd., Reading.

93 94 95 96 / 10 9 8 7 6 5 4 3 2 1

CONTENTS

INTRODUCTION

Among the great thrills of my life were two trips to Eastern Europe with Sammy Tippit, twice venturing into Romania—once before the overthrow of dictator Nicolae Ceausescu and once after. How stark it was to see the memorials to recently slain revolutionaries outside a hotel where we had been just a few years before! To think a historic revolution had occurred on the very streets we had walked.

Yet this book is not about only Romania or Eastern Europe. It is about a man who would rather speak about his God than about himself. It may be the most unusual autobiography you will ever read.

Have you ever wondered what God might do through a person wholly sold out to Him? D. L. Moody was challenged by that type of question more than a hundred years ago, and the results of his ministry remain to this day.

Some people may see Sammy Tippit as a throwback to another era. Can anyone with ability and talent remain unaffected by fame, wealth, materialism? If not, how does he deal with the attendant pride?

Already God has packed into Sammy's experience a lifetime of amazing events. He seems a lightning rod for outpourings from heaven, a dynamic preacher and bold personal witness whose hallmark is obedience.

The kinds of results Sammy has seen in his worldwide ministry have ruined many ministers. They become enamored with success, begin to see themselves—rather than God—as the key, and start the slow, sure slide to pride and sin.

Sammy is not above sin, but God has done more than shower him with amazing experiences. He has also done a deep work in Sammy's heart, breaking him, keeping him humble, keeping him in the Word. God has shown him that humility is the trademark of the true man of God. To be an obedient and effective man of God is the deepest desire of Sammy's heart.

He lives what he preaches, straight from the Bible. No doubt other Christian workers have the same burden, the same trust, the same zeal, the same talent to move people's hearts. But few are so dead to self or so honored to be used of God.

You will praise God for Sammy Tippit, who wants only to glorify Christ. More importantly, you'll learn to glorify God yourself by entrusting to Him every area of your life.

Jerry B. Jenkins

PART 1

THE CALL

CHAPTER ONE

THE DAY THE CURTAIN TORE

I was in Nigeria and sick as a dog, but the news made my Saturday.

It wasn't unusual for me to be in a remote area of the world. Strange as it may seem, that has been my calling ever since I gave my life to Christ as a teenager in the 1960s.

People call me a full-time Christian worker, a self-supporting missionary, an evangelist, a preacher, a personal witness, a prayer crusader, an international traveler, you name it. I don't care much about titles and descriptions, but if I have to say, I prefer to be known as a servant, an ambassador of Christ.

That might sound overly pious, and I confess I'm not comfortable talking about myself. It's not that I don't enjoy being appreciated, but I'm happiest and most fulfilled when I'm drawing attention to Christ and not to Sammy Tippit. I struggle with pride as much as anyone does. Like the apostle Paul, I must "die daily." At the end of my life, when it's all said and done, I want Christ to have been glorified, not that I had been remembered.

If I truly want my life to count for God, I must try to get out of the way and let Christ shine through. I have had ups and downs, learned hard lessons, and suffered failure and setbacks. But before God, I want my life to be a grand experiment that proves that total commitment, fully selling out to Him, is worth any discomfort or sacrifice.

Don't get me wrong. Even pretending that I have succeeded in becoming selfless proves that I have not. Yet I believe obedience is a worthy goal. Obeying has not come without pain and suffering, and yet God has granted me one overriding gift—besides the perfect mate and a certain ability for public speaking. That gift, which has grown each year as I have tried to follow God, has been a burden—a burden for lost people.

Plain and simple, I believe the Bible. I believe that, according to John 14:6, Jesus Christ is the only way to God. He is the Truth and He is the Life, and no one comes to the Father but through Him. Just knowing that isn't enough. Believing the truth of that does not necessarily weigh on you and spur you to action. Somehow, in His own dynamic, supernatural way, the Lord has laid that burden heavy on my heart. It works on me all the time, stirring my soul and my mind to use whatever He has entrusted me with to win people to Christ.

My style, my method, and my approach have evolved over the years—as you will see. I have learned much about myself and about the nature of God. I have learned the hard way that some of my personality traits that are strengths in an international ministry can be weaknesses in a marriage, in a family, in interpersonal relationships. I have been through deep water in my own spiritual life, realizing at a strategic time that my burden and vision had far outdistanced my spiritual maturity and my devotion to Christ.

God has at times pressed the burden so heavily upon me that it didn't seem like a gift at all, but rather a weight that drove me to give up any fleshly ambitions. Where it might have seemed natural for a young evangelist to want to be the next Billy Graham or to have a big organization or to be widely known, I found myself drawn to and pushed to the hard places in the kingdom.

Occasionally there is a stadium crusade in a large city, a TV opportunity, or something newsworthy that happens in our ministry. But you should not be surprised or feel uninformed if you have not heard of me at all over the past two-plus decades. Most often God leads me to out of the way places, to the struggling church behind the Iron Curtain or in the bush where there are no media "opportunities" and little fanfare, only hungry souls.

Perhaps God knows that too much attention would not be good for me. Surely He knows I'm most effective where my heart is: in telling lost people about a personal Savior. A few years ago, when our ministry seemed to be growing and pointing to more citywide crusades, and I had preached on every inhabited continent, my small board began investigating what it would take to meet the demands of a new direction.

Did we need a bigger staff? More money? More training? New techniques? I praise God He led my advisers the same way He was leading me. I came to realize that I would be just as happy telling one person on the street about Jesus as I would be to see thousands come forward at a huge crusade. I'm grateful for every opportunity in both of those scenarios, but I want always to be ready to go wherever God leads.

Now in my forties with a marriage twenty-five years old, a son in college, and a daughter in high school, I can say that I am glad our ministry has gone as it has. We're compact and mobile and able to be flexible. We don't have a huge operation; it doesn't take us months and limitless dollars to take advantage of ministry opportunities. We work with the national people and, as God provides the funds, we go.

That's the only other thing you should know about our ministry before I tell you the story of how God has worked in our lives over the years: We never ask for money. In this day when it has become almost embarrassing to be known as an evangelist—because of the excesses and public sins of many—there is as much of a spotlight on the financial side of things as there is on the moral and ethical. We are so averse to even the appearance of being in the ministry for any financial gain that we have come to view income only as a barometer of God's will.

In other words, if I feel led to consider an invitation to preach in some part of the world, I accept it on the condition that God provides the funds for travel and expenses. We keep our small mailing list of friends and supporters aware of what we're doing, but we never ask for—or even mention—finances. If God provides, we go. If He doesn't, we don't.

God provided for that trip to Nigeria in November of 1989, and so I went. Usually I try not to go alone, but I had run out of people willing to tag along. I had traveled thousands and thousands of miles already that year, and Nigeria didn't sound like a plum assignment to anyone else.

I nearly always regret going alone because travel is hard work. With cultural and language barriers, unsanitary conditions, weather differences, and potential illness, I can quickly become vulnerable to loneliness and homesickness. Even homesickness is preferable to what I came down with in Nigeria.

My system wasn't acclimated to the food or water, and suddenly I suffered from nausea, diarrhea, and dehydration. I hated the thought of making my way to the center of town and waiting a couple of hours in a steamy, filthy phone office for a long distance line to the States. But I needed to hear my wife's voice. I needed her support. Most of all I needed her prayers and those of the wonderful women in her prayer circle.

As I sat waiting, chastising myself for venturing out in my condition and wondering what in the world I was going to do if I became violently ill right there in public, the word finally came that my call had gotten through. Nearly doubled over with cramps, I shuffled to the phone.

"Tex?" I said, "Sweetheart, pray for me and get your ladies to pray for me. I'm not feeling well."

Of course she wanted all the details, and after she encouraged me, she asked if I had heard about the Berlin Wall.

"The Berlin Wall?" I said. "No. What about it?"

"It's come down."

I was sure I hadn't heard her right.

"It's what?"

"It's come down. People are dancing in the streets."

"You've got to be kidding!"

"I'm not, Sammy. The wall has come down."

Sick as I was, I hardly slept. So much of my life and ministry revolved around the Eastern bloc that my heart and soul and mind yearned to be there. I'd had the indescribable privilege of preaching all over the world, but my international ministry began in Europe, a place God led me to from my first few months as a Christian.

I had prayed since my college years for the downfall of atheistic communism because I knew it was Satan's greatest weapon against the gospel in Eastern Europe. Since beginning to minister there in the 1970s, I prayed more specifically for the end of oppression of the beloved brothers and sisters in Christ I had grown so close to over the years. I had heard great, elderly saints cry out to God for this day, yet I can't say I truly had the faith to believe it would happen in my lifetime. I knew it was a worthy prayer and that people imprisoned by godless dictatorships were victims of spiritual warfare, but I was as shocked and thrilled as anyone when the news came.

After a couple of hours of fitful dozing in a remote, dilapidated hotel, I awoke dehydrated and doubled over. The only people I knew in the hotel were two guys from New York I'd met in the restaurant. They were in Nigeria doing mission work. In the middle of the night I woke them.

No communication system worked in the hotel, but somehow they got to the local pastor and brought him to me. As soon as he saw me he knew I needed to get to the hospital. The first thing they wanted to do was to pump liquids into me, and much as I hated to offend the woman preparing me for the IV, with AIDS rampant in Africa, I had to ask. "Has this needle been used before?"

"Why, of course not," she snapped.

There seemed to be only one person on duty in the entire hospital, and no one on my floor. When my IV ran low I had to get up and carry it with me, calling for someone downstairs to come and help me.

They tried to convince me it was natural that my stomach began to bloat. I was scared and uncomfortable. Never had I been so sympathetic to my wife, who had twice been pregnant. I thought I was going to burst. I began praying in earnest. "Lord," I said, "I hate to put out a fleece, but I've got to have an answer. If what they're doing to me is wrong, don't let my stomach go down. If it's right, let the swelling reduce within twelve hours."

I had a plan. If my stomach was still swollen twelve hours later, I was going to take the needle out, get dressed, catch a taxi, and pay whatever it cost to get me to Lagos (about three hours' drive). From there I would fly to London and find a hospital where they could help me. I knew that would sound offensive and condescending to the people in Nigeria, but when you're that sick, your mind starts playing tricks on you.

Fortunately, the swelling reduced, but I was still very sick. The local pastor visited me for about a half hour a day, but otherwise I was lonely. He kept telling me, "You'll be okay, brother Sammy. God has given us assurance. God will take care of you."

I appreciated it, but in truth just then I wanted divine help that was concrete and visible—help and comfort in the form of people who would stay with me.

I knew how important the Berlin Wall news was when I realized that in spite of all my pain and sickness and fear and loneliness, I was occasionally overcome with joy. Lying in that hospital bed, wishing I could be anywhere but there, I began thinking about the wonderful news from Europe and praised God for His mighty work.

As usually happens with intestinal distress, the antibiotics gradually began to work against the bacterial infection, and the pain and discomfort slowly started to lift. I was eventually able to preach the last couple of days of the Nigerian crusade, and I couldn't wait to get back to the States and to see about getting to the Eastern bloc. Before having been detained, deported, and blacklisted July 22, 1988, my main area of ministry focus for a decade had been Romania. Tex told me as soon as I arrived home that everyone wanted to know if I thought Romania would be the next place to break free of totalitarianism.

I told her, "Tex, it will not happen in Romania without a bloodbath. The Securitate [si-kyoor'-i-ta'-tay, the government police force] is too strong. With transportation and communication so limited, no one could pull off a coup without bloodshed."

Just a few weeks later, after stepping out on faith and adding Bill Smyth, a businessman, to our San Antonio office to help with the crushing load of administrative details, I took my family to Louisiana to visit my widowed mother. We were enjoying the Christmas holidays there, the adults chatting in the kitchen, when my son Dave came in. "Dad, you need to come and watch the news. Something is happening in Timisoara [tim'-mee-schwa'-ra]. There's been a massacre."

I rushed to the TV where CNN had sketchy reports about the Romanian city of more than 300,000 people, the city that had become so dear to my heart. I strained to see and hear. People had been killed. The multitudes had taken to the streets. Could any of them be my treasured loved ones in Christ, the brave soldiers of the cross who had for so long lived out their faith under the tyranny of Nicolae Ceausescu? I was glued to the TV, praying I wouldn't hear numbered among the victims the names of layman Nelu Dronca or Pastor Peter Dugalescu—two of the many brothers and sisters in Christ in Timisoara who had become so beloved to me and my family.

Reporters had never been allowed into the country, so news was sketchy. The borders were closed and truck drivers were the only ones allowed out. I called Sam Friend, a former associate in Bothell, Washington, and asked what he knew. He told me the Securitate had come to arrest a pastor named Laszlo Tokes, who had spearheaded a demonstration. When government forces arrived, they found people surrounding his home to protect him. The Securitate had fired into the crowd, killing dozens. That was all Sam knew.

I called Josif Tson in Wheaton, head of the Romanian Missionary Society and former pastor of the great Second Baptist Church in Oradea, Romania, where revival had swept through years before. Josif confirmed the report from Sam Friend and bemoaned the plight of his countrymen. My concern immediately became the fact that the United States needed to take a stand. The Romanians were always low on food. They had no weapons, no money. We needed to come to their aid.

I became obsessed with the idea of doing something for the people of Romania. I told Tex, "I know it's our Christmas, but I have to do something."

"I'm with you all the way, Sammy," she said. "But what are you going to do?"

I had no idea. I thought of something drastic and noisy, as I would have done early in my ministry—maybe chaining myself to a cross in front of the United Nations building. Or maybe I would go to the great Romanian population in Chicago and call for a big rally in the civic center there.

But times had changed. Techniques that once were effective can make you a laughing stock and backfire today. I decided to call all my media contacts and encourage them to get the word out that the Romanians needed U.S. aid. I was worried that the Securitate would march through and massacre more people and it would be overshadowed by all the controversy in Panama at the time.

I knew that if there was one thing the communists hated it was adverse publicity. So every chance I got I accepted interviews as a Romania watcher who had spent years in ministry there. I called for the American people, particularly the Christian community, to raise a loud cry against the atrocities. "We need to protest every killing. We need to stand for the Romanian people."

Within days the stunning news arrived. The army had pulled out of Timisoara. The communists had been booted out, and a transitional government was in control. From what he knew of the passion of the resistance and his years as a Romania watcher, Josif Tson predicted that within forty-eight hours Ceausescu would be dethroned.

"Are you sure?" I asked. Coming from anyone else, that was a remark I would have dismissed as foolishness. I had spent enough time in Romania to know how powerful Ceausescu was, how he had surrounded himself with security and staged parades in honor of himself.

Yet Josif was a Romanian, a powerful expatriate. Could he be right? Perhaps his contacts in-country had passed on inside information. But was it possible? I was skeptical. "I believe it will happen, Sammy," he said. "We need to prepare."

I was so excited with the possibility that I might be able to return to Romania that I could hardly think of anything else. After years of ministering there and being blacklisted, told never to return, and miraculously being allowed back in time after time, I was finally detained at the border, held overnight, and deported. It had been seventeen long months since I had been to that precious country whose people I grew to love so much.

I helped arrange for a colleague, evangelist Steve Wingfield, to preach in Timisoara the next month, and for Dr. Joe Ford, chairman of the board of our ministry, to go. Both of them wanted to know if it was too dangerous and whether they should still try to go. "It's dangerous," I said, "and I can't tell you what you should do. But I can tell you right now, I'm making plans. I don't know when, but at the right moment, I'm going. If they open those borders and I can get in, I'm going."

The next thing I heard was that while Ceausescu was making a speech in Bucharest, he staged another of his demonstrations to show how the people loved him. But some university students, who had heard over Radio Free Europe what had happened in

Timisoara, began hollering from the back of the crowd, "*Jos cu Ceausescu! Jos cu Ceausescu!* [Down with Ceausescu!]"

The crowd picked up the chant, and perhaps for the first time since he had taken power in 1974, Ceausescu realized he didn't have the support of the people.

Ceausescu was the cruelest of all dictators. He spent elaborately on himself, even built himself an obscenely opulent palace, one of the largest buildings in Europe, despite the squalor of the people. The populace were starving and couldn't get bread or meat. They camped out to stay in line for gasoline. Yet Ceausescu lived like a king.

Most experts agree that at least a third of the population had been compromised by the Securitate. Family members would turn in each other for various offenses to gain favor with the guards. Yet all over the country were signs that read, "Long Live Ceausescu!" "The People for Ceausescu!" "Ceausescu Peace!" It was Orwellian.

One of my dearest friends in the world, a compatriot, a prayer warrior, my companion and translator when I'm in Romania, is a man named Titus Coltea. A young medical doctor who risked everything to serve Christ against the wishes of the communists, Titus and his wife, Gabi, were on our minds every minute. How I missed this dear brother and his deep, warm, affectionate, bold faith!

> **"My friend kept asking Titus how he was doing and was he safe and how was his family, but all Titus could say was, 'The glory of God has come to my country.'"**

Steve Wingfield came to me with the news that a friend of his had used a phone with an automatic redialer to finally reach Titus after thirty hours of calling. "It was strange," Steve reported. "My friend kept asking Titus how he was doing and was he safe and how was his family, but all Titus could say was, 'The glory of God has come to my country. The glory of God has come to my country. Tell Sammy that what we have prayed for for so long has come. Tell him he must come immediately.'"

The next day I was able to talk to Titus by phone, and he told me to get a vehicle and put a red cross on and drive to the border.

"They'll let you in if you bring medical supplies, no questions asked."

I arranged for a vehicle through a friend in Germany, and began planning to go. That Sunday morning my pastor, David Walker, asked me to update the congregation on Romania. After I shared what was happening and what our plans were, he added: "Sammy will not ask for money, but I will. If you want to help get him there or provide medical supplies, just give it directly to him after the service."

It reminded me of similar experiences earlier in my ministry where God simply had His own ways of providing for us. One man asked me how much I thought my flight would cost, then wrote a check to cover it. By the time I left church that morning I had been handed more than four thousand dollars!

On Christmas Day I heard the stunning news that Josif Tson had so precisely predicted: Ceausescu was put to death by firing squad. There was no longer any doubt in my mind; I knew it was time to go. I flew into Vienna January 1, 1990, and was met at about noon by Don Shelton, pastor of a church I had pastored years before in Hahn, West Germany. He and a few other laymen were there with a van and medical supplies. Though my luggage never arrived, I didn't want to take the time to buy clothes. We had nearly an eight-hour drive ahead of us to the border at Oradea, and I couldn't wait to get there. Titus told me there would be a church service that night, and though he wouldn't tell anyone I was coming, I wanted to be there for that more than anything.

The night I was deported a year and a half before, I enjoyed a special peace in spite of my heartache and sang "Great Is Thy Faithfulness" all the way home on the plane. Now that same song was on my heart as I realized that truly God is faithful. Even when everything else fails, God is faithful. No government, no dictator could keep me out if God wanted me in.

We drove as fast as we dared across Austria and Hungary to the Hungary/Romania border. About an hour outside of Romania we started praying. Both Don Shelton's and my name were in the computer as having been blacklisted and not allowed back in the country. The question now was who was in charge of the border. Who would be in control of the computer and how would they respond to us, red cross, medical supplies, or not?

First we had to pass through the Hungarian border, where they welcomed us with open arms and insisted we enjoy a lengthy meal. We kept trying to beg off, but they wouldn't hear of it. We finally got to the Romania side, and in the dark, desolate, dead of winter a border guard approached our car.

"Please get out," he said.

We got out. In the past, the first question we had always been asked was whether we had Bibles. And if we did, we were in big trouble. The Romanians believed that Christianity was an illness. There was no law against people inflicted with its disease meeting together, but bringing a Bible in from the outside was like pushing drugs. I didn't try to smuggle in even my own Bible, let alone Bibles for others. I always used one from someone in the country.

But this time the question was different. It wasn't, "Do you have a Bible?" but rather, "Are you a Christian?"

My heart raced. Where was that question coming from? I had always made it a practice to tell the truth, to not smuggle, to assume that if God wanted me somewhere, nothing could stop me. I had seen friends turned away because they were "in country with Sammy Tippit," only to be routinely processed through myself a few minutes later.

"Yes," I said, "we are Christians."

With that the guard smiled, threw open his arms, and said, "Welcome to Romania. There is a man in the customs office waiting for Christians to arrive."

We looked up and here came Titus and Gabi running to embrace us. What a joyous reunion! We knelt in the same spot where I had been told by a Securitate guard that I would never be able to return to Romania again. We prayed and praised God, and then Titus said, "We must get you to the church. The service has already run two hours."

We got there at the end of the meeting. I became so endeared to the people of that great church that they even had a typical greeting just for me. When I showed up, whoever was leading the service would say, "Tonight we have with us . . ." and the people would say in unison, "Sommy Teepeet."

Now they saw me arrive after my exile, and Titus's brother-in-law was at the microphone. Though they had been about to close, he said, "Tonight we have with us . . ."

How sweet it was to hear that congregation say in their unique accents, "Sammy Tippit!"

Peter said, "Brother Sammy, would you preach?"

There was nothing I'd rather have done. Titus and I mounted the steps to that platform, and my heart burst with love and joy as I looked into the two thousand plus beaming faces of newly freed people. I couldn't wait to tell them the details of my deportation and then open to them the Word of God. Titus and I could only weep as we spoke, praising Him for the mighty miracle He had wrought in their land.

The great question on all our minds was what this would mean for the rest of the Iron Curtain countries. With the tearing down of the Berlin Wall and the execution of the Romanian dictator, what could be next? From the massive Soviet Union came rumors of demonstrations, threats of secession, and Kremlin strong-arm tactics.

Clearly we had burst into a historic period. The mammoth Iron Curtain had been rent, and the world would never be the same. Neither would our ministry.

CHAPTER TWO

NEVER ASHAMED

No one predicted I would grow up to become an evangelist. I was a stranger to the things of Christ until junior high school in Baton Rouge, Louisiana. When I heard that an all-America and all-pro football player was going to speak at a church, I couldn't wait to see him. Football players were my idols.

I hung on his every word, and I still remember what he said: "All my awards don't amount to a cup of coffee compared to what Jesus Christ means to me." When that great athlete said, "Come and receive Christ," I hurried down the aisle.

The counselor assigned to me was more interested in getting me baptized and made a member of the church than in getting me saved. Before I knew it I had filled out a card and been dunked. I got wet, but I didn't come to know Christ. It wasn't until the summer after my junior year in high school that I even considered God again.

Meanwhile, even as a junior higher, I took an interest in public speaking. I took speech courses in seventh, eighth, and ninth grades, and I loved every minute. Now I can see that God was preparing me for what I do today, and I know why some of my preparation and delivery skills seem to come naturally.

I enjoyed wide success as a speaker and debater. By the summer before my senior year in high school, I was chosen as one of thirty students from Louisiana to study at the United Nations in New

York. On the way there our group stopped at the famous Gettysburg battlefield in Pennsylvania and sang patriotic songs and spirituals. As I stood gazing at the eternal torch, I began to wonder if there really was an eternal God.

I won an oratorical contest for the southern states, and later was named outstanding high school speaker for North America. I had no idea that the course of my life was being determined. I gained a global perspective from my study at the U.N., and being recognized as an orator even as a teenager now shows that God was working in my life even before I gave myself to Him.

I returned to Baton Rouge that fall with the world by the tail. During my senior year I traveled to several cities to speak about world peace. It was also a good year for parties, girls, alcohol, you name it. I graduated in the top few percent of my class and excelled in college testing exams, finishing in the top 1 percent in the nation in math. Representatives of Harvard and Tulane recruited me and told me about possible scholarships, and I accepted two separate scholarships to Louisiana State University.

My future seemed set, at least for the next four years. I had success, popularity, a girlfriend, and was rushed by the LSU fraternities during the summer. But something was missing. I could speak of global peace, but I had no inner peace. I was empty and at times even wondered whether life was worth living. I never went so far as to plot my own death, but I was one frustrated and confused young man. Nothing filled the aching void in my life.

One night my girlfriend's father, a deacon in a big local church, told us we couldn't go out unless we went to church first. That was a laugh. I knew she didn't care that much about church because we had gotten drunk at a party the night before. But her dad was serious, so we went.

A soloist sang old-time gospel songs, and I didn't like it at all until a young evangelist named James Robison stood to speak. I couldn't ignore him. He was excited, bounding all over the platform, smiling and shouting, happy about life. My plan to ignore the message went out the window. I didn't have half what this guy had. Even with all my success and popularity, I sensed I had nothing without Christ. I had walked forward in church six years before, and it made no difference in my life, but I was ready to give God another try. It didn't make any difference what my friends or even my girlfriend might think. I talked with Robison and then I prayed, "Jesus, if You're real, be real to me tonight. I'll give up anything, I'll do anything, but come into my heart and be my Lord." I knew for the first time that Jesus Christ was in my life. He forgave my sins, and my emptiness was gone. I knew immediately that God wanted me to use whatever abilities I had for Him.

> **"You must be willing to give Him everything, no matter what the cost. Even if it means going to jail, or losing your friends, you must be willing to pay the price."**

I told James Robison I felt a call to the ministry, and he gave me some advice. "Sam," he said, "Jesus didn't have to leave heaven to die for you. He chose to. He suffered and bled and was ridiculed and tortured. He gave His life for you. If He's called you to preach, you must be willing to give Him everything, no matter what the cost. Even if it means going to jail, or losing your friends, you must be willing to pay the price."

I had no idea, of course, that I would eventually be called to do those very things. I didn't know either that in spite of being willing to pay those prices, I would be blind to my own ego and pride. The day would come when God would have to search me and break me and mold me if I truly wanted to continue to grow and be of service to Him.

As young as I was in Christ, I was thrilled with my Lord. I wanted to tell everyone. There were meetings every night that week at church, and a few nights later one of my buddies was there —Freddie, a real boozer. During the invitation to receive Christ I told him, "I want you to know Jesus."

He laughed. "I've tried religion. It'll wear off in a few weeks. Tippit, this weekend we're goin' down to Grand Isle with all the girls you want and plenty of booze. Come with us."

"No," I said, "I've changed."

"I'm not listening," he said.

I was hurt and discouraged. I had failed.

Monday morning Freddie called. "I got loaded at Grand Isle last night, but all I could think about was what you said. Can you come over and pray with me?" A few minutes later Freddie and I were praying. I was so thrilled to lead someone to Christ that I couldn't wait to do it again.

Another friend, Don, had received Christ at one of the meetings too. The three of us started meeting for prayer and going to church together. The pastor took us under his wing and helped us grow.

I got my first opportunity to preach at a nursing home where the young people put on a service every Sunday. The only thing I knew to preach was my own testimony. I preached it each week in a different way.

Freddie and Don and I found the courage to go into nightclubs and bars to share our faith. We were scared to death, especially the first time. We recognized a lot of people there, and our mouths seemed glued shut. We had a private prayer meeting in the bathroom, but when we came out, we still just stood there unnoticed. Suddenly Freddie shouted, "I can't hold it any longer! I've got to tell you what Jesus has done for me!" The place fell dead silent and two bouncers came for Freddie. While they ushered him out, Don and I started quietly sharing Christ with anyone who would listen. That gave the three of us the courage to just go to those places and witness one-on-one, without causing a scene that would get us thrown out. Soon we were doing that several nights a week.

While we didn't see scores come to Christ, the exercise was great for us as new Christians. We learned the value of boldly, and often not so boldly, obeying the Lord when He led us to share His gospel.

One night a local pastor told me he felt led of God that I should go and witness for Christ in the nightclub across the river. That was a bad place, the scene of stabbings and even bombings. I said, "Well, if you feel led, then maybe *you* should go."

He asked me to pray about it, and I learned that prayer can be dangerous. Sure enough, God told me to go. Fred and Don and another friend, Charlie, went along. I carried my little red Bible and, directed by the bartender, went to a cubby hole in the back. Don, Freddie, and Charlie decided to stay in the hall and pray while I knocked hard. The door flew open to reveal six glaring eyes. The manager looked up at me from a pile of cash, flanked by two bouncers.

I said my friends and I wanted to tell the people about Jesus.

The manager looked at my Bible, into my eyes, back at the Bible, and back at me. "All right," he said.

"All right?" I gasped.

"Yeah," he shrugged, turning back to his counting. "You can have the stage when the band takes its next break."

I walked out, stunned and grinning, but my friends didn't notice. As I passed them in the dingy, dim hallway they stood there with their heads bowed, one of them fervently praying, "Lord, please be with Sam."

A few minutes later the band unstrapped their instruments and wandered from the little platform. I knew if I waited I'd lose my nerve, so I hurried to the microphone.

"Listen," I began, "I don't know what y'all think about Jesus Christ . . . " and a hush fell over the place. "But let me tell you what He's done for me."

After I told my story, the four of us split up to share Christ individually with people. Several gave their hearts to Jesus that night. We were thrilled, but we didn't tell anyone because we didn't want to become egotistical about it. That week in church the pastor said he had heard that some young people had shared their faith in the nightclub. One of the deacons had been approached by a man who heard us and wanted to know how to receive Christ. That was as exciting as the night I received Christ. I thought of Romans 1:16: "For I am not ashamed of the gospel of Christ, for it is the power of God to salvation for everyone who believes." As I looked forward to college I prayed, "Lord, help me *never* to be ashamed."

Near Louisiana State University I found a little hill where I often prayed and studied my Bible. I found it beautiful to spend time alone with Jesus, and God convicted me of many things. One was my girlfriend. I knew I had to get away from the kind of lifestyle we had enjoyed, and that meant staying away from her.

"Sammy, I'll change," she promised. "I'll give my life to God."

I said, "If you mean that, let's not see each other for two months." I knew that if she truly gave her life to God, she wouldn't want the party life any more than I did.

We had discussed marriage, so being apart from her for two months was going to be tough. But just two weeks later she was back to the old life, and I was convinced God would not bless our relationship. We were through.

Though I knew the break was the right thing for me, still I was lonely. Like most young men, I longed for a loving relationship. In my loneliness I developed a hunger for the Word of God and wanted to really dig into Scripture and increase my Bible knowledge. I knew what I had to do, but I also knew no one would understand. I felt God wanted me to leave LSU at the end of the first semester and transfer to a denominational Bible school. I gave up a scholarship at a prestigious university for what others considered "religious" training.

I had no idea how I was going to finance my new education, but I was excited about studying the Bible and knew God was in it. That knowledge kept me going when my enthusiasm was quenched at the new school. When some classmates and I witnessed on the streets, we were told we were embarrassing other students who considered us Holy Joes. I couldn't believe that reaction from a Christian school. Sure, at LSU we would have been laughed off the campus, but here?

Soon some of my clothes were missing. Students stole them just to bother me, and it worked. I soon talked myself out of being so radical and quit witnessing on the street. I justified that by accepting invitations to speak at youth revivals, but I had no power. Nothing was happening. My faith was lukewarm, and I was miserable.

My father had suffered for years with severe arthritis, and when I heard his condition was worsening, I jumped at the opportunity to again transfer to another school. I moved to Southeastern Louisiana University, just forty miles from home. I have to say, though, that one thing positive had happened at Bible college. One of the guys in our young preachers organization read a passage of Scripture one night that burned in my soul. I went to my room and looked it up and re-read it. It was the Old Testament passage where God puts His call on Jeremiah:

> Then the word of the LORD came to me, saying:
> "Before I formed you in the womb I knew you;
> Before you were born I sanctified you;
> And I ordained you a prophet to the nations."

Then said I:
"Ah, Lord GOD!
'Behold, I cannot speak, for I am a youth.'"
But the LORD said to me:
"Do not say, 'I am a youth,'
For you shall go to all to whom I send you,
And whatever I command you, you shall speak.
Do not be afraid of their faces,
For I am with you to deliver you," says the LORD.
Then the LORD put forth His hand and touched my
mouth, and the Lord said to me:
"Behold, I have put My words in your mouth.
See, I have this day set you over the nations and
   over the kingdoms,
To root out and to pull down,
To destroy and to throw down,
To build and to plant. . . .
I am ready to perform My word. . . .
Therefore prepare yourself and arise,
And speak to them all that I command you."
(Jer. 1:4-10, 12b, 17a)

That Scripture worked on my heart for days and I have never been able to get away from it. No matter where I go or what I encounter, I claim that passage. Even if I didn't feel called of God to preach all over the world, I would take great comfort and encouragement from the promise to Jeremiah that God is ready to perform His Word. Even to those who are not preachers, the Great Commission is still in force. We are commanded to tell others about Christ, and as scary as that can be, God promises to go before us and prepare hearts.

At Southeastern Louisiana State University I got in with a bunch of nominal Christians who emphasized that God allows Christians freedom to live as they choose. Frankly, in my youth and naiveté, this grace of God business sounded pretty good to me. I used it as an excuse to go back to social drinking, partying, and even smoking a pipe—not realizing that I had fallen into a trap. Of course the grace of God is not a license for sin, and I was miserable, knowing down deep I was kidding myself that I could stay close to God in spite of my lifestyle. I was still a Christian, of course, and I wanted to serve God. In the midst of the turmoil caused by that spiritual lapse, I met someone who would become the most important person in my life.

Because of the student government elections, one of the more publicized names on campus was "Tex." That was the nickname of Debe Ann Sirman, a Texas girl who ran for office and also came to our Bible study meetings. I was the first person who sat down with her and explained what it meant to receive Jesus Christ. With my inconsistent Christian life it was a wonder she even listened. Thank God some girls in her dorm were living examples of what I talked about. One night Tex went to her room and gave her life to Christ. The next day I saw in her the newness of life I had experienced at the time of my decision for Christ. It really shook me. Down deep I envied her and realized how far I had strayed from my first love.

Tex was excited about Jesus and often cried when she thought of all the girlfriends with whom she wanted to share Christ. I missed that kind of passion and zeal for the lost and realized I had really blown it. I knew I had to ditch all the habits I had regained. Tex and I started to date, and I gave up drinking, partying, and even my pipe—not for her, but to break down the barriers to fellowship with God.

Tex and I began dating and were in love by the time I got a phone call in March of 1968, telling me my father was dying. I didn't even have time to tell Tex. I drove to Baton Rouge in confusion, yet with a puzzling sense of peace. I drove slowly, thinking about death, life, my father, and how I had failed him so many times. Dad had rededicated himself to God not many months before, so I didn't worry where he would spend eternity.

I was holding his hand at four in the morning when I saw life leave his body. It hurt me to see my family go through such heartache, but I knew my father was with Christ and that God was with me.

Back at school, Tex and I began to think about marriage and the future. God had forgiven me for my stagnant Christianity and gave me a burden for the world—not just for a few souls. After hearing about mission efforts in Eastern Europe, my mind returned to that region often. For some reason I felt the conviction that I would one day preach the claims of Christ behind the Iron Curtain. I felt a deep desire to further His cause throughout the world, but I didn't know what I could do as a student. I sent a little money to evangelistic concerns in communist countries, but that didn't lift my burden.

Like any groom, I could only hope I knew what I was getting into when Tex and I married on June 8, 1968. I was deeply in love, and I knew Tex to be a spiritual woman with a loving, compassionate heart for me and for God. Neither of us was aware of what would be required of us in the future, and it's only with hindsight that I can say that God provided me the perfect mate. Though I had more to learn than I could imagine and areas of my life that needed a deep work of change from the Lord, He blessed me with a woman of character who cared about lost souls and would go with me anywhere to see them come to Christ. Unaware that Tex was often more of a victim than a partner during the early years, I plunged ahead into ministry. I had the right motives, and she saw that, but eventually God would use her to minister to me in painful but necessary ways.

A few months after Tex and I were married, God spoke to me in a way He never had before. No one else saw what I saw in a restaurant in Baton Rouge that day. As I sat there munching a hamburger and gazing out the big glass windows, my mind carried me far beyond the borders of Louisiana.

Strangely shivering on a warm evening, I stared straight ahead. Chairs scraped the floor, mothers scolded rowdy children, and Tex brushed her lips with a napkin. But my mind was somewhere else. It was as if the restaurant had been transported across the ocean. My soda had become some sort of a hot drink. The people around me spoke a language I didn't understand.

I realized that in my mind I was behind the Iron Curtain, surrounded by people in a godless vacuum. I bled for them and burned to tell them the forbidden news. The experience was so real to me that it stayed with me for several days and I knew it had some special meaning. I felt God was calling me to a specific ministry behind the Iron Curtain.

I had read about the persecution of believers in Eastern Europe, and God seemed to constantly lay it on my heart to pray for them. I wanted to go, but how could I? I was just twenty-one, and our home in Walker, Louisiana, was a long way from Europe. Besides, we were practically penniless.

After not having shared the vision with anyone but Tex for several months, I related the story to a group of young people at the Walker Baptist Church, and they were thrilled. They held a car wash to raise money to send us overseas. They made seventy-two dollars. I cherished it as an expression of their love, but after about a year I put the money away and dismissed the idea of going to Europe. When I discovered what it would cost to go, I even began to wonder if my vision had really been a vision after all.

I badly wanted to reach people for Christ, but for some reason I was seeing no fruit. Regardless of how I preached or witnessed, I was again in a spiritual desert. There was no power. Nothing was happening. It took a fiery redhead with a heart full of love to turn me around.

CHAPTER THREE

IN THE CASKET

L eo Humphrey was a muscular, stocky man in his mid-thirties, a rough and tumble guy you wouldn't want to mess with. A student at New Orleans Baptist Theological Seminary, he worked sharing his faith in the famed French Quarter. This fireball didn't pass anybody without saying, "Jesus loves you!" He was happy and joyful and seemed to live by the power of God. Most impressive to me was that his witness was fruitful—something I couldn't say for my own. I was determined to find out what made him tick.

I started going down to the French Quarter in my spare time to work with Leo. One of his ploys was to tell nightclub owners that he was praying they wouldn't sleep until they gave their hearts to Jesus. Then he would write their names in his little prayer book and walk out. I told him, "You can't witness that way. You'll turn those guys off."

But more than one came to Leo and asked him to quit praying for them. "I haven't slept for days."

"Receive the Lord and you'll sleep like a baby," he'd tell them. And some did. I was learning that even techniques that border on the extreme can work in some situations.

The French Quarter was shocking to me. I saw public immorality, people high on drugs, knife fights, and even murders. Kids talked about death the way you and I talk about the weather. I saw runaways and teen girls selling their bodies. I saw men embracing and kissing each other and dancing. It was a world ready to explode in its sin. I developed a tremendous burden for a dying world. I was a college senior doing well academically, but my heart was heavy. The sin of the French Quarter haunted me daily. I prayed that God would let me help people find Jesus.

Finally the burden became so strong that I couldn't concentrate. Every minute I sat in class seemed like time I should use to spread the word about Christ. So I dropped out. That was no small decision. My father's last request was that I stay in school. Now my whole family was concerned about me and hurt. Friends reminded me that without a college degree I would never preach in a large church or gain a ministerial reputation. And where would I go? What would I do? I had no source of income.

Somehow I knew that if God had put this restlessness in my heart, He would take care of Tex and me. My reputation wasn't as important to me as it had once been. Though it has worked out that I have preached in some of the country's largest churches and in stadiums all over the globe, I would be satisfied to simply share Christ on the street with one person at a time.

Tex was beautiful about it. "Sammy, wherever God calls you, I'll be with you." She has kept that spirit for a quarter of a century, even though she knew better than I did that the young man God was calling had as many blind spots and weaknesses as he had strengths.

The first thing I did was call Leo and tell him I wasn't waiting for some mysterious door to open. "I'm coming down to witness with you in the French Quarter." Tex and I loaded up everything we owned in a truck we borrowed from Tex's dad and drove to Leo's office. The first real test of our faith came immediately. While we were upstairs talking to Leo, someone ransacked the truck. There we were, two kids with nothing but a borrowed truck, a burden, and the clothes on our backs. We didn't know where we'd sleep or when we'd eat, but we knew we were in God's will. He just wanted us to start from scratch.

Leo signed me up and got us a room at an evangelism conference at the seminary, to which pastors and evangelists had come from all over the country. I didn't have a razor or even a change of clothes, but I wanted to learn more about sharing Christ. I heard a lot of ideas, some good and some not, and suddenly I felt the urge to speak up. I fought it, not sure I wanted to draw attention to myself. Already I stood out as one of very few people there without a tie and coat. Certainly I was the only one with a couple of days' growth on his chin.

Men addressed the group from where they were by simply raising their hands. Finally I couldn't contain myself. I told the nearly three hundred pastors and evangelists that we have to take Jesus to the people and not expect them to come to us. We must get out on the streets and present the claims of Christ to anyone who will listen. I got a little carried away and began preaching. While I had the floor I shared my burden for the sin and degradation of the French Quarter.

After the session, several pastors crowded around and asked if I would come to their churches and speak. I was floored. God had opened the door for me to share my burden in churches all over, and I had stepped out in faith only a few days before.

Those speaking engagements helped meet our financial needs, and it became exciting just to trust God when we needed money. Tex and I moved into a house in Hammond, Louisiana, for eighty dollars a month. One night I was scheduled to speak at a church, but we didn't have the money to put enough gas in the car to get there. The rent was due and I needed clean clothes and a haircut. We didn't know what to do except to pray.

We knelt in our little living room and claimed the promise in Philippians 4:19: "And my God shall supply all your need according to His riches in glory by Christ Jesus." We rose believing God would take care of us. I went to the post office to pick up the mail, and there was a gift, a check for a hundred dollars. That paid the rent, cleaned our clothes, cut my hair, put gas in the car, and even paid for a few groceries. The speaking engagement gave us enough to live on for a while. God has met our needs many times just like that.

My burden grew, and I began to minister in many cities. We witnessed on the street and I preached in churches, but still I wasn't satisfied that I was doing all I could. There was a lack of power in my witness. I was bold, but I was bearing little fruit. Again it would take Leo to head me in the right direction.

I got another chance to work with him when we were both

invited to a youth crusade in Gulf Shores, Alabama. I confided in him that I felt a lack of power, a void in my ministry.

"Sam, do you really want the power of God in your life?"

"I sure do."

"Let's go to the shore and pray about it."

> **"To tell you the truth, Sam, I thought you were in this whole thing for yourself."**

I had a feeling of great anticipation as we headed for the Gulf of Mexico. I was glad I had opened up to Leo, but before we prayed I knew I had to admit my misgivings about him when we had first met. He laughed. "To tell you the truth, Sam, I thought you were in this whole thing for yourself."

"Sometimes I think I *am*," I said. "But I want to get right with God."

We prayed that God would empower me and multiply my ministry. Then I wandered along the beach by myself. I lay on my back in the sand and gazed at the stars. I heard the waves crashing and was awed by God's handiwork.

"God," I prayed, "I see Your magnificent power before me, but I'm not experiencing it. I want so badly to bear fruit in my ministry. I need Your power." I poured out my heart, confessing my sin. He searched me and brought unconfessed sin to mind. He exposed some of my bad attitudes, and I begged His forgiveness.

I could feel his cleansing, and when I began to thank Him I couldn't praise Him enough. I worshiped Him and lost all track of time. I didn't have what some would call a charismatic experience, but I felt the Holy Spirit doing a deep work in my life.

Four hours later Leo came to me. "It's almost dawn, brother. Let's go."

I grinned at Leo. "Praise God," I said. "Praise God." Jesus had taken control of my life. I couldn't even sleep. I just kept praising Him.

You may wonder where Tex was in all of this. She was thrilled for me, of course, and she knew I earnestly sought to serve God. But without realizing it, I still treated her as an accessory. I was in charge. I guided her. When we disagreed, I won her over. When we argued, I showed her I was right and she was wrong. I was so confident I didn't have a clue to what I was doing to her.

During that week of meetings we saw over 130 saved, mostly through personal witnessing. God had given me His power. Before the first meeting the weather was so bad that our tent on the beach was about to be blown over. Leo said, "Guys, we aren't going to be able to hold the meeting if this weather doesn't let up. Let's ask God to stop the rain."

A few of us formed a circle inside the tent and knelt to pray. I asked God to stop the rain, but to be honest, my faith was weak. I had the power of God to witness and to preach, but meddling in the weather was something new for me, and I was skeptical. Somebody in that group must have had more faith than I did because God stopped the rain.

Unknown to us, Kelly, a girl from Louisiana, stood in the back and had heard us ask God to stop the rain. She thought we were nuts. She was a biker who prostituted herself for a guy in the American Breed cycle gang from New Orleans. Leo had witnessed to her in the French Quarter and had invited her to the meeting. She also had a girlfriend in the choir.

We learned later that Kelly had been selling her body since she was thirteen and was kicked out of her house by her father. She saw him kill her brother with a knife. Now she was seventeen, and God was working on her.

She had come only to get away from New Orleans for a while and to look for drugs on the beach. She sat listening to me preach that night with a lot of things on her mind. I spoke on the second coming of Christ. She thought about that, and she thought about Leo witnessing to her, and she thought about the girlfriend in the choir who had also shared Christ with her, and she thought about the rain stopping. But she didn't come forward to receive Christ.

After the meeting I saw her in the parking lot. "Kelly," I said, "Jesus loves you."

"Don't give me that, man," she spat. "If Jesus loves me why am I strung out on dope and running with a cycle gang?"

"I don't know," I said. "All I know is that Jesus wants to give you a new life."

She turned and ran toward the beach, calling over her shoulder, "Just leave me alone!"

Later Leo and I found her on the shore and sat on either side of her. We talked and prayed for hours. Finally, at three o'clock in the morning, Kelly asked Jesus to show her His love. She asked Him to forgive her sins and to come into her life. She wept and softly repeated again and again, "He's real."

The next day she went to church in the only clothes she owned, and everybody talked about what had happened to her. That night I scheduled her to speak before my sermon in the tent. After she gave her testimony she walked out, and I wondered if anything was wrong. I watched as she approached two young men across the street. When she came back she told me she had gone to share Christ with them.

Kelly didn't have a home to go to, so for the next three months she traveled with Tex and me. I saw her personally lead more than 150 people to Christ. When she went to church with us she would stand at the door afterward and ask people if they had met the Lord. She barred no one. She asked deacons and elders and even pastors, "Are you saved?"

When she finally returned to New Orleans to finish high school her biker man told her, "Forget about this religion. You're ridin' with me tonight." She refused.

The next day she had a black eye. I said, "What happened to you?"

"I got beat up for Jesus," she said.

Kelly faced her problems and temptations and often met with failure and frustration, but she always got back up and lived for the Lord. God showed me, partly through her, that His power can change lives. Finally I had the power to go along with my burden.

When I got back to Hammond, Louisiana, I told an old college buddy, Ramsey Gilchrist, what God had been doing in my life. He was especially intrigued by what I told him Leo had said about a man named Arthur Blessitt. Arthur ministered to dopers and hippies at His Place on the Sunset Strip in Hollywood, California. Ramsey and I decided that the best way to learn from Arthur would be to go see him. Our wives agreed, so we pooled our money, made sandwiches, and made it to California in thirty hours.

After telling Arthur about ourselves, we asked him to tell us some of his experiences, but he just looked at me and said, "You've got to get right with God."

I told him I had already gotten right with God, but he said, "You need to die daily. What you experienced the night you say you got right with God you can experience continually if you die daily."

He showed me Galatians 2:20: "I have been crucified with Christ; it is no longer I who live, but Christ lives in me; and the life which I now live in the flesh I live by faith in the Son of God, who loved me and gave Himself for me."

Right there in Arthur's living room a strange thing happened. Again I prayed for the power of God, but this time I figuratively placed my desires in a casket. I placed my wife in that casket, along with my car and my few belongings, and yes, even my secret desire to be another Billy Graham. I placed all the things I could think of in that casket, and then I climbed in and asked God to shut the lid. I told God I was willing to die to self. Though there were no tears, I knew deep in my heart that I had Christ's control *and* the Holy Spirit's power to go along with my burden for souls.

I thought the French Quarter was bad, but the Sunset Strip was really something. Cycle gangs roared up and down wearing chains and carrying blades. We spent only a few days in Hollywood, but it was long enough to give me a burden to serve Christ in a large city. For some reason I felt God drawing me to Chicago, so I started praying about it. Chicago was about as far from my culture as I could get, and the Lord had a lot to teach me first.

My first lesson was in south Louisiana, where I preached in a church where revival broke out. The pastor took me aside and said, "If you don't change your methods, you're going to have to leave."

I was shocked. "What do you mean?"

"You're using psychological tricks to get people emotionally stirred up."

"Man, I'm just preaching about God's changing power."

"And stop preaching that this church can't save a person. You and I know it's true, but you're causing people to doubt their salvation."

"I didn't intend to," I said, "but if they're doubting, maybe they should be."

He had heard enough. "Change your style or leave."

I prayed, "Lord, please show me in some way that I'm letting

Your Spirit preach through me. If it's me who's doing this, then I'll quit."

At about two in the morning I was still up, pacing and praying, seeking God. The phone rang. It was the church youth director. "Sammy," he said, "revival has come."

A full-time Christian worker, with whom I had gone to college, had come to his house in tears. The young man confessed, "God won't let me sleep until I return these shirts I stole from Sam when we were in college. I saw in the meeting tonight that he has something real. I was wrong to make fun of him."

That was all I needed. I knew God blessed my preaching and that I dare not change. I told the pastor the next day that I loved him and his church but that I would have to leave the revival if I couldn't preach the way I felt led. He told me to leave.

It would have been easy for me to be bitter and turn my back on the institutionalized church, but I couldn't. God showed me that the church was His idea. There's no substitute for it. I realized that if revival could come within the church, we wouldn't have to worry about the heresy that is so widespread. God showed me that I must relate the kids to the church and the church to the kids. Kids may get saved on the street, but if they can't relate to the church they'll blow away with the wind. Many kids don't like church because too many church services are like funerals. I longed to see revival within the church.

God proved in a practical way what He had taught me when I was invited to speak at a week of meetings in the twin cities of Monroe and West Monroe, Louisiana, early in 1970. It was to become another turning point in my ministry.

CHAPTER FOUR

THE MONROE SEVEN

The night before the first service at Calvary Baptist Church in Monroe, Louisiana, only four young people showed up at the prayer meeting with Pastor L. L. Morris and me.

"We might as well forget it if the young people aren't even interested," I said.

But L. L. Morris wasn't a quitter. "Sammy," he said, "before this week is over, I believe God is going to shake Monroe for His glory, and people are going to be saved."

The meetings were to run from Wednesday through Sunday night, with a group from Northeast Louisiana State University singing. There was a fair crowd the first night and a few decisions for Christ, but the next night—even though I'm not a charismatic —I felt the presence of God in a dramatic way. During the invitation a Sunday school teacher came forward to pray with Pastor Morris, then came to the pulpit and all but pushed me aside.

"I'm supposed to be an example," he announced, "but I've been a poor Christian, and I want you to forgive me."

Suddenly the Holy Spirit seemed to fall on that place. The singers from the university confessed that they had grown lax in personal witnessing and committed themselves to do nothing but glorify Jesus. Many came to Christ over the next few days, and the crowds kept getting larger. By Sunday night attendance was so great we decided not to end the meetings. The next night we moved into a larger building, and by the next week we had to move yet again.

Local college kids asked for time in class to tell what God had done in their lives. Ray Mears, a music teacher in the local high school, shared Christ with his classes. He couldn't give an invitation right there, so he asked those interested in hearing more to see him after class. All but two stayed.

We set aside a room in the local Christian coffee house, Your Place, for prayer around the clock. We prayed that God would touch the heart of former Louisiana Governor James Noe, owner of one of the television stations in Monroe, and that he'd give us free time to tell about the revival. God gave us more than we asked for. Noe gave us all the free spot announcements we wanted and two fifteen-minute shows besides.

> **"You're having trouble holding all the people, right? . . . How would you like to have the civic center?"**

"You're having trouble holding all the people, right?" he asked. "How would you like to have the civic center?" We nodded with mouths hanging open, and he wheeled around in his chair to call the mayor. "I want you to donate the civic center to these boys. They're doing something positive and constructive, so let's give it to them free. If they have to pay, I'll cover it."

One night about midnight a girl named Connie McCartney came into Your Place stoned on speed. She had been raised in a Christian home and had received Christ as a youngster, but when she grew up and saw what the world had to offer, she rebelled. Now twenty, she was out on bond after being arrested for selling. Now she was in line for a sure prison term.

"Sam," she said that night, "speed is my lover. I've tried everything, even astrology and witchcraft. I want out. Can Jesus set me free?"

It was a thrill to tell her yes. "God has promised to deliver you from anything, even speed, if you'll give Him your life. Jesus says the truth shall make you free."

That night Connie committed her life to Christ, and to my knowledge she's never since been strung out on dope. She said she went home and flushed her drugs down the toilet in the name of the Father, the Son, and the Holy Ghost.

Connie and a local football star testified at the next meeting, and the crowds kept growing. I was interviewed on the evening news on TV and the anchorman said, "We understand something is shaking the Twin Cities."

"Jesus is shaking them," I said. "People are finding that Jesus Christ is the only hope for the world."

I called Leo to tell him how God was blessing. "Sam," he said, "God is getting ready to do a mighty work in America. I just got a call from Arthur Blessitt on his 'Which Way, America?' walk for Christ." Arthur was carrying a cross from coast to coast, preaching in meetings and witnessing along the way. Leo said that at Arthur's meeting in Albuquerque there were a thousand decisions for Christ.

As I put down the phone my heart burned to see America turn back to God. I knelt and asked God what I could do to glorify Him. He seemed to say, "Sammy, walk. Walk, walk, walk."

Outside of Arthur, I had never heard of anyone walking for Jesus. "God," I prayed, "I have a wife to think about. I'll go if you want me to, but You'll have to make Tex willing to trust You in this."

A few days later, when I finally discussed the idea with Tex, she was excited. God had spoken to her less than a half hour before, impressing upon her that she must be willing to follow Him, regardless of where He led. "Had you come up with this an hour ago, I would have thought it was crazy," she admitted. To my shame, I have to admit that if I had not waited for God to work in her heart on that issue, I would have somehow badgered her into going along.

When Ray Mears, the music teacher, heard of our plans to walk from Monroe to Washington, D.C., he came to me. "I believe God is calling Charlotte and me to go with you," he said. But Ray was five hours from his college degree, and Charlotte was pregnant. Besides that, they were $1,100 in debt. Ray wanted to pay off his debts before the walk, so he put his car up for sale. A dealer told him he'd never get more than $800 for it, but Ray trusted God. Holding out for several days, he finally took it to an auction, where it sold for—you guessed it—$1,100.

Ken Hall, a college freshman, felt God wanted him to go with us too. His decision was made difficult by his father, who drove up from Shreveport to talk to Ken and Ray and me.

"Son," he warned, "if you go you may never see me alive again. I don't have long to live."

I figured we'd lost Ken until he looked his father in the eye and said, "Daddy, I love you, but I love Jesus more, and I have to do what He has told me." (Today Dr. Ken Hall is a pastor in Texas.)

Richard Medaries was a former rock drummer who turned his life and his talent over to God. I felt led to approach him about the walk. Little Richard, as he came to be known, was hesitant at first. But through prayer he felt God burdening his heart. He would bring along his drums.

And then there was Connie, the former speed addict. She would have to come back to Monroe to stand trial in April, but she wanted to go anyway. She expected several years of prison, and she wanted to learn how to share her faith with other inmates.

There was nothing exceptional about any of the seven of us. We all simply wanted to be used of God.

I finally got hold of Arthur and told him of our plans. He was taking a northern route to Washington, D.C., carrying a huge wooden cross. We prayed over the phone, and he suggested a Bible as our symbol. That rang a bell with me. The Word of God was where the nation should look for answers. We decided that the seven of us would push a wheelbarrow full of New Testaments to give to people along the way, and we would meet up with Arthur in the capital.

We were all ready to go when the deacons of a large local church informed us that walking for Christ just wasn't done. They said they had never heard of people selling their belongings and dropping out to follow Jesus, except, of course, in the Bible.

We said, "Praise God, that's right."

Next several local pastors met with us. They told Ray that he must not love his wife. The very idea of taking a pregnant woman on a march across the country!

"I don't understand it myself," Ray told them. "I love my wife and I love Jesus. All I can say is that God has called us, and we're going."

Finally one of the pastors spoke up. "If God has called these boys, we'd better not stand in their way."

Arthur called to warn me to be sure God was in the decision. I almost thought he was trying to talk me out of it. He said his life and the lives of those with him had been threatened and that they may never make it to Washington. "You might not either. Pray again and be sure God wants you to do this."

But before we could even meet and pray about it a young man came to us and told us that God had given him a vision. "God showed me that if you go ahead with this, you will be struck dead on the first step."

The seven of us prayed that God would lead us. While we prayed, Arthur's wife called to ask if we'd made a decision. We said no, we were still praying. In fact, we wouldn't get back to Arthur until we were under way.

All we had were two cars, a little food, our Bibles, a trailer-tent, and a wheelbarrow. With about $100 among us and the blessing of God, we planned to leave the morning of March 16, 1970. We were too excited to sleep well, but the lack of rest wouldn't take its toll until we were far down the road. Dozens of local Christians and several members of the news media gathered to see us off. Many of the kids who had received Christ during the revival joined us in a 7 A.M. prayer meeting. I'd made many new friends in Monroe, and I wondered if I'd ever see them again. It was one emotional morning.

After we were interviewed briefly by the press, Tex, Ray, Charlotte, Connie, and Little Richard drove ahead in two cars. Ken and I walked the first leg of the journey. The only thing definite on our schedule was a speaking engagement at Mississippi Baptist College in Jackson. Past that we were trusting God to open doors.

As I bent over to grab the wheelbarrow, my mind raced. Was I wrong to ignore the death vision? Would I ever see Leo or Arthur again? Would we make it to D.C.? I looked at Ken. "Praise God, brother. Let's walk for Jesus."

With the first step my whole being was flooded with the love and joy of Jesus. God filled my soul, and I could only praise Him. I knew we were in His will. Ken and I walked sprightly all morning, reaching the cars in time for a lunch that had been brought out by friends from Monroe. We were high on the excitement of being used of God in this unusual way.

Publicity preceded us so townspeople gathered and little kids ran along shouting, "Those guys with the wheelbarrow are coming!" It was bright and unusually warm for March in Louisiana. A man working in a cornfield in Rayville was the first to come to Jesus as a result of our walk. We just shared the love of Christ with him, and he prayed to receive Christ. We witnessed to people all along the way and saw revival in many lives before we finally called it a day. We set up our tent in the country away from the highway. Ray, Charlotte, Connie, Tex, and I slept in our clothes in the tent while Ken and Richard climbed into their sleeping bags on the ground outside. It had been a beautiful day.

Then the rain came.

By the time Ken and Richard gathered up their sleeping bags and splashed to the Toyota, they were soaked. They had to sleep sitting up all night. It was still exciting and fun, but when we were greeted in the morning by mud and wet equipment, our spirits were dampened. So it wasn't all going to be a joy ride. Already we were down to the nitty-gritty. There wouldn't always be crowds and excitement. We needed a special blessing.

Walking twenty-five miles a day, we made it to Jackson, Mississippi, in a week. We stopped at a restaurant just inside the city limits and looked forward to ministering at the college. But we couldn't wait. We started sharing the claims of Jesus right there in the restaurant.

The next morning we held an outdoor meeting during the break after the regular campus chapel service. Little Richard cut loose on his drums and, just as we figured, that drew a crowd. Ray sang a solo and I preached, and many students got right with God. Afterward two local pastors asked us to hold services in their churches. When they learned we were marching to Washington for Jesus they took up a love offering for us. God was providing.

On our way through Jackson we took a break and knelt to pray at the side of the road. A car pulled over and a man came to ask what we were all about. He was a minister, thrilled with our mission to call America back to God. He invited us to have a service at his church, and from there we were invited to several other churches and another local college. We saw many come to Christ during four days of ministering in that city.

We left the next Monday, headed for York, Alabama, and—to our surprise—a chance to witness to Governor George Wallace. He was in town for a rally, and I was curious to know of his relationship to Christ. We detoured to the rally, and I was referred to one of his aides. I told him we'd like to give the governor one of our Bibles. He said he would see what he could do. I had just about resigned myself to not seeing Wallace when the rally started and an aide told me, "We're going to let you do it."

From the platform I heard a flowery introduction of the governor as a Christian man who believes the Bible, and I realized I was being used as a political gimmick. I silently prayed for forgiveness, assuring the Lord that I had not intended to be used that way. "If I've made a mistake," I prayed silently, "I'll leave right now. Tell me what to do."

As I was being introduced and asked to come to the platform, the Lord impressed three verses on my heart: "And you will be brought before governors and kings for My sake, as a testimony to them. . . . But when they deliver you up, do not worry about how or what you should speak. For it will be given to you in that hour what you should speak; for it is not you who speak, but the Spirit of your Father who speaks in you" (Matt. 10:18-20).

As I walked toward the platform I told the Lord I was claiming that promise, and I couldn't believe what came from my mouth. "People," I began, "the solution to the problems that face our nation today is not found in any politician, but only in Jesus Christ! Mr. Wallace, I'd like to give you the Word of God because in it is found the solution to the crises in America."

He responded politely, and I had no impression he had tried to use me for his own gain. So the crowd would know we were not there for political reasons, we left immediately. Back on the road, we headed for Livingston. My presentation to the governor was broadcast on statewide television. Unknown to us, the president of Livingston University had state troopers looking for us up and down the highway all night, wanting to make sure we didn't pass through without stopping to speak there.

As we neared the University of Alabama at Tuscaloosa a few days later we passed a chain gang on the other side of the highway.

Holding a big Bible aloft, we yelled, "Jesus loves you, brothers! Jesus loves you!" A year later I learned that one of the men on that gang met a friend of mine in Baton Rouge, told him that story, and eventually received Christ.

At the University of Alabama we shared Christ with a couple of young men on the steps of the student union building. One of them said, "Man, you've really got something. You should tell this to the whole student body."

He got permission from the university president for us to hold an outdoor meeting at nine on Monday morning, two weeks to the day since we had left Monroe. We had no time for publicity, so we prayed that God would bless Little Richard's drums. Those drums had been used in nightclubs for Satan, but Richard had turned them over to the Lord. God used them in a mighty way. When Richard cut loose Monday morning, the kids started coming. I spoke to two thousand that day, and many gave their hearts to Jesus.

We had nothing planned when we strolled into Samford University later in the week. Dr. R. G. Lee, the Baptist preacher of "Payday Someday" sermon fame, was scheduled to speak in chapel, so we went to hear him. He was ill and unable to be there, so the students were asked to share testimonies. The first kid who stood said, "Those guys we read about in the paper are here, the ones with the wheelbarrow full of Bibles. Let's let them tell us what they're doing."

I told of the revival in Monroe and of all that God had already done on the trip, and students began to confess sin. Many prayed to get right with God. Another student stood and moved that the students give us a hundred dollars for more Bibles. That more than replenished our supply.

The police stopped us at the border of Sweetwater, Alabama, and told us it was illegal to pass out tracts and that they wouldn't let us walk through their town. We had no room for the wheelbarrow in either car, so we didn't know what to do. A young boy we had been witnessing to told us he was the nephew of the mayor. "Let's go talk to my uncle," he said.

The police were already talking to the mayor when we got there. One of the councilmen told the mayor we were saying something the country needed to hear and that we should be allowed to continue. The mayor agreed.

We got about a mile down the road with our wheelbarrow when a squad car pulled up. "Hop in," a cop said. I started to tell him that the mayor said we could proceed, but he clearly wasn't in the mood. The policemen put the wheelbarrow in their trunk and drove us to the other side of the city.

They ordered us out of the car at the edge of a woods, and I remembered the young man's death vision. "Sir," I said, "we weren't trying to give you any hassle. We just want people to know the Lord. If you don't know Jesus—"

The cop interrupted: "I'm telling you, son, you'd better not ever show your face in this town again. Just start walking."

I said, "All right, sir, we'll do that. But we want you to know that Jesus loves you and that He died for you. And we love you too."

As we walked, I prayed, "Lord, You got us through Louisiana, Mississippi, and Alabama, and You've worked in marvelous ways. We don't know what lies ahead, but we know You're going to do something really great in Georgia." I was right.

There we were contacted by Murray Bradfield, a local youth director. I never dreamed that two years later Murray and I would be walking for Jesus, carrying a cross across Germany. Murray invited us to a rally at his church, but Ken and Richard and I felt led to a prayer room upstairs to seek the Lord. As the meeting started below we knelt and cried out to God for revival in America. Psalm 46:10 came to mind and I quoted it to the others:

> Be still, and know that I am God;
> I will be exalted among the nations,
> I will be exalted in the earth!

We stopped praying aloud. We waited, expecting the presence of God. On our knees and elbows, hands covering our eyes, we suddenly broke into uncontrollable sobs. I felt I was in the presence of Jesus, and I have never felt so unclean, so unworthy. I was broken. Each of us asked God for forgiveness for failing Him so often, and for cleansing and filling, despite our unworthiness. I can't speak for the other guys, but I was filled with peace and joy and power.

God chose to meet our needs in that room, so we expected great things in Atlanta. I'm convinced that none of the amazing things that were about to happen would have come about had we not waited upon God that evening.

I was scheduled to speak at the mammoth Rehoboth Baptist Church on Sunday, and the night before we held a youth service at the church. Several adults showed up also and talked us into going to Underground Atlanta, the big nightclub district beneath the city. Thousands crowded the streets, nightclubs, and shops. We set up Richard's drums and prayed, "Lord, here goes." When those drums echoed off the walls, people streamed out from everywhere. I started preaching, and the crowd was huge. People at the edges couldn't hear, so laymen preached to little clusters of their own. We blitzed the place with the gospel.

A few days later we arrived at the University of Georgia in Athens, where a rally was planned to memorialize the students killed by National Guard troops at Kent State. Two thousand students gathered, and someone tried to get me on the program. The leader said I could have a few minutes but said, "Don't mention the name of Christ. We also have a rabbi on the platform."

I said, "Well, then count me out. Jesus is what we're all about."

He finally consented, but as it turned out, neither I nor the rabbi got a chance to speak. Radicals stormed the platform and urged the students to take over the administration building, abruptly ending the memorial rally. As I stood watching the kids leave I could see the steeples of the surrounding churches of the community. We were in the Bible belt, but I wondered where the Christians were.

Thousands were involved in peace demonstrations the next day, but there were also twenty-five Christians marching in and out, passing out Jesus stickers and carrying posters that read, "Real Peace Is Jesus" and "Get Back to God."

I worked my way toward the platform, where a radical was shouting obscenities and calling for the destruction of city hall. I was talking about Jesus to the guys behind him when he suddenly turned and handed me the microphone, obviously thinking I was the next radical in line.

"Here we go again, Lord," I prayed.

"There has been a lot of talk about peace here," I began. The crowd cheered. "But let me tell you, there won't be any peace until we get the Prince of Peace, Jesus Christ, into our hearts!" Silence. As I continued I expected a brick or a tomato, but the students applauded. As TV cameras moved into position, I prayed silently, "Lord, here is a real opportunity to glorify You."

For the next ten minutes I preached Jesus and challenged the students to commit their lives to Him. I was often interrupted by applause, and God broke through to many of those radicals. The next speaker said, "Well, what *would* Jesus do if He were here?" The riot had turned into a revival. The guy who had asked me not to mention Jesus now asked me to pray there would be no more violence on campus. An hour later the whole demonstration had blown over.

That year the University of Georgia yearbook carried a picture of Tex and Connie holding a big sign, "Real Peace Is Jesus."

CHAPTER FIVE

LESSONS

As we slowly made our way from Georgia into South Carolina, our minds focused on Washington. It seemed as if we were almost there, but we had a long way to go and many lessons to learn first. One day Ken and I heard a huge trailer truck roar up behind us. The driver pointed at us and pulled onto the shoulder, barreling straight for us. At the last instant we realized it was no game. We took one quick step and hurled ourselves into the ditch, wheelbarrow, Bibles, and all. The truck missed us by inches and nearly tumbled into the ditch itself. We knelt right there and thanked God for sparing us.

Another day Little Richard and I were walking when someone drove by and fired a pistol out the window at us. There was no time to duck. I'll never know whether the the bullet was a blank or just missed us.

Another time Richard and I walked past a high-fenced kennel housing two German shepherds. A man came out and unlocked the gate, pointed at us, and said, "Get 'em!"

The dogs came bounding at us, snorting and growling. We froze, and I thought I was about to die. I pointed at the dogs and shouted at the top of my lungs, "I command you in the name of Jesus Christ to go back!" The dogs skidded to a stop and scampered back.

The owner shook his head and pointed at us again. "I said, 'Get 'em!' "

The dogs charged us again, and louder than before I shouted, "In the name of Jesus Christ, I command you to go back!" When they trotted back again, the man finally gave up. We walked on with rubbery legs. I have no idea whether that was a satanic attack or if my authoritative tone just intimidated the dogs, but I'm glad it worked anyway.

The greatest lesson God taught us was love for one another. That was tough on the road. Because we had to sleep in our clothes we were dirty and hot and tired and miserable. God provided money and food all along the way, but at one point we were down to just some Kool-Aid, peanut butter, and bread. At the end of a day of walking, when all you've had was a scoop of grits, you need more than half a peanut butter sandwich and a couple of swallows to drink for supper.

As I sat wearily trying to make that little sandwich last longer, I noticed another half cup or so of Kool-Aid in the pitcher. I thought, *I'll bet ole Ray wants that, and I'm not going to get it.* It sounds petty and ridiculous now, but at the time it seemed important. God had to teach me to die to myself daily. Other, even deeper, lessons were needed but wouldn't come for years. After four months and fifteen hundred miles, the day finally came when we could see the capital city across the bridge over the Potomac River. We praised God for the adventure. We'd had some rough times but most of all great, blessed times with the Lord. But our walk wasn't finished. Three black guys stopped us as we neared the city, and one pulled me off to the side. "I'm going to kill you," he said.

He pulled back to hit me, and I said, "Jesus loves you." His hand stopped. Something held him back.

"I hate you!" he snarled.

"Jesus loves you," I said.

"Don't tell me that!"

"Jesus loves you," I said again and again. He kept cocking his arm, but he never swung.

"Is Jesus white?"

"I don't know," I said. "I've never seen Him. The Bible says that those who worship Him must worship Him in spirit and in truth. I used to hate black people. I thought they were lower than whites. But when Jesus took over my life, He took away that prejudice and filled me with love. That's why I can tell you I love you."

His face softened. "You mean it?"

"I sure do."

"Honest?"

"I'm not just talking."

He stuck out his hand. "Man," he said, "you're okay."

"No, Jesus is okay. I'm rotten. Jesus changed me."

It was great to see Arthur again. He filled me in on all the plans for meetings and a march across the city with hundreds of Christians. Murray Bradfield met us there, and he and another friend and I decided to do some witnessing by car. At red lights we'd jump out and pass out tracts to everybody around, trying to get back to the car in time for the green light. We were having fun and sharing Christ at the same time. Once I didn't get back to the car in time. The traffic was terrible, so the guys couldn't wait. The way the streets were laid out, it would be a long time before they could get back to me. I was disoriented, but I didn't want to waste time. I trusted the Lord to lead me wherever He wanted me to go.

I walked fast, passing out Jesus stickers and tracts, witnessing as I went. After several minutes I came to a gate and a big, black iron fence. There, between the bars, was the White House. In my youthful idealism I wondered if the Lord might give me the opportunity to share Him with Princess Grace, who was visiting that day.

I knew that thousands of people peered through that fence every day, so I started pasting stickers on about every fourth bar. People gathered around to read, "Real Peace Is Jesus."

I had covered one end of the fence when two guards came running. "Hey, you! Come here!" They produced a knife. "You're going to take this and scrape off all those stickers, or we'll arrest you for defacing government property!"

"Yes, sir," I said. "Forgive me. I had no idea it was against the law."

The guard followed me to make sure I'd do it, and I got a good chance to witness to him. I scraped all the stickers from one end, and he asked, "Is that all?"

I said, "There's some on the other end too."

"I'll trust you to scrape them off," he said. "You're a good Christian."

Later I was ushered into the security office at the White House and asked what I had been doing. I told the guard I hadn't realized I was doing anything wrong. "I'm a Christian too," he told me. "We need more young people doing what you're doing."

While I waited to be interviewed by the top guy, the Christian guard showed me pictures they had taken of me outside the gate. They entered my driver's license number in a computer and ran an FBI check on me. While I waited, the guard kept directing me to people he knew who needed Christ. I witnessed to lots of people in there.

Still I felt stupid for having done something wrong, and I could feel the animosity from everybody except the Christian guard. The top security officer told me, "Tippit, if we can get you on anything, we will."

I apologized profusely, but I started thinking: *If this guy is in charge of security, he probably has access to the princess.*

"Sir," I said, "could you do me a favor? Could you have one of your men give the princess one of these?" I held out a tract.

"*What!?* Don't you say anything about the princess around here! You're not going to get near her!"

When my record came back clean, the top man said, "You can go, and you can hand out literature, but don't stop and talk to anyone. Understand?"

I promised, and they watched as I walked away. I handed a tract to two girls and kept walking, but the girls looked at it and came running back to me. *Oh, no!*

> **"I've been lying awake nights worrying about whether I'm going to heaven. Can I know for sure?"**

One of the girls said, "I've been lying awake nights worrying about whether I'm going to heaven. Can I know for sure?"

I talked without looking back. "Do you want to know Jesus?"

"Yes."

We knelt right there on the sidewalk in the shadows of the White House, and she and her friend prayed to receive Christ. I kept expecting someone to interrupt us, but no one did. I never looked back, but I do believe God sent me to the White House for that purpose.

On July 17, 1970, we were to have a big rally at the Washington Monument after marching to the Capitol and back. People flooded the area as we proclaimed to the nation's leaders that Jesus was the only hope.

About a thousand people gathered, and we had a great time. Afterward Arthur felt led to fast for forty days at the corners of Constitution and 15th Avenues, praying for revival in America. I'll never forget pushing that wheelbarrow as he carried a cross to the corner where he would spend the next six weeks of his life.

I spent a little time with him there, and usually there was a crowd during the day. At night things were pretty quiet. One evening as he dozed, I prayed that God would use me that very day to spark revival in America. The pay phone rang nearby. (Arthur had released the number to the local press.) The caller was a guy from Boston. He said he wanted a little more information on what we were doing. I told him and asked him if he was a Christian. He said he was Jewish. I told him Jesus was Jewish, and I shared with him the plan of salvation. I led him in a brief prayer of acceptance, and he asked me for the phone number again. I told him I'd send him some follow-up material so he could grow in the Lord.

A few minutes later the phone rang again. It was a girl from Pennsylvania. I couldn't believe how widely the number had gotten around. "I praise God for what you guys are doing," the girl said. "I just heard you on the radio, and—"

"The radio? No, you didn't hear me—"

"You weren't just on the radio?"

"No."

"You didn't just pray with a guy from Boston?"

"How did you know that?"

"He was a disc jockey and you were live on national radio!"

Several more people called that night, including a truck driver who was crying. "I heard you as I was driving through the mountains," he said. "I've been searching for God for two years." I led him to Christ over the phone.

I found out the next day that the deejay had not received Christ but repeated the prayer so his listeners could hear it. God had used him as an instrument to get His message to much of the nation.

God answered my prayer in a surprising and unique way.

CHAPTER SIX

GOD'S LOVE IN ACTION

God had been impressing on me that I should set up a headquarters and start a street ministry in Chicago. So after a week with Arthur in D.C. and a visit to my home in Baton Rouge, I named our ministry God's Love in Action and headed north on September 1, 1970.

The only person with us was a huge man named Roger McKim. We called him Bear. He had received Christ in Tulsa, where I had given my testimony at a rally. Despite a history of drugs, knifing, stealing, and even a hitch at Leavenworth, Bear wouldn't hurt a flea. He was truly a new creature.

Chicago reduced Bear to a scaredy-cat. He was even afraid to sleep alone and always wanted to drag his bed into our room. "I know what kind of people live here," he said. "Now that I'm a Christian I have to turn the other cheek instead of smashing them."

We were praying in a church one night with the lights off when Bear heard water dripping in the baptismal tank. "Sam, do you think that's the devil?"

It kept getting louder. "Sam, I'm sure that's the devil."

"No, Bear. It's just water."

When footsteps came down the aisle, Bear jumped up and

shouted, "Devil, I command you in the name of Jesus to get out of here!"

The lights went on, and it was the pastor!

We lived with some Moody Bible Institute students in a big house in Uptown, then Chicago's North Side ghetto. When the Moody kids returned to school that fall we were left renting the upstairs. With no steady income and only the knowledge that God wanted us to start a work in Chicago, we trusted Him to provide.

Our support came almost exclusively from individuals, and rarely from the same ones. A couple of Sunday school classes sent us about fifteen dollars a month each. We never asked for a penny, and that remains our policy to this day. I believe that income is a gauge of God's direction. If He wants us to do something, He'll provide for it without our begging. If He doesn't, that means He's not in it. We do include a return envelope with our newsletter, and gifts to our ministry are tax deductible, but we never ask for anything from anyone but God.

Response on the streets was discouraging. People didn't trust us. One girl said, "Why doesn't your Jesus get you some shoes?" We hadn't noticed that Northerners didn't run around city streets barefooted.

I had been spoiled by seeing God work in mighty ways in the South and in Washington, and now it was time for a lesson in patience and persistence. For the first time in my ministry I saw no results. I knew we were in God's will because He kept supplying our physical needs, but the lack of fruit was getting to me. If I'd ever had a problem with pride, it was cured in Chicago when I saw clearly that no one comes to Christ unless the Holy Spirit of God works in his life. Whether my effectiveness was hindered while I was getting acclimated to the North or it took a while for people to get used to a Southern preacher, I don't know. All I know is that while I was in that wilderness with no fruit, God was teaching me —yet again—that it is only He who draws people to Himself.

Finally, after three months of barrenness, Big Mike came to Jesus. Mike Logston said he came to Chicago from Oklahoma because the thieving was easier. The six-foot, four-inch, 280-pounder always carried a sawed-off shotgun. He ran into Bear one night in Old Town, and the next day he was a babe in Christ. Within twenty-four hours a runaway Jewish girl named Cindy gave her heart to Christ, and after that God seemed to pour out His blessing.

We started a Monday night Bible study class, but the first time Tex and I were the only ones there. Neither of our new converts could make it, and Bear had been called home. His wife, who had left him the year before, had gotten right with God and wanted him back. We were happy for him, but now it was the two of us against the city with no choice but to turn to God for everything. We worked with several area youth pastors and their kids, I spoke throughout Chicago, and we kept holding our Bible studies no matter how many people showed up. Within a few months we filled our attic with seekers every week.

We brought on four other full-timers who knew that we didn't pay salaries as such. I helped finance the operation with speaking engagements, and people who knew what we were all about sent a little support. Mostly we all lived in that big old house, witnessing, teaching, speaking, and trusting the Lord to provide for our needs.

The big daily papers in Chicago became aware of us and called us the originators of the Jesus Movement in Chicago. We were often referred to as Jesus Freaks or Jesus People. There were parts of the movement we didn't want to be associated with, but we never said so publicly. We weren't into the fads. We were really just old-fashioned Christians.

Within a half year our Bible studies averaged sixty kids each week, and by July of 1971 we saw six hundred kids in four weeks. We simply studied, sang, and prayed, but the new Christians were hungry to learn about and worship Jesus.

As I preached in a church one Sunday on how God had promised Abraham a son, I had trouble keeping my train of thought. God was trying to tell me something. As I tried to tell the people that they should trust God in the same way Abraham did, God was trying to tell me that I would have a son and that he would be used of God in a mighty way.

I didn't necessarily prefer a son, but there was no doubt in my mind that God had promised me one. Tex was skeptical. Neither of us knew she was already pregnant. When we found she was, we prayed about a name. No names for girls even entered our minds. Slowly Tex came to be convinced, but she wasn't too excited about my announcing it before 2,000 people at a city-wide crusade in East St. Louis, Illinois.

That summer Arthur came to Chicago, and we held a giant rally in the Civic Center Plaza. More than a thousand people gathered and many turned from drugs and alcohol to give their lives to Jesus Christ. Our Bible studies grew, and we saw more and more results on the streets. When the famous acid rock group Sly and the Family Stone played for about ten thousand kids at Northwestern University in Evanston, we went to share Christ. It was wild. Kids lay naked on the beach, and drugs were passed around openly.

We passed out little red stickers that read "One Way, Trust Jesus," and carried our name and address. We called them reds, the word for downers in the drug culture. When one of our guys stood in the middle of the crowd and yelled, "Free reds!" you should have seen kids flock around him.

A lot of people thought we were fanatics when we painted "Jesus Loves You" in our upstairs window. One girl is glad we did. She stopped in one day to tell me she had run away from her home in Washington, D.C. "I thought I would find out what was happening if I came to Chicago, but I've already been raped, and now I'm addicted to drugs. I saw your sign and felt like Jesus touched me."

I asked her if she wanted to give her heart to Christ and get her sins forgiven and her life changed. She prayed with me, then we contacted her family and arranged for her to return home. She believes God led her down our street that day. So do I.

> **Tex and I heard that there was a huge contingent of Satan worshipers in Chicago, and we knew if we were serious about doing battle with the enemy, we would have to confront them head-on.**

Tex and I heard that there was a huge contingent of Satan worshipers in Chicago, and we knew if we were serious about doing battle with the enemy, we would have to confront them head-on. We stopped at their coffeehouse to share Christ with one of their leaders. He was not receptive. He said, "Tippit, I have more power in my little finger than all the Christians in Chicago."

That line must have intimidated other people and left them

speechless because he looked surprised when I said, "I challenge you on that."

"What do you mean?"

"I challenge you to prove that." He didn't know what to say. Tex and I left, praying that God would remove the power of Satan from the neighborhood. The next night there was no satanic literature being distributed, and the leader was nowhere to be found. One month later that coffeehouse burned to the ground (and we had nothing to do with it!). Praise God we worship the victorious Christ.

In the nightclub district, centered around Rush Street, we met many people who weren't true nightclubbers. They were lonely people—people who walked the streets and went into clubs to find something, any kind of peace or love or happiness. The nightclub owners didn't appreciate our coming around. One night I got a phone call from an owner who refused to give his name. "I don't want to see you down here anymore," he said.

"Well, sir," I said, "we're not doing anything but talking to people, and only if they want to talk. We're not going inside your club; we're staying on the sidewalk."

"People don't want to hear about your religion, and you're hurting our business. People come down here to have a good time, so stay away."

"I'm not trying to be obnoxious, sir, but God has told us to go where the people are. There are people down there who need the ministry God has given us."

"You come down here and I'm telling you I'll have you thrown in jail." That ended the conversation, but it didn't end the trouble.

Our most serious hassle came from My Place, a club just off Rush on Delaware Street. Arthur Blessitt's ministry on the Sunset Strip was called His Place, and the coffeehouse ministry in Monroe, Louisiana, was called Your Place. How appropriate that this ungodly establishment was called My Place.

The doorman there, LeRoy, tried to intimidate one of our full-time guys one night. He said he had rumbled in Chicago and was used to knifing people. "I wouldn't mind cutting you guys up if you keep coming down here."

On September 1, 1971 (a year to the day since we arrived in

Chicago), I returned from a week of meetings in Florida. I was excited to see Tex, but I could tell immediately that something was wrong. She was eight months pregnant and didn't need any more stress. "What's up?" I asked,

She told me that two of our high school volunteers had been arrested for witnessing. They had been hustled into a paddy wagon by two plainclothes detectives, just before Tex had come to get me. They had been charged with disorderly conduct. I couldn't believe it and worried about the future of our ministry. I believed we had been called to share Jesus in that area, and we weren't going to be intimidated. Friday, September 3, my associate Lloyd Cole and I went down to witness on Delaware Street. We weren't looking for trouble, but the same thing happened to us. The first person I handed a tract to was a plainclothesman. "I'm sorry," he said, "but you aren't going to be able to do this here tonight. It's not legal."

"Sir," I said, "if we're doing something wrong, we'll leave. I believe in obeying the law. What are we doing wrong?"

"I'm telling you, you'll have to leave."

"If this is illegal, I'll leave."

He pulled me off to the side. "Listen, I'll tell you what you're doing wrong. You're taking food out of a baby's mouth. The man who owns this place supports his family by providing entertainment and selling alcohol. Do you think it's right to deprive a man of his job?"

"I believe that if a man seeks God's will in his life, God will provide him with a better job. If we have revival in America, a lot of nightclub owners will be out of work."

"Well, you're hurting this man and a lot of other people down here."

"That's your opinion," I said, not unkindly. "There are pushers and prostitutes on these streets, and we certainly aren't doing anything illegal like they are. We're offering something positive, and they're ruining people's lives. We're just sharing Christ with lonely people."

"Why don't you do this downtown?"

"If it's wrong here, why wouldn't it be wrong there?"

He glared at me. "If you don't leave, we'll get something on you."

I believe God let me know we were doing the right thing when the next person I talked to received Christ. He knelt right there on the sidewalk and prayed with me. Then I noticed LeRoy, the doorman, emerge from My Place and produce a knife from his pocket.

I moved quickly up the sidewalk, staying as close to the street as possible. LeRoy approached and flipped open the blade. I decided that if he attacked me I would drop to my knees and pray. I wasn't prepared to defend myself against a knife. I broke into a jog, and LeRoy didn't follow. Lloyd and I kept witnessing up the street, keeping an eye out for LeRoy. I saw the two plainclothesmen come out of My Place, and assumed I should tell them about LeRoy.

"Could I talk with you a minute?" I asked,

"We have nothing to talk to you about. You're the one who's doing everything right."

"Someone pulled a weapon on me."

"A weapon," one said loud enough so LeRoy could hear. "Where? What did it look like?"

I pointed at LeRoy, who hurried into the alley next to the club. One of the cops brought him to the front of the club before searching him, and when he found no knife he accused us of trying to cause trouble. "No, sir, we're not," I said. "We feel our rights are being infringed upon. We just want to speak freely for Christ." I couldn't back down now.

"You've got five minutes to get off the street."

"Why? You haven't told me what we're doing wrong."

"I'll give you a law. Loitering."

"We can't get them on that," the other policeman said. "They're not loitering."

They argued between themselves, one suggesting disorderly conduct, the other littering. One turned to me. "Don't worry, son, we'll get you on something."

"But why? You still haven't told me what we're doing wrong."

"All right, you're under arrest."

"Sir, we don't have to go through all this."

"Just shut up. I don't want to hear any more."

We got to the station near the corner of Chicago Avenue and LaSalle a little after 10 P.M. The plainclothesman encouraged the booking officer to let us keep our Bibles and tracts. I was confused. His attitude seemed to have changed. "Sir," I said, "do you know that Jesus really loves you?"

"Yeah, I know. For God so loved the world and all that."

"Do you know Jesus?"

"I wouldn't exactly call myself a Christian."

"Jesus could come into your heart."

"I know. You fellas go ahead and make your phone call."

Tex almost cried when I called her. We would have to wait in a cell until someone came from our headquarters with the bail money. And despite the attempt of the arresting officer, we were not allowed to take our stuff into the jail with us. We were led down a gray corridor with cells on either side. The noise and the stench were terrible. Drunks slept on the floor in one. Blacks and whites were separated in the others. Prisoners yelled at each other.

Lloyd and I were put in an empty cell at one end, out of the range of vision of the other prisoners. We sat on either end of a steel slab and looked at each other. "I can't believe it," I said. "Before I got saved I never went to jail. All the testimonies I ever heard went the other way." Neither of us laughed.

We prayed and God filled our hearts with peace. We were reminded of Philippians 4:6-7: "Be anxious for nothing, but in everything by prayer and supplication, with thanksgiving, let your requests be made known unto God; and the peace of God, which surpasses all understanding, will guard your hearts and minds through Christ Jesus."

There were people in there who needed Jesus. First we sang. Then we shouted our testimonies. Things were quiet for a few seconds, but when the prisoners heard what we were doing, they banged on the bars and hollered for us to shut up.

We testified to the power of God to change lives. The men would get noisy and then quiet and then get noisy again. After about fifteen minutes of sticking with it, we noticed that the noise had all but subsided. From the other end of the cell block a voice called out, "Hey, are you a preacher?"

"Yes, sir, I am."

"What're you doing in jail?"

I told him, and that seemed to give us a common bond. A man in the cell next to us said, "You talk about peace, man. I've been searchin' for peace for six years."

I couldn't see him, but I knew he was just inches away, listening as I talked about Jesus. I told Lloyd I wished I had a tract to give him. Lloyd fished in his back pocket and beamed. One had been overlooked when he was frisked. He reached through the bars to try to hand the man the tract, but it slipped from his fingers and floated to the floor. Lloyd stabbed at it with his comb and carefully slid it as far as he could toward the other cell. Finally the man could reach it. The whole place was quiet as we waited for the man's reaction.

After several minutes I asked, "What's happening, brother?"

"This says a lot," he whispered. "I want to know God."

"Are you willing to pray with us right here?"

"Yes."

"Even in front of all these guys?"

"Yes."

We prayed for him, and then he prayed. He admitted that he was a sinner, and he thanked Jesus for dying for him. Then he invited Christ into his life. We told him that when he got out of jail he should look us up so we could help him. "I'm gonna be in here a long time," he said. "I cut up a guy and they found the knife on me." But still, he had been saved, and Lloyd was bubbling over. He told me it was near midnight and we were reminded of how Paul and Silas saw a man come to Jesus in prison at midnight.

"Sammy, let's lead these guys in singing with us," Lloyd said.

"This isn't a church crowd, Lloyd. These are bad people. You're not going to get them to sing."

"Let me try," he said. "Y'all know 'Amazing Grace'? [It was on the pop charts at the time.] We'll sing and you follow!"

I can hardly carry a tune and Lloyd wasn't much better, but we started singing and sure enough the men knew the song. It was an indescribable thrill. Here were these criminals, none of them real singers, growling and mumbling along, off-key and sour, but enjoying singing "Amazing Grace." It was a sweet, discordant sound. When we finished I preached on Acts 16 and told the men how they could have peace with God even in jail.

When one of our guys showed up from headquarters with the bail money, we left, grateful for the opportunity to preach at midnight. It was a relief to both Tex and me to be reunited, but now we had the future to worry about. We had seen four staff members arrested in three days. If nothing else, we were running short of money to bail ourselves out.

CHAPTER SEVEN

AT A CROSSROADS

I t didn't take long to realize how far-reaching those arrests could be. Not only were we being denied our right to freedom of speech, but all the other ministries that witnessed on the streets would be in trouble too. I thought of the Open Air Campaigners, the Salvation Army, and the countless dedicated individuals who shared Christ on their own. Our entire ministry, outside my preaching, was on the street.

My heart broke as I thought of the trouble that lay ahead. How could we be denied the right to share Christ, especially when we were careful to never force anything on anyone? As we poured our hearts out to God, pleading for an answer, I began to get the distinct feeling that I should fashion a huge wooden cross and take it to the civic center, where I would fast and pray until our trial. Immediately I tried to tell myself this wasn't of God, but I couldn't shake it. "Lord," I argued, "I believe You promised me a boy, and he's due this month. I have to be with Tex. I can't leave her now."

I felt God telling me, "Sammy, you must." I knew deep in my heart I had to do it. How I longed for my son to grow up in a country where he had the freedom to share Christ anywhere. I promised my obedience. In the wee hours one morning, another staff member and I found some lumber in the garage and fashioned a crude eight-foot cross.

Tex was with me all the way. The next morning she knelt with me near the cross as the staff put their hands on our shoulders and prayed for us. The burden welled up anew inside me and tears came. A long month lay ahead.

I called the newspapers that had done stories on us in the past, and the word spread quickly throughout the media. Surrounded by members of the print and broadcast media at the civic center, I explained what I was doing. We received tremendous response from all over. The Wheaton (Illinois) Bible Church held a twenty-four-hour prayer vigil for us, which was characteristic of many reports we received. Petitions flooded the mayor's office. One afternoon I vainly tried to see him, but an aide said, "We know who you are. You're the one responsible for all these petitions."

We received calls from dozens of lawyers who must have figured our case would be a bandwagon of publicity. The more I prayed about it the more convinced I became that God wanted us to have a Christian lawyer. We waited for the right man. Meanwhile, our civic center ministry was in full swing.

As I sat on a bench near the cross one day a girl sat down a few feet away. I looked up from reading my Bible and felt led to take a direct approach. "Hey," I said, trying to be pleasant, "do you know Jesus?"

"No, and I don't want to talk about it."

I never press the subject. I figure if a person doesn't want to talk or listen after I've opened the conversation, I have no right to continue. I went back to my reading, but after a few minutes the girl turned to me in tears. "I need help," she whimpered. She had run away from her home in the suburbs and said she had messed up her life. In fact, the police were looking for her.

"Jesus promised to give you abundant life," I said. I told her the testimonies of other runaways I had known and how God had saved them. "They still have the same problems they had before they came to Christ, but Jesus has given them the strength to face them." Eventually I asked her if she would like to know Christ, and we prayed right there.

I told the staff members and the winos in the area what had happened and asked if they could donate a little money toward getting the girl home. Several of the drunks, who themselves had been panhandling, gave a few cents each, and we raised enough money to get the girl back to the suburbs. A few weeks later the girl's mother called to tell me that her daughter had been truly changed and thanked me for sharing the claims of Christ with her.

The vigil and fast quickly became one of the most beautiful physical and spiritual experiences I'd ever had. Subsisting only on liquids, I lost twenty-five pounds and felt as if I was in the presence of Jesus most of the time. Once, however, I lost my temper. Several well-meaning Christians often joined us to help witness. One such man from a large church in northern Indiana stood around hassling blacks. I had enough trouble winning the confidence of blacks without this professing believer doing that. Finally I leaped from the bench and grabbed him by the shoulders. I stuck my face close to his. "Listen here!" I said. "You need to get right with God! You need to let Jesus take that hate and prejudice out of your heart and fill you with love!" I let go and he hurried off, obviously shaken.

When he came back a few minutes later I apologized. "I still think you need to get right with God on this," I said, "but I shouldn't have reacted the way I did."

Murray Bradfield joined me at the cross one night when the winos were out in full force. I'd had many opportunities to witness to them, but it was often chaotic when several were around. This night was no exception. A huge, muscular drunk staggered up, fighting mad. He broke a bottle and stumbled around with the jagged neck in his hand, looking to cut somebody's throat. Everybody kept out of his way until he threw the bottle away. Then he grabbed Murray's hair in one hand and mine in the other and smacked our heads together several times, screaming that he wanted to kill us. We just kept shouting, "Jesus loves you, brother!" When he finally let go we dropped to our knees and prayed for peace in the midst of confusion.

One night about nine o'clock I heard cheering and shouting in the distance. Suddenly a group of sixty or seventy students from Moody, Wheaton College, Judson College, and local churches came around the corner. They carried posters and shouted Christian slogans. We had a great time of fellowship and prayer together. Ironically, they had marched down the sidewalks on Rush Street without any problems. Two of us at opposite ends of the sidewalk were arrested for blocking pedestrian traffic where now more than sixty of them walked, some spilling into the street.

The day finally came that I received word from Moody Bible Institute that my case had been discussed at a meeting of the Christian Legal Society. They gave me the names of several Christian lawyers, a real answer to prayer—especially since I had been contacted by the American Civil Liberties Union. The ACLU believed in free speech all right, but they were so identified with the help they'd given to radical groups that I didn't want anyone to think we were associated with them. From the list the Christian Legal Society provided I called George Newitt, who had offices near the civic center.

I was impressed with him right off the bat. Most of the lawyers who approached me were slick talkers and pseudo big shots. Newitt sounded sincerely interested. I told him we were just genuine Christians who weren't out to cause trouble. "We just want our freedom to share Christ."

After meeting with Lloyd and me, Mr. Newitt became excited about the case. He took it on at no charge, which was the only way we could do it. God was providing for our needs, though we now had ten full time staffers living with us, and we tried to pay according to their needs. Even with that our total salaries for eleven people were less than $600 a month, and we had postage, literature, and food bills besides. Our staffers really gave of themselves.

We planned a rally at the civic center for noon on Saturday, September 25, 1971, four days before the trial. We spread the news by word of mouth, not wanting to tell the media until that day. That morning it rained for hours with no break in sight. When the noon chimes rang in a church steeple across from the center, the rain stopped and I praised God. About a thousand showed up for the rally.

Tex was past due about a week, and as I continued to pray for her it entered my mind that our son might be born the day I went to trial. I churned inside, and I'd have to say that if the same situation faced me today, I'd probably insist on my lawyer seeking a continuance. But back then my choice had been to spend a lot of time away from my very pregnant wife, and Wednesday morning I awoke at the civic center with tremendous anticipation. I knew this would be the most important day of my life.

Tex was in labor when I got to the house. By the time I left for court she was being taken to the hospital. I worried most about whether I'd be free in time to be with Tex in the hospital. My first stop was at Moody Bible Institute, where Lloyd Cole and I were interviewed on the radio. Then we went to the office of a local Christian artist who had offered his place for a pre-trial prayer meeting. About 150 friends joined us there, and a hundred more joined us a few blocks away at the little precinct courthouse. It was wall-to-wall people, many of whom I had never even seen before.

After the usual hearings over prostitutes and drunks—which broke my heart because it was clear these people were merely being processed without being helped—it was finally the City of Chicago vs. Tippit and Cole. A million things raced through my mind as I followed Mr. Newitt to the front.

He started boldly, referring to the charges as spurious. When the judge refused to dismiss the case, Mr. Newitt insisted on a jury trial. The judge was unimpressed.

"Counselor, your clients are not entitled to a jury trial."

"Why not, Your Honor? These boys' constitutional rights have been violated."

The judge countered with: "In this state a misdemeanor would not require sentencing to a penitentiary and is thus not afforded a jury trial."

Newitt was shocked. "Your Honor, this is fundamental! Are you telling me I can't have a jury trial on a question as vital as this? The Constitution sets forth certain rights as inalienable. If Illinois law takes away this man's right to free speech and to exercise his religious prerogatives, then that law cannot stand."

The crowd seemed about to cheer, and the judge appeared taken aback. He reserved judgment until he could consult with the city attorney. We left immediately, and Mr. Newitt checked with his office to reaffirm his position. Then he was surrounded by news microphones. "I felt like the president," he said.

The city attorney agreed we had the right to a jury trial, and when the judge set the date for October 13, everything went up for grabs. Mr. Newitt, Lloyd, and I were surrounded by the press. One reporter asked if I had heard any news from my wife, and suddenly all the emotion of the past month washed over me and I broke down. I wept as I announced I was on my way to the hospital.

"Sammy!" a voice yelled from the crowd, "you're a father!

You've got an eight-pound baby boy!" Then the questions really started flying. I was drained.

I hurried to the hospital and asked where I could find my wife and baby, only to find that Tex was still in labor! I didn't know if the person I heard at the impromptu press conference was a prankster, a prophet, or just wishful.

> **For the first time in months my faith wavered. "Lord," I prayed, "what if I'm wrong?"**

I spent several hours with Tex, praying for her as she endured the contractions. The experience drew us closer, and I appreciated her more than ever. When I took a break to get something to eat, I picked up a copy of the *Chicago Tribune* and noticed our story on the front page. It told of my going to trial and becoming a father the same day, and it even carried the name of my son, Paul David. The only problem was, I didn't have a son yet, and for the first time in months my faith wavered.

"Lord," I prayed, "what if I'm wrong?"

Then I felt ashamed. "Lord, I believe you promised me a son, and I'm still claiming it." Tex's labor was prolonged and suddenly it was getting late. I was scheduled for a TV interview at eleven. Gail Cole, Lloyd's wife, would be there with Tex, but I didn't want to leave her. Tex talked me into it. "You can tell a lot of people about Jesus tonight," she said.

When I left she was in deep labor. I knew it wouldn't be long. It was hard to concentrate, and at a break in the show at 11:30 I took a call from the doctor. "I wanted you to be the first to know," he said. "You have a healthy baby boy, a little over eight pounds."

A fantastic day of emotional strain ended for Tex and me, and soon we just held each other and cried. I finally got to see the son God had promised us. It was a sweet, unforgettable day.

The two weeks between September 29 and October 13 were long and busy. Mr. Newitt prepared the pretrial brief as if it were a federal case. He called the lawyer on the other side and warned, "If you go to trial, you are going to lose. The city of Chicago and the police department are going to have a black eye. People are going to get the impression that all your policemen do is knock people off the streets when they are passing out gospel tracts. There's been a lot of publicity on this case, and there's going to be a lot more. The best thing that could possibly happen to the city would be for you to let this case be dismissed and slink off into the background."

Mr. Newitt also told him that he contemplated filing a counter suit in federal court for the violation of our civil rights to free speech and the exercise of our religion. The case had become a personal matter to our lawyer.

When the case was called and the judge asked if the prosecution was ready, the city attorney requested a continuance of an hour to meet with the defense. Newitt knew then that they were ready to quit. When you're confident, you answer, "Ready, Your Honor," he explained. When you ask for time, you're in trouble.

We went into the office of the chief enforcement attorney for the city. He was a tough, cocky guy who wound up conducting a mini-trial of his own and then lectured all involved. Mr. Newitt knew all along that he was just trying to save face, but he got to me. While interrogating me he insinuated that I wouldn't know the difference between a knife and fingernail clippers. Then he asked why I didn't simply sock LeRoy in the nose if he was hassling me. "You don't understand how we live around here."

I was insulted. He was trying to make me look like a hillbilly who'd found himself over his head in the big city. "Sir," I said, nearly in tears, "if you think I'm lying, then let's just go ahead to court." I didn't want the charges dropped. I wanted the freedom to witness on the streets.

Newitt motioned me close and whispered, "Now knock it off. We're going to get out of this all right. We've got them over a barrel and they're giving up."

"Well, I'd rather go to trial and prove I'm innocent."

Newitt insisted there was no need to go to trial to win. In the end we agreed not to file a federal suit against the officer, and the city agreed to drop the charges against us. I didn't know if we really had gained our freedom or just played a little game with them. I didn't realize how big a victory we had won until we were threatened again a couple of weeks later. I went to the district commander and told him we'd been threatened by a nightclub owner again.

"Don't worry, Tippit," he told me. "None of my men will arrest you boys when you're out there telling people about Christ. If more young people were doing that I wouldn't have half the problems I have today."

George Newitt felt good about the outcome. He told us: "We gave the city a whipping. The personal satisfaction I received from defending the rights of Christians to share their faith without intimidation will last much longer than any payment I could have received."

CHAPTER EIGHT

HEADING EAST

I t was good to get back to the Uptown streets and re-establish friendships with kids who had come to Christ through our ministry. Our Bible studies were booming, but somehow I still felt drawn to minister behind the Iron Curtain.

When Arthur Blessitt visited Chicago for a rally that summer, I planned to train counselors at a college in the northern suburbs. No one showed up for the training, but as I waited alone I noticed that the only thing in the room was a map of the world. I knelt and prayed that God would lay a deep impression on my heart if He had some sort of an international ministry for me. "I'll do anything to further Your Kingdom," I prayed.

I felt I needed to talk to Arthur about it, but I was afraid his advice would be to stay in Chicago. I would have done that if I thought it was God's will, but the idea that God wanted me to someday preach in Eastern Europe had led me to sign up for Russian language courses in college. Each time the courses had filled, and I was bumped into German classes. I didn't want German, so I dropped each course, wondering why God wasn't opening the door for me to learn Russian. I would soon find out.

Hurrying to consult with Arthur at the Holiday Inn in Home-wood, Illinois, I got off the interstate at the wrong place and drove around looking for the way back on. I found a Holiday Inn and asked if they could direct me to the one in Homewood. "I need to talk to my friend, Arthur Blessitt."

"Blessitt? He's not in Homewood. He's here."

God had led me directly to him. "Lord," I prayed, "speak to me through Arthur."

Proving my fears unfounded, Arthur was excited. "If that's what God is telling you to do," he said, "you'd better do it." We prayed about it, but there was no time to plan an overseas trek while the vigil and the trial were on. Once everything had blown over, my world burden began anew.

Murray Bradfield and I often stayed up until the wee hours praying that God would show us distinctly what He wanted us to do. One morning at three o'clock we were on our knees in my little office when we felt impressed that God wanted us to walk across Germany for Him. God tried to prepare me by having me take German in college, but I didn't listen.

As we got down to the details, we saw that God would have to help us overcome three major obstacles: first, we needed twenty-five hundred dollars for transportation alone; second, we knew no one in Germany; third, though Murray took a year of German in college, neither of us could speak the language. My dream was to hold a prayer and fasting vigil and rallies in Berlin to call all of Europe back to God. Without contacts or an interpreter, prospects looked dim.

We felt led to go in December of 1971, which didn't give us much time. "Lord," we prayed, "we have to know. If You want us to go we should be getting our passports and reserving our flights. We need twenty-five hundred dollars."

As he prayed God touched his heart and he felt led to come and give us a check. He had no idea what our financial need was, but God did.

That very day a man came to the house and identified himself as a school teacher. He said he had saved money for years, but that morning as he prayed God touched his heart and he felt led to come and give us a check. He had no idea what our financial need was, but God did. The man handed us a check for twenty-five hundred dollars, and what a blessed time we had, sharing with him how we had prayed for that amount.

We left for Germany November 28, 1971, and one of the great surprises of my life came at the Frankfurt airport as we waited for a flight to Munich.

"Sammy Tippit? Sammy Tippit?" The accent was German, but I knew no one in Frankfurt. "Sammy Tippit?" I heard again. For sure that's what the stranger was saying. He was a well-dressed man in his late twenties, and he was smiling at me. "Are you Sammy Tippit?"

"Well, yes, I am," I said, rattled.

"My name is Volkhard Spitzer."

I was still nearly speechless as I shook his hand.

"I've heard of you and read about your trouble," he said. "Our church in Berlin has been praying for you since your arrest."

"How did you know me?" I finally managed.

"You looked American, and when the girl [Tex] said 'Sammy' in an American accent, I wondered if you could be Sammy Tippit." I told him we had been praying for a contact in Berlin. "Don't worry about that," he said. "I'll arrange a rally for you, and we'll have several thousand there."

God miraculously directed Volkhard and me together. He had been on a nonstop flight from Berlin to Munich but was rerouted through Frankfurt. Now we were scheduled on the same flight to Munich, so we spent the entire time planning for the Berlin rally. Volkhard's church was large and nationally known for its youth outreach. I was grateful for his involvement as soon as we got off the plane in Munich. The press was waiting for us, and with Volkhard interpreting I was able to share both our faith and our burden for Europe.

Our first personal contact with the Germans came at the University of Munich when Murray and I went there to witness. I was scared, praying that God would give me the words and help me understand the German students. The Marxist party was in control of student government, and the communist leaders of the country were pictured on the walls in the student union. It was an eye-opener for me.

Two of several guys I witnessed to prayed to receive Christ. They understood only a little English, so it was my quoting of Scripture in German that made the difference. They soon got involved in a Bible study group on campus and began to grow spiritually.

As we were leaving the university I stopped to talk to a girl. I handed her a sticker that read "Real Peace Is Jesus."

"*Nicht Jesus,*" she said. "*Zondern Marx.*"

I knew only a little German, but God gave me the words. "*Marx ist tot,*" I said. "*Jesus lebt noch.* [Marx is dead. Jesus still lives.]" The Word of God pierced her heart and her face fell. Later I thought about the importance of the words God had given me, and they became the keystone of our ministry there.

Our walk across Germany took us from Augsburg to Kassel through Stuttgart, Frankfurt, and Giessen. The first night of the walk was the first time I ever preached with an interpreter; I was nervous and couldn't sleep the night before. The meeting was to be held at the Augsburg Evangelical Free Church, where we were warned to not be too loud or get too excited or give an invitation. We were informed that the typical German was sophisticated, intellectual, and formal. I prayed for wisdom.

An hour before the meeting the place was packed, yet people kept coming. It was people on top of people. I'm sure many were just curious about these American Jesus People, and that much of the crowd could be attributed to Volkhard arranging the meetings, but mostly we credited the work of the Holy Spirit. We believed God was moving upon the continent.

As I preached I had little idea of how the people received my message until I came to a sentence that stumped the interpreter. When he paused, several men on the edges of their seats blurted the translation so I could continue. Despite the language barrier, that made it clear to me that they were with me and God was helping me communicate. That night about thirty young people responded to the claims of Jesus Christ. They weren't emotional. They talked to God as a friend. They confessed sin and repented. It was refreshing to see such honesty, though it was a new experience for me to see people take such a sober, intellectual approach to God.

The next morning I spoke to the entire student body of the local high school. I preached on what Christ could do for a young person, and concluded, "If you would like to turn from your sin and give your heart to Jesus, I'd like to meet with you right now in this corner."

To my amazement, more than half the students rose and started for the corner. "Wait," I said. "Let me explain." I went through all that it meant to be a Christian, that it was no trendy, faddish thing. I explained that it meant sacrifice and discipline and dedication. Again more than half started to move. "Okay," I said, "I'll have to talk to you right where you are."

Until then we had noticed little conviction of sin in Germany. Promiscuous sex was widespread among young people, and they seemed to have no second thoughts. But now, as I explained the forgiving power of God, kids asked, "Is this wrong? Is that wrong?" It was hard to leave as kids swarmed us with question after question about the Christian life. Those kids were starving for the Word of God.

The trip continued through one outpouring of God's power after another: through Fellbach where, before we ate, each stood and turned to the one next to him and said, "I love you in Jesus Christ, and may God's blessings be upon you"; through Mannheim, where with little publicity nearly fifty kids committed their lives to Christ; through Neu Isenburg where a plot by the communists to take over the service was turned into a great outpouring of the Spirit; through Giessen where God taught us that one conversion could result in a Bible study that would average sixty kids each morning.

In Neu Isenburg we were confronted by a group of students from the University of Frankfurt who were obviously well-organized. Our singing group was ministering to one of our largest crowds and then Murray was to give his testimony and I would preach. But a group of communist students drowned out our P.A. system by shouting, "We want discussion! We want discussion!"

When Murray stepped up to speak, the chanting grew louder and he could not be heard. He looked directly at the communists and spoke quietly. If they expected him to get into a shouting match with them, they were disappointed. He said, just above a whisper, *"Jesus liebt dich.* [Jesus loves you.]"

They fell silent, but when he finished speaking and the music began again, so did the chanting. "Power to the people! We want discussion!"

When the interpreter and I stepped to the microphone, the noise was deafening. A member of our singing group and two Christian soldiers quickly moved into the midst of the communists and knelt to pray. By the time the communists decided what to do, I had gained the attention of the rest of the crowd.

About a dozen received Christ that night, and when I returned to the auditorium from the prayer room the crowd had remained and was in an uproar. To an American who thinks his country has wide open political debate, this was a shock. The news media were there, and everyone seemed to be demanding debate. I don't generally allow debate of the gospel in my meetings; in America that would have wound up in endless, nit-picking discussion.

But this was a different atmosphere. This crowd was likely to come up with very direct, answerable questions, if God would give me His wisdom. I silently prayed for that as I said, "All right. We'll have debate, but we'll also have order. If there is disorder, we quit."

I had never studied dialectical materialism or even communism much, but God made me sensitive to their arguments and allowed me to see past the words to the real problems. I was wearing a vest with *Jesus Loves You* sewn on the back, and one of the first questions was about that. "I'll bet you supported a big, capitalist company when you bought that vest!"

"No," I said. "My wife made this because we wanted to share what we had with others." Much of the crowd, even some of the communists, applauded.

"Are there white churches in America that won't allow blacks in?"

"There may be," I said, "but not my church. A few years ago I hated blacks, but when I met Jesus He replaced that hatred with love. If you want to bring the races together, the love of God will do it."

For several minutes, questions were hurled, and I felt God gave me answers for each. The crowd applauded each answer, seeming to befuddle the communists. An American pastor later told the European Baptist Press that it was the greatest outpouring of the Spirit he had seen in his years of ministry.

God provided a rickety, old van that we nicknamed Aby Baby, for Abraham, an Old Testament model of stepping out in faith. We thanked God daily for that van, frustrating as it was. The only way we could start it was to push it and pop the clutch. It was hilarious when it stalled in traffic. We'd all jump out and off we'd go, running and pushing with Aby Baby spitting and popping and rattling and shaking.

Tex and Davey and I took a train toward Berlin. When the train developed a problem with its heating system we had to wrap Davey in everything we could find. The only times my faith was really tested was when I started having second thoughts about dragging my loved ones on an excursion like that—which was often. As the train moved from West Germany to East Germany, border guards checked our passports and luggage. We prayed that the rest of the staff—and Aby Baby—would make it.

Aby Baby must have looked a sight! On top of that old rattletrap was an eight-foot cross, a lantern, and a worn spare tire. We prayed the guards wouldn't find the suitcase full of Bibles and tracts. Some vehicles were searched for hours at the border.

Murray told us later that everyone had been ordered out of the van for the search. The guards could hardly stand the stench from the sleeping bags the others and I had used every night after walking all day. So they hurried through their search. Murray says they popped open his suitcase first, and when they got a whiff of his undershirts they scrambled out with an "Okay, go on."

It was good to reunite with Volkhard Spitzer. We set up our prayer and fasting vigil in downtown Berlin at the Wilhelm War Memorial Church. We witnessed beneath the cross, and many German Christians joined us. We had many opportunities to share Christ there and at our nightly rallies.

The day finally came that God opened the door for Murray and Debbie and Tex and Davey and me to go behind the Iron Curtain. Lynn Nowicki, a young American Christian guy studying in West Berlin, was going to visit some of the underground Christians I'd read so much about. By law, no home could entertain more than three people at a time unless it was an announced birthday party. With our guide there were six of us, so we went two by two. I'll never forget the first time I saw the Berlin Wall, and I wouldn't want to if I could. We climbed a little stand at Checkpoint Charlie, from which I could see the mine fields on the other side. Every seventy-five yards or so was a huge tower on the East side where a machine gunner watched. His assignment was to kill his own countrymen if they tried to escape.

I was helpless before this massive prison bloc. My head and heart raced with new emotions. I had never seen anything like it. What could I do, a nobody against the forces of communism, indeed the forces of Satan?

I paced, staring at the gut-wrenching scene, my heart crying, "O God, how can we reach this people for Jesus Christ? There must be some way we can reach them with the Good News." I had never been so moved.

We didn't cross the border there but crossed with Lynn by train through Friedrich Strasse. I could hardly believe the contrast between East and West. West Berlin was full of life and light, but the East side was tomblike. There was no noise in the dank, dimly lit streets, and everything was gray. My relief at making it across the border was replaced by a wave of emotions. I was afraid, anxious, burdened, and full of love for this mysterious country and its people.

Lynn took us to the home of an old gentleman I'll call Pastor Busch. When our guide introduced us as Christians from America, Herr Busch greeted us with a bear hug, tears in his eyes. He had been pastor of a Lutheran church but had refused to sign a document penned by the communist government which acknowledged that Jesus Christ was *a* savior but not *the* Savior of the world. By signing the document the man would have been agreeing that communism was the only true answer for the world. The communists had removed him from his church, and he was heartbroken. He sent an underground letter to other Lutheran clergy, urging them not to sign the document. None complied. He was the only one who had stood for his beliefs. Even his children had turned on him.

What a tremendous blessing this man of God was to us! Even then he was studying Russian so he could share Christ with the Russian soldiers, despite the risk of imprisonment again. Holy boldness.

Pastor Busch took us to a Lutheran church the next Sunday

morning, and I was struck by the lack of young people there. Here was a nation of lost souls who needed to be reached for Christ, and the church was full of old, tired, beaten people. I felt for them, but few were equipped to win their countrymen for God.

I was encouraged that evening when we went to an Evangelical Free Church. It was packed with young people full of life and joy. Defying the state and exercising their faith in a free church was a risk for them, but their enthusiasm and intensity were obvious.

As we rode the train back from the services, Pastor Busch pointed out a group of young people wearing blue uniforms. "They call themselves the Free German Youth," he said sadly, shaking his head. "They're not really free. They either sign up with the FGY or they cannot continue their education."

As the train rattled up to the border we could see Checkpoint Charlie. The old man gazed at the wall and his thoughts seemed far away. He took us to the Temple of Tears, the spot where you cross the border on the way back. It got its name from the tears shed there by countless parting relatives.

It was hard to leave Pastor Busch. He hugged and kissed us and our eyes filled. He looked up at the gun towers on the wall and said thickly, "Someday maybe I will be able to visit you on the other side." He tried to smile.

"I sure hope so," I said. In truth, I couldn't even imagine that possibility.

We left, not knowing what would happen to him. Would we ever see him again, and if we did would it be in the East or in the West, at his home or in prison? Through Pastor Busch the Lord showed us the real need behind the Iron Curtain. We assured him we would share his ordeal with praying Christians in America.

For days in West Germany I couldn't shake the rapid-fire experiences and emotions I had gone through during our visit to East Berlin: the things we had seen, the people we had met, the churches we had visited, Pastor Busch, the grayness of the streets, the feeling of oppression. The words of Pastor Busch echoed in my mind: "Someday, maybe I will be able to visit you on the other side."

I knew I needed to do more about my lifelong burden for Eastern Europe. I didn't know what form that would take, but love for that place exploded in my heart and lay heavy on my mind.

On Christmas Eve 1971, Tex and I were thousands of miles from home and family. "Let's go to the wall," I said, and we went back to Berlin to pray there. We were silent as we walked that night. I just cried. The wall had lost none of its intense impact on me, and I was shaken anew with the overwhelming need of these people— the believers and the lost.

The ugly monstrosity took on spiritual significance. It was more than a physical barrier lined with machine gunners and mines, separating a city, a race, a people, and a nation. I saw it as a wall of sin that separated people from God. My heart tore within me and I prayed, "O God, we must be closing in on the last days. Allow me to reach these people for Jesus Christ." The next day, as we stood out of the rain at the War Memorial Church, the cross was stolen, almost right before our eyes. It had been out of view for only a few seconds, and the next time we looked, it was gone. We couldn't imagine someone walking off with an eight-foot wooden cross in downtown Berlin, but it was gone. I felt as if my visit with the old pastor and our look at the Berlin Wall had been God's way of giving me a new cross to bear.

After visiting with Volkhard Spitzer that day at his church, I walked back to the War Memorial Church. It was chilly and damp and overcast, so I stopped to get some hot chocolate. As I sat sipping and looking out of the glassed-in restaurant I idly listened to the people all around me speaking German. Then it all came back to me. The glassed-in restaurant, the people speaking a foreign language. I looked at their faces. They were the people I had seen in my mind three years before! The Spirit of God came upon me and thrilled me. Here was the fulfillment of my dream. The Lord had provided one more sign to assure me that the walk and a worldwide ministry were part of His plan for God's Love in Action.

As we boarded the plane for Chicago the next day, I thought of Pastor Busch, the communist students, the loving brothers and sisters in Christ, and how God had blessed our walk and our meetings. We left Murray and Debbie there to carry on the ministry, and we planned to return in less than a year. I didn't know what God had in store for us, but something was in my heart for East Germany that would not leave.

CHAPTER NINE

TUMULTUOUS ASSIGNMENTS

I n Chicago we began turning over the Bible studies to new converts, and we saw on-fire believers take over the street ministry too. I sensed God leading us away from Chicago, but to where I wasn't sure. During a week of meetings in Miami, Florida, I learned of the demonstrations planned by radicals for the Democratic National Convention to be held there that fall. It seemed the convention would be an ideal place to witness and demonstrate for Christ.

In May God laid it on my heart to walk from Orlando to Miami a week before the convention. As I fulfilled final obligations in the Chicago area, Tex and a few other staff members went on ahead to Florida to set up our office and arrange for lodging. We were excited about the future, especially after I heard from an Orlando pastor who said he would set up rallies for us along our walk route. God had given us a tremendous burden and now an opportunity to call America and its leaders back to God. Now more than twenty years since that wild, tumultuous Democratic National Convention in Miami, it's hard to imagine what a scene it was. If it weren't for books and movies about that period, most wouldn't realize it was as volatile as the Chicago convention had been just four years before.

Ten different protest groups announced their intentions, including the Gay Liberation Front, the Southern Christian Leadership

Conference, Vietnam Veterans Against the War, and assorted Yippies and Zippies (Yippie offshoots). In Dade County the Ku Klux Klan burned seventeen crosses. Another right-wing group claimed that if Miami opened up to the radicals, it would bring thousands of KKKers, hard hats, and rednecks into the city to break up their campsites. The city council worked furiously to pass tougher laws against obscenity, vulgarity, and inciting violence.

I was oppressed by a feeling of impending personal disaster. I didn't want to be afraid, and I certainly didn't want a martyr complex. Yet the feeling made me stop and think, *What am I doing for Jesus every second? Every moment, every breath must be Christ living through me.*

Tex and I discussed what would happen to her if she and Davey were left without a husband and father. I didn't enjoy thinking about my own death, but it constantly plagued me, and I wanted her to be prepared. I couldn't turn tail and run from the convention or danger. I knew God wanted me there and that it would be the greatest opportunity our ministry had ever had. My burden for our work grew, despite the premonition. It lay deep and heavy on my heart.

God allowed us to witness for Him through the media and in speaking engagements to local churches and civic groups. The evening before the midnight, July 1, 1972, walk, more than seven hundred showed up for our rally at the Orlando band shell. Several joined hands in a circle to pray for us, and we surrendered our lives anew for the glory of God.

The eight-day walk was one of my shortest but most intense ever. The first night we covered only thirty-two miles because there were so many people—including the press—to talk to. We also felt eaten alive by mosquitoes. We heard snakes slithering in the grass at the sides of the road, and we saw several snake carcasses.

The next day, at about four in the morning, one of the guys brought a well-dressed but drunk motorcyclist to me and asked that I share Christ with him. As soon as we were alone the man pulled a huge pistol from his saddle bag, pointed it at me, and cocked it. I believed my premonition of disaster was coming true, and I thought of my young family and all that would happen if this guy murdered me. I wasn't afraid of death, but the dying part made my knees shake. I just kept talking about Jesus.

The man pulled a huge pistol from his saddle bag, pointed it at me, and cocked it. I believed my premonition of disaster was coming true.

The drunk made me strap on a holster. He said that if anyone came by, we should look like we were just talking. When one of our guys did arrive, I assured the drunk that he was a friend. With that he pulled out the gun and fired it. My friend and I each thought the other had been shot, but he had missed.

"That's the wrath of God upon you," the cyclist said. "That's power! Power!" He put the gun in the holster I had strapped on. He pulled out another pistol and challenged me. I finally talked him into putting them away. I tried to pray with him, but he was irrational. When the opportunity arose, I sprinted away from him and sped off in the van. We called the sheriff and left it to him to hunt down the gunman. It was hard to forget that brush with death.

Every few days, despite fatigue and sunburn and fear, God used someone or something to refresh me and give me renewed vigor. One night the deacons of a local church prayed for me after a service, and I felt the power of the resurrected Christ.

We walked all night July 3 and saw the sun come up. More and more people were showing up along the route, proving that the news media had spread the word. All I could think of was Davey and Tex and how much I missed them and wanted to see them again. I wasn't sure I would. One of the newspapers I picked up carried our story, including my testimony, why we were walking, what we were all about, and even quoting 2 Chronicles 7:14: "If My people who are called by My name will humble themselves, and pray and seek My face, and turn from their wicked ways, then I will hear from heaven, and will forgive their sin and heal their land."

At about three in the morning on July 5 the sheriff advised us to stop walking until daytime because there had been a prison break nearby. By stopping our van every so many miles and waiting for each other, we were sitting ducks for escaped convicts who needed hostages and transportation. We stayed in a hotel until the next afternoon and got some much needed rest.

The rest of the way was filled with encouragement and press

reports, all of which were surprisingly accurate and carried God-honoring truth. On July 7, with plans to reach Miami within twenty-four hours, we heard that the radicals had taken over a location and called it the People's Park, where anyone could say or do anything he wanted. That was good news to us; no one would tell us we couldn't preach and witness and pass out tracts. Or so we thought. When we showed up a couple of days later with our cross and our literature, the Yippies told us we couldn't stay, that we were too controversial and not preaching what everybody there believed. We reminded them that it was the People's Park, and Leo Humphrey—my old mentor from the French Quarter in New Orleans, who had just joined us—looked one of them in the eye and told him we loved him, and the guy walked away. We had a cross to set up and staff members to man it at each candidate's headquarters. We also placed one at the convention hall itself. When we brought a cross from the convention center to the People's Park, we didn't get fifteen yards inside before we were besieged by radicals, the press, and bystanders. The cross quickly became controversial. Some were drawn to it, while others were repulsed. As Scripture says, the cross divides.

The convention itself actually began July 10, and at midnight Leo and I began a prayer vigil at the center, which would last until the convention was over. With just snatches of sleep here and there during the six days, I still remember the entire time as one long day. Each morning at ten we made a daily walk with the cross around the convention center. The last day we would walk twice to make a total of seven trips, modeling our approach after Joshua's march around the walls of Jericho.

More than once that morning walk put us between rival groups of radicals or protesters. We walked back and forth between them, praying and singing and witnessing. God cooled down the demonstrators time and time again. When we knelt to pray in the middle of a potential riot, people from both sides assumed we were staging some sort of sit-in and asked, "What's happening here?" Of course, that gave us a chance to witness.

"Jesus is happening here," we answered. There were a lot of Christians in Miami that week, so we have no idea how many people were led to Christ. Our staff alone estimates we saw between fifteen and twenty people a day come to the Lord.

Each night we held what we called a soul session where we sang, cheered, witnessed, and preached. One night we were interrupted by a demonstration by the Gay Liberation Front. They marched along staging a kiss-in. What shocked me most was that their leader was a gay pastor who preached the blood of Jesus. I believed that was a dangerous, blasphemous thing for a willful sinner to do, and so I confronted him.

"The blood of Jesus has cleansed us," he said.

"What about repentance?"

"We have repented."

"What about your homosexuality?"

"Homosexuality is not a sin. Jesus and the disciples were gay."

To think this guy was advocating in the name of Jesus something the Bible clearly prohibited! "I rebuke you in the name of Jesus Christ," I said.

I confess I don't understand why some people have homosexual mind-sets even when they don't want to, and I believe that Christians can suffer from this. But Scripture is so clear that practicing homosexuality is sin and that those who do it will not enter the kingdom of God, that it is impossible for the believer to reconcile. I love the sinners and I long for their salvation, but I see no compromise on this issue in the Word of God. We should not be harsh or unkind to them, but neither should we countenance such sin.

What a chaotic week we had outside the convention center! It seemed every few minutes was a new crisis or opportunity. We shared Christ with leading politicians and special interest group leaders. We were hassled by radicals and embraced by others. Late in the week I met one of the most unusual personalities I have ever run into. His name was Hubert Lindsay, and he was known as Holy Hubert. Man, that street preacher in his late fifties had a holy boldness I have not seen since. In fact, at first I was turned off by his approach, but he became a model of fearlessness to me. He'd been hospitalized a dozen times after getting beat up, shot, and stabbed in demonstrations where he tried to preach. A Hell's Angel who had shot him was sent to jail; Hubert eventually bailed him out and led him to Christ.

We were praying with him when he noticed a group of Vets Against the War sitting near a dike they'd built. "I'm gonna stir 'em up," he said, a twinkle in his eye. He wasn't as crass as he appeared; he knew what he was doing, which was drawing a crowd so he could preach. He started by pointing at the vets and shouting, "You filthy, rotten sinners! You're headed for hell! Your souls are dirty . . ."

A crowd gathered, and old Holy Hubert began to preach. He softened his tone and used his head. He preached Christ and Him crucified. From the crowd of about three hundred someone tried to shout him down. Hubert got a special dose of wisdom from the Lord.

The heckler shouted, "Why don't you blow a little grass with us? God created marijuana, didn't he?"

Never missing a beat, Hubert shouted back, "God created poison ivy too. Why don't you chew a little of that?"

The crowd cheered.

"I'm gay!" another called out. "I believe God wants people to be gay!"

"You're not gay," Hubert responded. "Gay means happy, and you're not happy. Only Jesus makes you happy."

After our seventh walk around the convention center on the last day, we praised God for the revival He had sent, for the opportunities He'd given us, and for the growth in each of our lives. We went home and immediately began a follow-up program, mailing encouraging letters and literature for spiritual growth to those we led to Christ. I praised God that despite all the tense situations, including the times I felt I was near death, He had not allowed me any harm.

While the rest of the staff went to the Republican National Convention in August, Tex and I turned our eyes to Europe where we would return that fall for several months of meetings. I felt drawn back to Germany with a burden so deep that I knew God had a plan for me in Eastern Europe. He was not revealing it to me all at once, so I committed myself to following and obeying as I went along.

It was great to see Murray and Debbie Bradfield again, but when they left Europe to visit the United States for a month, Tex and I found ourselves alone for the first time in our ministry—except for the first few days in Chicago. It was a strange feeling, disconcerting at first. We had few contacts and still knew very little German.

We spent the first several days just resting and praying, seeking the will of God. One day I sensed the Lord impressing upon my heart that I should memorize my testimony in German. I didn't understand. Aside from the few times I had witnessed one-on-one on the streets, I had always used interpreters in Germany. But the message was clear; I began to memorize, eager to see when God might use me.

During the next several days we had joyous reunions with many of the people we had met and worked with a year before, especially Pastor Busch. One night we visited the Evangelical Free Church again, where only German was spoken. The pastor called on various ones to share their testimonies, a most unusual practice to Westerners like us. In the States we simply open the floor to testimonies, and anyone who feels led stands and speaks. I was thrilled to hear these German Christians, but I was intrigued that they were chosen.

My heart pounded. God seemed to be leading me to speak up. But I was scared. There were no interpreters and English was not even the second language here as it was in the West; it was a distant third behind German and Russian. I felt locked to my seat. Was I ready? Had I memorized well enough? Would the people respond?

Suddenly the pastor pointed at me. *"Du!* [You!]" he said. *"Du!"*

I stood and shared my testimony in German as God had directed. It was one of the great blessings of my life to be able to share with these people in their own tongue. Later I realized that one of the abilities God gave me was an ear for languages. Over the years I have had to adapt to many cultures and languages, and though I've had no formal training, I pick them up quickly. I have a distinct Southern accent when I speak English, but apparently that leaves me when I speak German and the smattering of other European languages I know, because people often ask me what part of their country I'm from.

I could tell by the looks on the faces of the people at the Evangelical Free Church that they felt honored, and also probably bemused by my very first effort. Later, by their words of encouragement, which I could barely understand, I sensed I had been as much a blessing to them as it had been for me to share with them. It was just another confirmation for me that God had plans for us in Germany.

The question, of course, was: What were His plans? I believe that the will of God is not usually hard to determine. Where the Scripture says, "This is the will of God concerning you," a person doesn't have to be a scholar to figure it out. And usually, if you love the Lord with all your heart and live accordingly, you will find yourself doing His will. But I believed God had a specific mission for our ministry behind the Iron Curtain, and I longed to know what it was. He had blessed our witnessing and my preaching. Souls had come to Christ. Now I wondered if God felt there was still more I needed to learn before He would reveal our next step.

That night, after the service at the Evangelical Free Church, we returned to Pastor Busch's home. It had been an exhausting day, and after a filling piece of cake, I nearly dozed while Pastor Busch fellowshipped with the others. Suddenly something he said shocked me back to full consciousness.

"I want you to pray about coming back here next summer to preach at the Communist Youth World Fest."

I bolted upright. "What?" I said. ""What's that?"

My heart raced as he explained. "There will be 100,000 young Communists in Berlin from every country in the world. These will be the elite Communist young people, many even from America and other free countries."

My mind reeled. What an opportunity!

"But surely they wouldn't let me preach the gospel there."

"Oh, but they might," the old man said. "Arresting a Christian for speaking out would cause an international scene, the last thing they would want. They claim they are for freedom of expression, so they will be tolerant for the few days of the festival." My soul burned with the realization that this was what God was calling me to do. Here was perhaps the greatest opportunity in history to minister behind the Iron Curtain, and possibly without being arrested.

Pastor Busch advised that I visit a travel agency at Alexanderplatz where I would learn more. "But be careful," he said.

That night in bed on the free side of the border I praised God. "Thank You for what You're going to do!"

The next day I went with three friends to the Communist side, so excited I could hardly concentrate. Still I felt compelled to first share my faith with people. Even before learning more about the Communist Youth World Fest, I was reassured that these people were hungry to hear the Word of God. At the three- or four-minute stops on the train I would stand and preach my testimony, then hop off and catch a train going the other way.

Not one young person turned us off or was rude. They had grown up in a country where it was normal for everyone to share his beliefs, as long as they conformed to communist ideology, but this was something new. They seemed more concerned with our safety than with theirs. One girl told a friend of mine, "You must not do this. If the police find out, you will be in very much trouble."

I sat next to one young man and asked, *"Kennen Sie Jesus?* [Do you know Jesus?]"

"No," he whispered in German. "I have been taught there is no Jesus." That broke my heart. Time and again I heard the same thing from young students. "We have been taught there is no God." Every time I heard that I felt a deeper burden to share Christ with the untold masses. Even as they warned me not to speak of my faith in public, I could see the hunger for God in their eyes.

Finally, it was time to find out more about the Communist Youth World Fest and whether there would be any way to get in. Our next few hours could have been the makings for a spy movie.

CHAPTER TEN

PREPARATION

We went through Alexanderplatz on the east side of the border to the travel agency Pastor Busch had told us about. From there we were sent to another office and finally to yet another building where a girl began asking us questions. I told her in German that we might be interested in attending the Communist Youth World Fest.

"Come with me," she said.

We followed her to the parking lot, where she told us to wait in a car. We had not met anyone in East Berlin who owned an automobile, and after we sat there for forty-five minutes we were nervous. Finally a man came out and got behind the wheel without a word. As he drove we looked at each other, wondering if it was a trap, wondering if they were on to us already.

Suddenly the driver spoke. He pointed to a building. "That's the Soviet Embassy." He pulled up to a building next door and escorted us inside. We were told to sign in and give over our passports. I wasn't eager to do that, but we were so far along in this crazy deal already I figured we'd better do what they said.

We were led down a long corridor where I noticed that every door had an alarm device. Covering almost the entire wall of one of the rooms was a huge photograph of American activist Angela Davis.

Finally we arrived at a beautiful reception room full of French university students who spoke fluent English and were assigned to talk with English-speaking people interested in the Fest. They made every attempt to make us feel comfortable, but they failed. I felt miserable and scared.

No one seemed the least bit suspicious, and they thanked us for our interest. We were never asked the exact nature of our curiosity, and of course we never offered. We got a lot of information, but I never wanted to get myself into that kind of situation again. I was glad to have my passport back.

As we stepped into the sunlight I noticed the girl who had told us to wait in the car. Before we parted I felt led to give her a "Four Spiritual Laws" booklet. I hesitated.

"Lord, I can't do that," I prayed silently. "She's part of the communist party."

Immediately I felt rebuked. If we came to the Communist Youth World Fest, everyone we encountered would be a communist. I handed her the booklet. *"Jesus liebt dich,"* I said.

She shot me a doubletake and stared. Then she smiled. *"Danke,"* she said, and she walked away.

I was both encouraged by her response and chagrined to have learned a valuable lesson. We had been given a glimpse of the wide-reaching tentacles of the communists. They seemed to know all and control all, and if we weren't careful, we might play right into their hands. We never again blindly followed paths unless we knew where they led.

Over the next several months in Germany, I learned a great deal more. At a rally in Walldorf, one of our young speakers was disrupted by a gang of youths who shouted down his testimony. Taking a page from Holy Hubert's book, I felt the boldness from God to confront them. I took the microphone and nodded to the interpreter.

"We've not come here to play games!" I said, and the translator echoed: *"Wir sind nicht hier gekommen um Spiele zu spielen!* [We've come here to talk about Jesus!] *Wir sind gekommen um uber Jesus zu sprechen.* [If you don't want to listen, get out!] *Wenn Sie nicht Zuhoren mochten, gehen Sie hinaus!"*

They respected our boldness, and they shut up!

Opportunities began to open for us to speak in local schools. We shared our testimonies, and then the students asked questions. What an educated population they were! They asked heavy, intellectual questions about things I would not have felt confident tackling without always referring to Scripture. Many young people received Christ through those sessions.

When I was invited to speak at a meeting of the youth workers in the evangelical churches in Germany, God opened doors throughout the country. We made friends and contacts that would last a lifetime.

While on a mountain retreat with several Christian brothers and sisters, I sensed a new call of God. About ten of us were fasting and praying, seeking the will of God for our lives. At one point we all concentrated on what God would have me do next, and one of the brothers read aloud from the Bible: "Your eyes will see the King in His beauty; They will see the land that is very far off" (Isa. 33:17); and

> Look upon Zion,
> the city of our appointed feasts;
> Your eyes will see Jerusalem,
> a quiet habitation. (Isa. 33:20a)

As I prayed I could almost hear God speaking to my heart, telling me to visit Jerusalem. I first felt a tug toward Israel when I spoke to some students at a Chicago synagogue. But this seemed to me a definite call. It was exciting and I was intrigued that He seemed to be leading me not to the whole nation, but specifically to Jerusalem. I assumed He would lead me there sometime in the future, so I expressed my willingness and put it out of my mind.

Until two weeks later, that is. At three in the morning I couldn't sleep. I woke Murray and we began to pray. Our wives wondered what was going on. They know anything can happen when we pray in the middle of the night.

Go to Jerusalem kept echoing through my mind, and I believed God wanted me to go soon. Murray didn't feel the same leading, but we knew that if God wanted him to go, He would give a definite indication. I believe in the biblical model of ministers traveling in pairs, so having him with me was my preference.

A few days later Murray received a check in the mail from the

States. It was for $100 and was designated for the Holy Land. That would pay for a one-way ticket. About two weeks later an undesignated check for the same amount arrived. On January 2, 1973, we flew to Jerusalem. I half expected to travel about the region, but for some reason God wouldn't let me leave Jerusalem. We were there for twenty-eight days, and I marvel twenty years later at what He taught us during that time.

We spent the first twenty days in prayer and Bible study. He instilled in me a love for the Scriptures I had never known and have never lost. He opened the prophetic passages to me so that I understood not only the completeness of Christ's first coming, but also His second coming.

Murray and I spent hours at the Garden Tomb, and we made friends with the Dutch warden stationed there. Praying there for hours, I became impressed by God that now, more than ever, the church needs to be rooted and grounded in His Word. I sensed a leading from the Lord that I should not concentrate solely on evangelism, as I had been doing lately. I felt He wanted me to exhort and educate and train believers to help with the work, to get them back into Scripture and holy living and then motivate them to share their faith.

By January 6 enough extra money had come in that our wives were able to join us. One day while on an errand for Tex I was taught an invaluable lesson that graphically illustrated the trials of Jesus in His ministry. I got lost and drove into the Orthodox section on the Sabbath. Immediately our rented car was surrounded by angry Jews. They set up human barricades, shouting and pounding on the car as I furiously shifted gears, trying to find a way out of the neighborhood.

The nerve of someone to drive a car on the Sabbath! I learned later that I was lucky I had not been stoned to death. God delivered me, but only after I got an idea of what Jesus went through when He "worked" on the Sabbath.

The last week we were there, Murray and I walked to each of the gates that surround the city, praying and speaking to people about Christ. What a blessed experience that was, one that will likely never be duplicated in my ministry. The sweet joy of the Lord often drove us to our knees. There was no fear and no opposition; in fact, we didn't even have to seek out people to talk to. God kept sending them to us, and they had questions. We never approached one person to tell him about Christ. It was as if we were in a heavenly situation where God did all the work and all we had to do was the fun part—tell people about Him. Can you imagine the joy and ease of having God put the listeners right in front of you, eager to hear the gospel?

On the sixth day we had no one to witness to. A spiritual battle was going on. It was the Sabbath, and over loud speakers the entire city heard the eerie cry in Arabic: "In the name of Allah, the merciful and compassionate, praised be Allah. . . ."

On Sunday morning the Lord impressed upon me that I would give my testimony at the Garden Tomb. Murray and I had planned to go there for communion before our last walk. When we arrived we discovered that the warden, John, wanted to see us. "Would you take the service this morning?" he asked. "And give your testimonies?" I shouldn't have been surprised.

It was a beautiful experience and a thrill to be able to commune with believers that day. Later, when we arrived at the Golden Gate, one of Jerusalem's closed gates, we felt victorious. Though there was no one there to hear our witness, I was overwhelmed with the power of God and seven times I shouted, *"Yeshua Hamashiach!* [Jesus the Messiah!]" All I could think was that Jesus is coming soon. Hallelujah, praise be to God! My eyes shall behold the King!

As I've been able to reflect on that strange, wonderful trip from the perspective of two decades, I'm struck by the fact that it was primarily a work of commissioning in my life. God was taking me away from my usual ministry and teaching me, focusing my mind and heart on His essentials. There was still ministry there, of course. In fact, that five-day period during which He sent people our way instead of requiring us to seek them out remains one of my sweetest memories. But most of all, I was learning history, Old Testament, the big picture. God had much, much deeper work to do in my life and character—work I had no idea was needed—but right then He was preparing me for a ministry he had not yet revealed. I lived in a constant state of anticipation, eager to see where He would lead me next.

Slowly the Lord was teaching me lessons about spiritual matters. I had been empowered to witness and preach, and I had learned the importance of dying to myself daily. But I had been making the mistake of *putting* myself in the position of authority without submitting *to* any authority. I felt like a traffic cop without proper authorization. I needed a church, a local body of believers to whom I was spiritually accountable and who would pray for me.

Once while witnessing with Lynn, the friend who had introduced us to Pastor Busch, we were chased by Soviet soldiers and barely eluded them on a train. That was my closest call since visiting Europe, and it made me think twice about my family and our ministry. God began to speak to me about my lack of willingness to count the cost.

I had been threatened, run off the road, run out of town, held at gun point, shot at, arrested, and even jailed during my street ministry in the States. I've always felt I would be willing to die for my Lord. But dying is one thing. Living in prison is another. I have to say truthfully that I am more willing to die for Christ than to live for Him in prison.

> **In death my family would be left without a husband and father, but if I were imprisoned they would be subjected to constant anxiety.**

In death my family would be left without a husband and father, but if I were imprisoned they would be subjected to constant anxiety. In human weakness, I decided to be more careful. I believed I was more likely to be imprisoned than martyred in Europe.

My German was improving from ministering in and around Frankfurt, but as the time grew near for the Communist Youth World Fest, I felt the need to go back to America and submit myself to a local body who believed in our ministry and would send us out. I had met a Texas pastor at an international conference and felt led to move to San Antonio, Texas, and become accountable to the Gateway Baptist Church. We would have a home base, and I believed God would grant our ministry all authority in heaven and earth if we would submit ourselves. That authority can tear down the gates of hell, and that was the type of authority we would need to combat communism, atheism, and Satan behind the Iron Curtain.

I wrote to Fred Bishop, a pastor from southern Illinois who ministered with us at the Democratic convention the year before. He was a bold witness with a good youth work going. Just before leaving for the United States I learned that he felt led of God to help us in Europe, so we started making plans for him to go with me to the Fest.

Meanwhile, I had to make one more trip to Berlin before leaving for Texas. If I needed one more confirmation that we needed the backing of a local body, I got it on that trip.

Somehow Lynn got hung up in Poland and was unable to meet me in East Berlin. We prayerfully decided to temporarily rescind our policy of no smuggling for this unique opportunity. I was loaded down with Bibles and tracts concealed all over my body. Still, we would never lie. If we were asked whether we had Bibles or tracts, we would say yes. We always prayed that we would not be asked and that if we were searched our materials would not be found.

Now I stuffed Bibles in my pants, my shirt, and everywhere else. Tracts were up my sleeves and in my shoes. I was not questioned or searched, so I made it across the border without a problem. My plan was to go to the men's room in a restaurant near the Soviet military base and transfer all I was carrying into a brief case. I had done it before, but never alone, and I was nervous.

I noticed two Russian policemen and wondered if they were suspicious. I followed a sign to the men's room and, trying to look nonchalant, walked through the door and shut it quickly before realizing I wasn't in the men's room at all. I was in a laundry closet, and there was no inside door knob!

For an hour I sat there helpless, praying. I didn't want to make any noise with the police outside and the Soviet military base nearby. I imagined they had surrounded the closet, and there was nothing I could do but wait.

Suddenly the door opened and a waitress put something away. I bolted upright and she gasped, but before she could say anything I stepped past and kept moving. It seemed everyone was staring and wondering where I had come from, but I just kept walking, right out the door and down the street. It seems funny now, but it wasn't then. That hour seemed like a week.

I had always depended on Lynn, who knew some Russian and spoke fluent German. Now I was all by myself, and when I needed my poor German, it wouldn't come to me. I could hardly get simple sentences to make sense. I can't describe the loneliness.

Somehow the Lord helped me to get more specifics about the Fest, and I was never so glad to get back to the West. Tex and I felt good that we were going to submit ourselves and our ministry to a body of believers in San Antonio that was not just another church but people who would love us and care about us and pray for us.

Fred Bishop and his wife left their church in Illinois and moved to San Antonio to prepare for the ministry at the Communist Youth World Fest. He and I met every morning for prayer and Bible study, then we memorized Scripture, "The Four Spiritual Laws," and some choruses in German. Once we had the basics down, it was time for God to show us the strategy for the Fest.

CHAPTER ELEVEN

STRATEGY AND PROVISION

One morning Fred came by with the news that someone at church had given him two twenty-dollar bills, one for him and one for me. "He said the Lord led him to do it and seemed to be telling him we would need it today."

Neither of us had any immediate needs, so we prayed about it and decided to rent a hotel room for the day to just seek God. There He spoke to our hearts and led us to various Scripture passages, including Acts 13 where Saul and Barnabas were sent out and John Mark was commissioned as their helper.

I certainly didn't see myself as a modern-day apostle Paul. But I would be proclaiming the gospel as he did, and Fred would be helping me, as Barnabas helped Paul. I also felt that there was another lesson in that passage for us, and it was that three of us should plan to go. Fred Starkweather, a young man who had come to Christ through Fred Bishop's ministry, would serve as our John Mark.

I couldn't elude the impression that God wanted me to preach publicly at the Fest, even though that seemed impossible. I assumed we would minister to people secretly, individually, trying to stay out of trouble and not get anyone else in trouble either. We would witness and pass out as many "Four Spiritual Laws" booklets as we could get across the border. I didn't see how I could possibly preach to 100,000 communists without getting arrested or at least deported.

God led me to Isaiah 58:6-8 where He talks about loosing bonds of wickedness to let the oppressed go free, breaking every yoke. We were to

> Share [our] bread with the hungry,
> And . . . bring to [our] house the poor who are cast out.
> Then your light shall break forth like the morning,
> Your healing shall spring forth speedily,
> And your righteousness shall go before you;
> The glory of the Lord shall be your rear guard.

That thrilled my heart. God was going to bless in a way we couldn't even imagine. I believed He was going to pour out His Spirit and do a tremendous work if we would just obey. With the glory of the Lord as my rear guard, how could the gates of hell prevail against us, even in an unthinkable situation?

It was June 1973, and we were to leave in about six weeks for Germany. I was certain we were ready to go except for last minute Bible study, memorization, and brushing up on the language. It turned out that God had another lesson for me. A brother from our church came over one night to pray for our family because we had all been down with the flu and colds. He prayed with such compassion that I realized he knew something about prayer that I didn't. He seemed to be willing to take our sickness upon himself, if that were possible. I asked him to teach me about intercessory prayer.

He told me that a true intercessor is a bit different from a regular prayer warrior. He not only identifies with the need he is praying for, but he is also willing to take that burden upon himself. The greatest example of intercession, of course, is Jesus, who knew no sin, yet became sin for us. It moved me deeply to think that we can know some of the suffering of Christ on the cross if we are willing to take the problems of others upon ourselves.

That was an important lesson because it revolutionized my prayer life. I had been praying for months about the lives I wanted to see changed and the souls I wanted to see saved for God's glory.

But was I willing to face the persecution these people would face as a result of their decisions?

God promised to work a spiritual miracle at the Fest. But was I willing to pay the price? . . . I battled with that question for days.

God promised to work a spiritual miracle at the Fest. But was I willing to pay the price? Was I willing to go to prison for any or all of the people He would draw to Himself through my preaching? I battled with that question for days.

Was I in it for the glory of marching into the Fest and being able to say I preached there? Was I on some spiritual high or ego trip? Was I ready to lay my freedom on the line for Christ? God taught me a hard lesson. He showed me that this ministry was His and not mine. If I wanted to play in this league, with this much at stake, then I had better get myself in gear and get close to Christ. That would mean joining in the fellowship of His sufferings, according to Philippians 3:10-11: "that I may know Him and the power of His resurrection, and the fellowship of His sufferings, being conformed to His death, if, by any means, I may attain to the resurrection from the dead."

Was I ready? I searched my soul. In the flesh, Sammy Tippit was not ready to give up his freedom for anything or anyone. But I wanted to be obedient. I wanted to serve Christ. I loved Him and wanted to share Him. I wanted more than anything to say that I would do that at any cost, but I knew only He would be so perfect in His love as to give Himself. I prayed He would give me that supernatural love for lost souls. That was not a part of my natural self, so it would have to come from Him.

I also knew it was no game. If I prayed for souls, expressing my willingness to go to prison for them, God might require me to do just that. He is not in the business of providing a cozy life for Sam and Tex. He's in the business of drawing people to Himself. If I wanted a part of that ministry, I had to count the cost.

This was not just a spiritual exercise. This was ominous. Fred Bishop, Fred Starkweather, and I drew up wills and made arrangements in the event we never returned.

A week before our departure date we were flat broke. We had deposited money with a travel agency, and God promised to bless our ministry, so I knew we were supposed to go. But, being new to Texas, I was not known widely enough yet to be speaking regularly. We needed at least $1,100 more to get us to the World Fest, and I didn't have it.

There was nothing in our bank accounts, nothing stashed in a cookie jar, not even pocket change. The gas gauge in my car sat on empty. I even considered swallowing my pride, admitting my lack of faith, and borrowing the money to obey God. Fred Bishop insisted that he didn't believe God would have us borrow it. "If He has called us to go, He'll provide."

I was to speak at the crusade of an evangelist friend (David Stockwell) and then at a seminary class, but I didn't have the gas money to get there. The day before, my pastor invited Fred Bishop and me to a ministerial luncheon. We went along, not knowing how we would pay for our meal. The pastor paid, though he was unaware of our plight. On the way out I was greeted by a man from the Billy Graham team I had met a few years before. "It's good to see you again," he said, pressing a five dollar bill into my palm.

That gave us enough to put two dollars' worth of gas in the car and three dollars to eat on that evening. Later, in the restaurant, I thanked God for providing. When I opened my eyes a man approached us. "I'm a pastor on vacation," he said. "God touched me when you were praying. We need more young men who will stand for Jesus Christ. Allow me the privilege of paying for your meals." I was beginning to see that, as always, God will take care of His own. There we were, paupers eating as children of the King.

That night, at the end of the evangelistic meeting, people came by to greet me and chat and pray with me. On the way to the airport I discovered they had stuffed more than seventy dollars into my shirt pocket.

The next day at the seminary a girl came to me, telling me she had heard me preach the year before. "I didn't do it then," she said, "but I must do it now." And she handed me a check for $100. God had told her to do that the first time she heard me preach, and she had been battling it ever since.

David Stockwell said the Lord had laid it on his heart to give me $250. I was overwhelmed. When he and a few others joined me at a nearby restaurant, I was overflowing with the goodness of God. We joined hands around the table and softly sang, "God is so good, God is so good, God is so good, He's so good to me." I knew it, and I meant it!

On the Sunday evening before we were to leave for Germany I was invited by a member of the First Baptist Church of Castle Hills to go with him to the airport to pick up Haralan Popov, author of *Tortured for His Faith*. Popov, who had been imprisoned for years by the communists, was to speak that night at Castle Hills, and I was thrilled by the idea that I could meet him.

Popov's flight was delayed, and I was asked to speak until he arrived. There were over a thousand in the service that night, all excited about hearing Popov. I spoke for just twenty minutes, sharing what God had told us to do at the Communist Fest and what He had done for us in recent days.

The congregation then turned as one and knelt to pray for us. When the last *amen* was heard, Popov arrived. It was perfect. An offering was taken, then the regular service took place, and another offering was taken for Popov. That made it even more incredible later when people began stuffing my pockets with money.

When I got home I almost forgot about the money. I told Tex all about the service and the people who had promised to pray for us, when I began pulling wads of money out of my pockets. I counted $350, and with what had come in the mail that week we had a total of $1,000, exactly $100 short of what we needed the next day. By now there was no doubt in my mind that God would provide.

We planned to get a good night's sleep and leave the next morning at eleven for our flight to Germany. At seven I was awakened by a phone call from a man who had heard me speak the night before; he asked if I could meet him at the union stockyards. "Not really," I said. "We're going to be on a tight schedule today."

But he insisted, promising it wouldn't take but five minutes, so I left early. When I arrived, this brother said, "All I know is that the Lord laid it on my heart to give you this." He handed me two fifty-dollar bills. Fred and Fred (as I came to call my compatriots) and my family were on our way, with the Lord providing what we needed right down to the last penny.

CHAPTER TWELVE

ATTACKED

A few days before the World Fest I heard the news. The communists had decided to close the borders to the Fest. No Westerners would be allowed. We had prepared for months and months and had seen God provide for us to come all this way. In a matter of hours Satan hurled woes our way in a frantic attempt to discourage us. But he did not succeed.

God gave us a Scripture passage as we poured out our hearts to Him. He impressed upon us to read Revelation 3:8: "I know your works. See, I have set before you an open door, and no one can shut it; for you have a little strength, have kept My word, and have not denied My name."

When God opens a door, we don't have to worry what any earthly government says or what the media say. God said the doors would be open, and so they would. We didn't know how He would do it, but we trusted that He would.

The night I decided to take Fred and Fred to see the Berlin Wall for the first time proved to be an unforgettable experience for me too. I was as impressed as always by the wall, but I also encountered three strange events that I think were calculated to shake me up. And they did.

First I ran into a weird man with wild eyes who tried to speak to me. I sensed the Lord telling me to stay away from him, so I told him my German was not very good and moved away. Then a woman let loose a German shepherd from more than a block away, and it ran straight past everyone else and leaped to attack me. Fred and Fred dropped to their knees to pray that the dog would leave me alone, and it scampered off. I was nearly scared to death.

Then the weirdo approached me again and said in German, "How would you like to go across the border with that dog?"

We finally asked the guards what they knew about the border being closed to Westerners during the Fest, and they told us the order had been rescinded.

Later, on the way back, we twice found ourselves on the same train as the weird man. We finally lost him and I tried to share my faith with a young woman, partly to get my mind off the experiences at the wall. The woman seemed interested but I got the clear message that she was coming on to me while she was giving me her address. Weirdos, dogs, and now the flesh. I tore up the information and was glad to get away. The whole evening had been a nightmare.

Two days before the Fest we woke up excited. This was the day we would make a dry run, giving Fred and Fred the experience of crossing the border, checking out the area, and getting a feel for what we might encounter. Tex would be our daily prayer warrior. If anything happened to us, she would get the ball rolling to inform Christians in the States. Within hours, many of the news media in the Christian world would know a Christian had been imprisoned by the communists.

Fest delegates had already begun to flood the city, and it took us more than two hours to get across the border. Waiting in tension was exhausting, especially since we were laden down with tracts and some 20,000 Russian language Jesus stickers stuffed in our shirts, pants, shoes, and jackets. The crowds were a blessing in disguise because the border guards were lax. We were quickly processed and given twenty-four-hour visas.

I took Fred and Fred to Alexanderplatz, which was to be the center of evening activities at the Fest. Everywhere we walked we stuck the Russian *Jesus Loves You* stickers on anything and everything. Alexanderplatz was bustling. Fest organizers set up the huge sound system that would boom communist teaching to the hundreds of thousands of delegates. Estimates were that a half million people would visit the Fest daily and that 100,000 would fill Alexanderplatz every night.

An air of expectancy surrounded the area, but no one could have been more excited and eager than we were. We had something no one else had, and we were going to share it. We realized that this was not political warfare. The solution to the problems of these people was not an anti-communist crusade. The solution was an outpouring of the Holy Spirit. The Bible says we wrestle not with flesh and blood but against powers and principalities. It would be spiritual warfare. Our weapons would be prayer and witnessing and preaching, in the boldness of the Spirit.

What an air of expectancy washed over the city of Berlin the day before the Communist Youth World Fest! Hundreds of thousands of the elite communist young people from all over the world poured into the city, and the news was filled with stories of the activities to come.

It was a perfect day. The sun was shining. The air was cool. The borders were jammed, and the city was geared up and ready. Somehow I knew God would give us an idea of what to expect at the Fest when we crossed the border that day, one of the most important days of my life.

Every fourth or fifth person was pulled from the line and searched thoroughly. As the line inched forward we prayed we would not be chosen.

Every fourth or fifth person was pulled from the line and searched thoroughly. As the line inched forward we prayed we would not be chosen. The eyes of the border guard passed over us as he chose those who were to be searched.

I knew the city would be crowded, but I was not prepared for what I saw. I just stood gaping. Thousands upon thousands upon thousands of young people jammed into the main train station, and hardly anyone could move. I'm not exaggerating when I say there was a uniformed policeman every ten feet. I hadn't seen so many men in uniform anywhere, including in Israel during a war!

I was struck with an overwhelming sense of defeat. The Fest had not even officially opened yet. The crowds would get bigger! How could we possibly minister? How could I possibly preach? My faith was small. I was in over my head, and I knew it. All I could do was continue to trust God that with Him nothing is impossible.

The task seemed more ominous by the minute. I thought I had counted the cost when I learned about intercession, but now I gave up trying to be prepared for every obstacle. I felt as if I were walking through a brick wall, blindly trusting that God would somehow open the way. We no longer had a choice but to trust Him because even if we wanted to try this mission on our own, we had run out of ideas. We knew God would have to move in some mighty way to glorify Himself in this situation.

We rode trains from station to station, passing out tracts and stickers. Finally our boldness grew, and we began speaking loudly to each other about Jesus right in the middle of a packed car. When the communist young people got quiet to hear what we were shouting about, I'd take over and start preaching.

We boarded one train with three Russian soldiers, and I debated with myself. We were going to wind up witnessing and preaching in front of the military at the Fest anyway, so there was no sense waiting. There was no sense to any of this really, except that God had sent us and we would obey Him.

The only Russian words I knew were *Jesus loves you.* I said that to one of the soldiers and handed him another tract in Russian called "How to Find Peace with God."

One soldier said, *"Jesus loves you,"* back to me and another patted me on the shoulder. All three looked at the tract, and one read it. When they got off the train they waved and smiled. I felt warmed and encouraged by their receptivity, especially knowing that anything could have happened.

We headed back toward Alexanderplatz, distributing more and more literature as we went. Not far away was Marx-Engles Platz where the huge statue of Karl Marx stood. The concrete base below it seemed like a good place to stick our *Jesus loves you* stickers. We arranged several in the shape of a cross, and as we walked away, we could see the luminescent stickers glowing in the dark. Two hundred yards away we could still see that cross of stickers glowing red under the statue of Marx.

Another cross that would come to mean much to us at the Fest was one that reflected from the huge television tower in Alexanderplatz. The Germans are proud of this huge tower, which can be seen for miles on both sides of the border. Strangely, the sun reflected the shape of a cross on the tower during much of the day. The communists tried to change the way the sunlight bounced off the tower, but St. Walter's Cross, as it came to be known, just kept shining. It was soon to become the banner under which we met as a body of believers during the Fest. Even in the midst of persecution we would be able to glance up and see the reflected cross and remember what Jesus suffered for us. It would make our impossible mission seem more possible.

We returned to West Berlin seeing no way we would be able to preach publicly the next day at the Fest. All we had was the promise of God, but as we continued to learn daily, that is all anyone ever needs.

CHAPTER THIRTEEN

THREE BEHIND THE CURTAIN

The Communist Youth World Fest officially opened on a Sunday evening. I thought I would never again see as many people as I had the day before, but that night proved me wrong. As far as the eye could see there was nothing but young people, policemen, and soldiers. Even from the third floor windows of surrounding buildings you couldn't see the ends of the throng. My eyes were wide as I tried to take in the scene, and silently I prayed, "Lord, there are just three of us. How? How?"

Suddenly I was not so overwhelmed with the impossibility of the task as I was with the burden God had laid on my heart. This wasn't just a massive crowd; it was tens of thousands of young people who needed Christ.

I realized that there would *never* be an opportune time to try to preach in this situation, so there was no sense waiting for one. Bands of young people from different cultures all over the world congregated in small pockets, singing, dancing, doing skits, playing instruments. Except for all the security, it was like a giant rock concert.

I was stunned to see a young person wearing a sticker that read "One way: Jesus."

I asked him in German, "Are you a Christian?"

"Oh, no," he said. "I found this on the ground."

As I shared with this young man what his sticker meant, a friend joined him and I witnessed to them, using *The Four Spiritual Laws*. It didn't surprise me to hear the typical response: "We've been taught there is no God, but this is interesting and we want to hear more." What did surprise me was that our conversation drew a crowd. Without our realizing it, our ministry at the Communist Youth World Fest had officially begun.

It was a hobby at such international gatherings to get the autographs of foreigners. Everyone within earshot could tell my German was heavily influenced by my American heritage, so kids gathered around, hoping to get an autograph from someone from the States.

When there was a break in the conversation, kids pressed forward and asked us to sign their kerchiefs. I pulled Fred and Fred close and told Fred Bishop, "Write in German, 'God loves you and has a wonderful plan for your life,' before you sign your name." I told Fred Starkweather to write, "Man's sin has separated him from this plan," before signing his name. I wrote that Jesus was the only bridge over the gap left by sin and told how to receive Him.

Curiosity over what we were doing drew more and more kids, and we sat there furiously writing the Four Laws on more than two hundred scarves. I felt the presence of God and became more and more bold as we answered questions. I kept being reminded that God had told me to preach and that His glory would be my rear guard. The time had come. There would be plenty of opportunities to share one-on-one. I had been called to preach.

I pulled Fred Bishop close again and said, "Stand here and don't say a word, no matter what I do."

"What do you mean?" he whispered. "What're you gonna do?"

"Don't worry," I said, and with that I shoved my face near his and shouted at him in German, preaching the love of God and the forgiveness of sin through the death of Jesus Christ. Fred stared at me as I continued, covering *The Four Spiritual Laws*, giving my own testimony, and then starting all over.

I was so loud that nearly a hundred kids crowded around to see what was going on. When I sensed I had their attention I pulled away from Fred and preached to them. Kids seemed interested and hungry. Even when we took a break after about an hour to get a bite to eat, young people sat with us in the restaurant, eager to know more. It didn't seem to me that they just wanted to debate.

It was as if, for the first time in their lives, they heard something appealing about a personal God they had been told didn't even exist.

I knew that one of the reasons we drew such crowds was that the kids at first assumed we were American radicals. After the Russians and the North Vietnamese military, American communists were among the most revered at the Fest.

I can't describe our joy on our way back across the border late that night. All we could do on the train was sing and praise God. We had worried and wondered and prayed over how God would open the doors for us, and He showed us that He was in charge.

We stayed up until about two in the morning, sharing with Tex all that had happened. I was so keyed up I could hardly sleep. But I wasn't sensitive to how Tex reacted. She was thrilled with what the Lord was doing, of course, and she was excited about the possibilities. But why couldn't I see how she might feel to get all of this secondhand when she had always been such an integral part of the ministry? The clock couldn't move fast enough for me. I wanted to get back to Alexanderplatz.

Fred and Fred and I felt like revolutionaries in the midst of the communist camp. We spent much of the next day in prayer to prepare for the evening at the Fest. I spent some time with Tex and Davey, but it was hard for me to concentrate on anything but the Fest. Here I was in the middle of the most thrilling and important ministry of my life, on a super-spiritual high, yet I was incapable of giving proper attention to my family. Any day could be my last on the free side of the border.

I was not being the husband and father I should have been. Later I would get some small idea of how neglectful I had been, but it would be some years before I learned the deep lessons I needed to learn in this area. The problem was that I didn't even know I had anything to learn.

Fred Starkweather felt led of God to not carry any literature or stickers across the border that evening. So Fred Bishop and I loaded ourselves up, and the three of us began the long process of being checked through the border. When we finally reached the guards they pointed at one of us to be searched: Fred Starkweather. My heart leapt! Truly God was with us and would bless us again that night!

Though the crowd in Alexanderplatz was every bit as large as it had been the night before, things were a bit quieter. There didn't seem to be any natural openings for witnessing, and I felt impatient and uncomfortable. "Guys, listen," I said, "I think we need to get off somewhere and pray."

Fred Bishop said, "Let's kneel right here and pray."

Ten feet from us stood six communist soldiers. "We could go to prison," I said.

"I thought we'd already settled that," he said.

"If you really feel led," I said, "let's do it."

We knelt in the middle of Alexanderplatz with thousands of communist young people milling about. Fred Starkweather prayed first, and people around us fell silent. Then Fred Bishop prayed. I was trembling. Feet shuffled closer to us and I could feel the eyes of dozens of delegates. I kept my eyes shut tight.

When it was my turn to pray my voice was weak and shaky, but I was afraid to quit. This had to be the longest public prayer in my ministry. It took all the boldness I could muster to say those last four words, "In Jesus' name, amen."

I knew a crowd had gathered, but I hardly noticed it as I rose. It seemed to me that the Spirit of God came upon me in such a way that I was lifted from my knees. Before I was even fully standing I began to preach the gospel, and I continued for four hours. That was a miracle in itself because I didn't know four hours' worth of German!

Few times in my ministry had I felt the presence of God as I did that day. He met my needs as I spoke, quickening every word of German I had ever learned or heard. I don't know where Fred and Fred got to, but as the crowd grew, I continued to preach. I shared my testimony, the straight gospel, the love of Christ, the need for confession of and repentance from sin, "The Four Spiritual Laws," and as much about the blood and power of the resurrected Christ as I could.

Suddenly the communist soldiers broke through the crowd, and I thought of Tex and Davey, of Siberia, and of my precious freedom. As the soldiers reached me I hesitated, waiting for those fateful words, "You're under arrest." I forgot the promise of God that His glory would be my rear guard.

When the soldiers began firing questions at me, they were not at all what I had expected.

"Who is Jesus?"

"How do you know He's real?"

"How did He come into your life?"

The crowd picked up on the questions, asking the same things, everyone seeming to talk at once. A young man called for silence. "I don't believe in God!" he shouted. "But this man has something to say and we must listen! Let's spread out and sit down so everyone can hear!"

I fielded questions, full of the joy of the Lord. There was no place in the world I would rather have been. These were non-Christians, ignorant of the things of God. A love for them welled up within me, and I felt an immense assurance that now, as never before, I was in the center of God's perfect will for my life.

This was not merely something I did that God decided to bless. Nor was it something He allowed as part of His permissive will. No, this was a divinely planned event to which I had been called. I believed it was a preaching opportunity that would not come again in this century.

I do not generally put much stock in actions based on emotions, but I felt such joy and love for these kids that I burst with compassion for them. I loved them so much that I knew it had to be of God because humanly I didn't have the capacity for loving on such a scale. God was loving lost souls through me. Though they were dedicated followers of a philosophy opposed to Christianity, He loved them.

Their hearts were hungry. Their minds had been filled with the lies of Satan from the time they were born, and I wanted to give them all of Jesus that was in me. After four hours I could hardly talk anymore. My words wouldn't come fast enough to convey my thoughts. One boy asked me a question, and I missed part of it. As I strained to hear him better I noticed a young girl with a beautiful smile. Immediately I wondered if she could be one of the underground believers I had heard so much about. She caught my eye and translated into English the boy's question. Now I was convinced she was a sister in Christ.

When I was finally exhausted and the crowd began to break up, some stayed around to ask pointed questions. "How do I receive Jesus?" "How do I pray?" "I want to believe; what does it mean to believe?"

> **"My name is Ilse. I cannot talk to you now. If I am seen I will be in very much trouble. . . . Can I meet you tomorrow?"**

As I stood talking the girl came up and whispered, "My name is Ilse. I cannot talk to you now. If I am seen I will be in very much trouble. People are watching who could mean trouble for you. Can I meet you tomorrow?"

"At the fountain at 6:30," I said.

I looked for Fred and Fred, but I couldn't find them. As I walked the perimeter of Alexanderplatz, fatigue and the emotional drain hit me. I was spent. I saw the thousands running and singing and dancing and looking for causes, for purpose, and I knew what the gospel writer meant when he said that Jesus saw the multitude and felt compassion for them.

All I could do was weep. For an hour I walked in a daze, unable to contain the depth of my feeling for these young people. "How can we reach them, Lord? There are just three of us and 100,000 of them." God reminded me that Gideon's army was not big either. I felt that God would do with us what he had done with Gideon if we would remain committed to Him and trust Him.

While threading my way through the crowd I came upon Fred Bishop preaching! A little way away, Fred Starkweather was preaching too. The crowd had gotten so large when I was preaching that Fred and Fred went to the edges and got communists to interpret for them!

Fred Bishop was arguing with a black man, and when Fred saw me he asked me to take over. "I'm bushed," he said.

"Where is your Jesus?" the man said. "I can't see him!"

I turned to a boy and girl holding hands. "Do you believe in love?" I asked.

They giggled and nodded.

"Then where is love? " I said. "Show it to me. I can't see it."

The man said, "You Christians hate blacks."

I said, "Eight years ago I would have hated you just because you are black. Now I can say honestly that I love you in Jesus Christ."

He was taken aback.

"Do *you* love people?" I pressed.

"Yes!"

"Do you love communists?" I said.

"Of course. I'm a socialist myself."

"Do you love capitalists?"

"Well, uh—no."

"That's the point," I said. "Communists love communists and capitalists love capitalists, but only a believer in Jesus Christ can love every man. Only a person who knows God can even begin to understand love."

The first night was the happiest of my life, but the second night even topped that. After telling Tex all about it and praying for every face I could remember, I finally fell into an exhausted sleep. The next day we would meet Ilse, the underground believer, and who knew where that might lead?

CHAPTER FOURTEEN

OPPOSITION AND SUCCESS

The next evening we waited in excited anticipation by the fountain. Young people from all over the plaza recognized us and asked if we were going to talk about Jesus again. It thrilled me to know that they wanted to hear more. An article in a communist women's magazine warned delegates about Jesus People types and even advised them how to debate us, but all that had done was stir up more interest.

It was rarely the young who resisted us but rather their older leaders. The young people seemed to want to let us have our say. If this World Fest was supposed to be a showcase for the communists' freedom of speech, the young people seemed to want to see that happen.

A young person pointed out other kids lounging on the grass, talking and playing. "When the Fest is over and they return to their own countries, they will not be allowed such leisure time again. The only reason they are allowed now is because the news media from all over the world are watching."

More and more kids came to see if we would preach again that night. We assured them we would. Finally, Ilse showed up. She had brought her brother and a girlfriend. What a joy it was to hear how they had come to Jesus, where they worshiped, and how glad they were that we were there. Hearing the name of Jesus in normal conversation brought communist kids from all over. "They're talking about Jesus again," some said. "They're going to start preaching soon."

It was amazing to me how God opened the doors each day. The first day it had been because of autograph seekers. The second day we risked our freedom by kneeling to pray. Now we had an audience of about a hundred just because we had mentioned the name of Jesus to our new friends.

I began to preach, and more young people swarmed around. Fred and Fred moved to the edge of the crowd and began preaching, breaking off clusters of communists to keep the groups small. Soon, however, each of us had a crowd too big to handle. Ilse and her friend and brother split up and took on groups of their own! Ilse told me later that she had been warned a year earlier by the authorities that she should never again talk about Christ in public. Knowing how scared she had been to talk with me briefly the day before, I knew this was a major step of faith and boldness for her now.

This was the night the communist leadership began to take us seriously. We had grown to six witnesses, with groups around each one listening to this new idea: a God who is and who loves. It was obvious the delegates listened intently. When the opposition came, it came from the adults, and they asked all the right questions.

A communist from Israel shouted me down and said he had worked for Christians in Chicago who were rip-off artists. "They took money from the poor and gave it to the capitalists!" I had lived in Chicago, so I knew I would be able to tell if he were accurate. When he accused the Chinese for Christ, a group I knew to be reputable, of taking money and not using it for ministry, I reacted in the flesh rather than in the Spirit.

I said, "Listen, I lived in Chicago and I know that organization is honest!"

"You calling me a liar?" he said, grabbing my shirt and pulling me toward him.

"Yes, I am!" I shouted, infuriated, but in that instant I fell under conviction. God spoke to my heart, showing me that I was wrong to react that way. "I'm sorry I yelled at you," I said.

"You calling me a liar?" he demanded again.

"All I want to say is that Jesus loves you," I said.

"Are you still going to say Jesus loves me when I smash you in the face and fill your mouth with blood?"

I was scared, but God was still with me. "If you hit me," I said, "I pray that every drop of my blood will remind you of the blood of Jesus that was shed for you."

"I ought to kill you!" he said, rearing back to slug me. The crowd backed away from us.

"Jesus loves you," I said.

"You *want* me to hit you?" he asked, incredulous.

"Go ahead," I said. "I'm willing to put my life on the line for Jesus Christ."

He turned and stomped off. I trembled. Two Free German Youth approached me. "We've never seen so much love," one said. "How can you get that kind of love?"

> **"We've never seen so much love," one said. "How can you get that kind of love?"**

"Jesus Christ can give it to you if you give yourselves to Him. If you want Jesus in your life, you can pray and ask Him."

To my surprise they said, "We would like to do that."

They didn't want to do it in front of everybody, so I told them how they could receive Christ at home. They said they would and promised to tell me about it the next day.

A couple of university students came up and asked if they could talk with me alone. "We want what you have been talking about," they said.

We walked away from the crowds and sat on some steps near Alexanderplatz. It was obvious that God had been working in their hearts. I told them that Jesus loved them and wanted them for His own.

"We want to know Jesus," one said, "but it costs so much here. When we were fourteen years old we had to choose to either join the church or join the communist party and become Free German Youth. If you join the church you cannot complete your education or get a good job. It was too big a decision and we, along with almost all our friends, joined the FGY. Now we feel terrible about it."

"God knows and understands," I said. "He can give you a new life in spite of your circumstances, but you must be willing."

"You don't know what it will cost. A friend of ours, a good student, stated publicly that she had given her life to Christ, and she was kicked out of the university."

"Jesus Christ gave His all for you. Are you willing to give your all for Him?"

I could never really know what it was going to cost them, yet I knew that if I asked them to pay the price, God expected me to be willing to do the same. In my heart, because of Jesus, I was ready to do that. And so were these two.

"Yes," they said solemnly, tears in their eyes. "We are willing." We bowed our heads and prayed right there. I prayed with converts who had more at stake than anyone I had ever prayed with before.

I was so proud of our new friends, Ilse and her brother and their friend. They faced imprisonment for speaking out for their faith. Most likely the worst that could happen to us Americans would be banishment from the Fest and maybe the country.

When things broke up Tuesday night, Ilse invited us to go with them to church the next evening. The organizers of the Fest had permitted one church service each night, as long as it was orderly and held in a church building. We agreed to meet them the next evening.

We were overjoyed at our first converts, and when we got back across the border we learned that Lynn Nowicki and his brother and a friend would join us for the rest of the Fest. His ability to speak both German and Russian would be great, as would the increased manpower.

Never should it have been more clear to me than right then that I had the perfect wife for me. She'd followed this preacher-boy all over the world, sometimes not knowing if I would return. Many times we had not known where our next meal would come from.

While we were out where the action was, Tex washed our clothes and had meals waiting when we got back late each night. We were on the front lines, seeing God work. She always got the news secondhand. Yet she was as important as any of us. While her ministry was a humble and selfless one with few obvious rewards, it was an indispensable one she persisted in diligently.

It was hard for Tex to have me gone every evening and most of every night. She tried to tell me in many gentle ways that I was neglecting her and Davey, and when I didn't pick up on it, she grew irritable. I was blind and self-righteous enough to consider her mood an attack of Satan to which she had fallen prey.

With the right motive, but little sensitivity, I looked her in the eye and told her I loved her. "But, please, you're going to have to bear with me for a while longer. This is the greatest opportunity we will probably ever have."

She admitted she worried mostly for my safety. Every night, sitting up waiting and worrying in unbearable tension, she would see us burst in with stories of how wonderful everything had been. I should have considered that she would worry and pray all the time we were gone, but she became simply an audience for us when we got home.

The next day we were invited to the home of a West Berlin pastor, Werner Schoch, before leaving for the Fest. He encouraged Tex to go on a boat ride with him and his wife and their cousin, who spoke English. I thought that would be a good diversion for Tex while I was gone, and it was. But I was still blind to her real need and would be until a few years later.

As my compatriots and I walked to the central train station in West Berlin, I finally succumbed to the pressure and the fatigue. Tex and I had had a difficult discussion about our roles, and I was short of sleep. I had been going on nervous energy and excitement, and I was suddenly struck with a wave of depression. I wanted to give in to Tex and spend an evening with her and Davey, and all I could see ahead was another night of communist leaders screaming in my face. I nearly stumbled as my strength drained away. I slumped and said, "Guys, I can't make it."

They were stunned. I had been the leader. This whole mission had originated with God's direction to me through Pastor Busch. Now here I was, the first one to break. Fred and Fred finally fully realized their roles. I needed them. Without them I never could have stood up to the onslaught of the evil one.

The guys gathered around and took me to a corner where they prayed for me. I was able to go on and I felt a bit refreshed, but I was acting only out of obedience rather than in the fullness of joy and enthusiasm I felt the first three days. I was, however, about to get a shot in the arm.

Six of us crossed the border that night, and only Lynn and Fred

Bishop were searched. They were the two of us who had been led not to carry anything across! We rushed to meet our new friends and join them at the church service, only to find it a dead, boring service. The kids seemed excited and ready to live for Christ, but the church had little to offer.

As soon as the kids got outside, about a hundred of them started singing and several played guitars. Lynn joined in and we all sang choruses. A church official came out and told the kids that such activity was not allowed outside the church.

"Okay, we'll leave!" one of the kids shouted. "Let's march to Alexanderplatz for Jesus!"

I could hardly believe it. I'd been involved in a lot of walks, but a Jesus march in the middle of the Communist Youth World Fest?

About halfway to Alexanderplatz a church leader and a government official met us and said, "This is an act of provocation and will be considered a criminal offense. You must decide whether you are going to confine your activity to the church or commit this crime."

A young man from the back of the throng shouted, "We have already decided. We are following Christ! Let's go to Alexanderplatz!"

Another said, "The Free German Youth say there's freedom at the Fest! Let's prove it!"

When they got to Alexanderplatz, however, some of the kids became fearful. They saw Party members eying them and writing their names, and they fell silent. One of their leaders suggested singing the songs in Hebrew or Latin so no one would understand. That kept the authorities away, but it also ruined the witness because the crowd that had gathered to see what the Jesus People were up to fizzled and broke up.

About fifteen of the Christian young people came to me. "Sammy, we want to go all the way for Jesus. Will you lead us so we can make an impression for Him?"

The six of us and the fifteen of them made a good sized little band, playing and singing praise to God. The communist kids thought it was some kind of a game, so several joined in. As we circled the plaza, we kept picking up more and more marchers, only a few of whom we knew were Christians. By the time we circled the place we were about a hundred strong and no one knew what to make of it. Their favorite argument had been, "Why should we trust Jesus? There's 100,000 of us and just a few of you?"

But now we had grown from three to six, then more than twenty, and now it appeared we were a hundredfold. When I spoke, one of the adult antagonists shouted, "You've been propagandized in America! This is a lie of the capitalists!"

Before I could say anything, one of the underground Christians stepped forward. "I'm from East Germany," he said, "and I want to tell you that Jesus Christ is in my heart and is real to me."

Every time we were shouted down, someone else stepped forward to testify of the work of God in his life. We convinced them at least that we had not been victims of propaganda, but that we had sincerely felt the work of God in our lives.

Later I ran into the two young men who had promised the night before that they would go home and receive Christ. "Did you?" I asked.

They beamed. "Yes!"

"And?"

"Jesus is in our hearts."

It was obvious they were thrilled with their new relationship with God.

By now word had spread so far and wide about us that delegates sought us out, asking how they could know Christ. We knew that if we were that well known, the authorities would soon find us too. Sure enough, a Fest official came to Fred Bishop and me and said, "If you do not stop this, you will be arrested."

The time had come for a decision. I had no fear for myself by this time, but what about the twenty or so new believers and the underground Christians? I didn't want to be responsible for seeing them go to prison.

CHAPTER FIFTEEN

THE CHOICE

I gathered our enthusiastic little band of believers and said, "Listen, we have to break up and quit, or we'll all wind up in prison."

A girl looked at me with sad determination. "Sammy," she said, "Jesus gave His all for us, and we are willing to give our all for Him. You can go back to West Berlin. We can't, and we don't want to. We are going to continue."

All I could do was pray, "God forgive me."

To avoid flagrantly antagonizing the authorities, we laid low for a while. We agreed to meet at a secluded park near the church where I would begin discipling the new believers. I knew we had been called not just to evangelize, but to also make disciples. I couldn't ignore that command just because we were pressed for time on a dangerous mission.

These kids drank in the teaching from God's Word, and the burden God gave me for the people behind the Iron Curtain exploded into such love for them that I can't describe it. Their boldness, their openness, their hunger for the Word endeared them to me. These were twentieth century young people living in the dark ages of oppression, yet they had decided for Jesus through the simple preaching of the gospel.

This was no joy ride. They had counted the cost. This was no decision they'd made under parental pressure or in the emotion of an evangelistic service. They made the most unpopular and difficult decision anyone in the world could make. I longed for them to know all there was of Jesus.

Satan had attacked forcefully, making me think I was too weak to cross the border that day. But he could not prevail against the cross of Christ. This was a day I would remember always, and I was humbled that God had chosen to make me part of it.

We learned from some of the new believers who had come out of the Free German Youth that the Party leaders had been teaching every morning how to combat our ministry. They watched us, then devised countertactics and taught the young people. What they didn't realize was that the Holy Spirit gave us the strategy, and He never gave us the same idea twice. We rarely knew what we were going to do before we did it, so whatever they thought they were prepared for, we disappointed them.

We didn't know what to expect on Day Five, Thursday evening. I considered concentrating on more discipleship to keep everybody out of trouble, but almost immediately I was convicted that was a cop-out. It would have been the natural thing to evangelize until the heat came on and then sneak off for discipleship. I sensed God was not in that cowardly plan.

We knew from the FGY that the party troublemakers were just waiting for us. We scored a major victory the night before, so they were eager to counteract our influence. Our first appointment, however, was at the home of an underground believer. We would then be taken to yet another underground group made up mostly of Catholic Christians.

At the first meeting I saw what communism had done for its people. I had lived in Chicago, so I knew what slums were. This neighborhood was worse than anything I had seen. And this was supposed to be an average neighborhood, equality at work. The families were equal all right; they all lived in squalor.

We felt immediate rapport with these believers and enjoyed beautiful fellowship and a wonderful worship experience. Then they took us to a little clearing in a nearby woods where we met underground Christians from Hungary, Poland, both sides of Germany, and Czechoslovakia. Someone from each country shared about the persecution in his land, but each rejoiced in the goodness of God in bringing him to this place of international fellowship.

> **As we stood in that wooded sanctuary we realized that our East German hosts could have been imprisoned because of our very presence.**

As we stood in that wooded sanctuary we realized that our East German hosts could have been imprisoned because of our very presence. In both East Germany and Czechoslovakia it was illegal to meet for any reason with people from the West. How we cherished that time. We imagined that this must have been the way the first-century Christians met during the height of their persecution. What beautiful fellowship we enjoyed, not as Catholics and Protestants, but as brothers and sisters in Christ!

We learned that when the chips are down and your life is on the line, you either hold a ceremonious ritual and turn your back on the Truth, or you get right with God. I had seen many Christians on the free side of the Curtain who couldn't take a little peer pressure; but behind the Iron Curtain were Christians who lived for Christ under the daily risk of prison. Over the years I've had to resist thinking that this necessarily makes Iron Curtain Christians more spiritual, yet I often wonder whether those of us who have been inculcated by the West could survive over there.

After someone shared from each country, we were asked to minister. We sang and testified, and then I preached. For a couple of hours our little church in the woods was the most precious place I had ever been in.

By the time we got to Alexanderplatz, the new believers were eagerly waiting for us. The communists also had to wonder where we had been. We banded together, formed a circle, and sang our songs. Immediately the communists surrounded us. The crowd was huge because we were the talk of the Fest by now. When I began to preach I was not challenged, but the three hundred or so communist young people surrounding us tried to drown me out by singing their own songs.

The Lord gave me the idea to have our kids sing "We Shall Overcome." That had originally been a Christian song, but was now used internationally as a theme for the oppressed. We had heard it often at the Fest; it had become the young communists' theme song. When we broke into that number they looked delighted, probably thinking they had caught us off guard. Since we were singing "their"song, they joined right in. Until, that is, they ran out of verses about peace and unity and we were still coming up with new ones. Now we had caught *them* off guard.

We switched from singing "We shall overcome" to "We shall be like Him" and then "Jesus Christ loves you," and the communists didn't know what to do. They had been lured into singing our song. When they dispersed to find out what to do, they made room for other curious delegates who wanted to hear what we were all about. As soon as we quit singing, we had the freedom to preach uninterrupted for the rest of the night.

More and more kids came to Christ. Whenever we broke into a chorus like "God Is So Good," it was thrilling to hear even brand new converts begin to make up new words, in their own language, like "He's coming soon, He's coming soon, He's coming soon, He's so good to me."

Soon there were at least a hundred of us, with more coming to Christ by the hour and putting their freedom on the line. I taught them a Jesus cheer: "Give me a J," etc. In America Jesus cheers had become meaningless fads, but when underground Christians shout for their Lord in public for the first time, it's like heavenly music. After they'd spell out His name, I'd ask, "What's His name?"

They'd shout, "Jesus!"

"Who is God's Son?"

"Jesus!"

"Who does the world need? Who loves everybody at the Communist Youth World Fest? Who is our Lord?"

"Jesus! Jesus! Jesus!"

By Friday, the day before the end of the Fest, we were exhausted and had to lean on the Lord for every step. We planned to meet some of the believers at a little church for some training before heading to Alexanderplatz, but when we arrived, the small room was packed. Among the young people was an elderly lady who approached me after the session. She gave me a small notebook and a plaque, which said in German, "We are truly brothers in Christ."

In the notebook she had written, "Blessed are you when men revile you and persecute you for My name's sake." It was a token of love, and I still cherish it.

I offered the young believers the opportunity to spend the whole evening in discipleship training, but they refused. "This is the chance of a lifetime," they said. "We may never get another chance to be missionaries. Kids from all over the world are at Alexanderplatz."

We headed back to the Fest, one hundred strong. One young man told me he would rather be a Christian in a communist country than in a free one. I asked him why. "Because we are like trees. Oppression pushes on our branches and makes our trunks and roots strong."

When we got to the plaza, the communists were waiting for us. More than five hundred surrounded us, booming, "Peace! Friendship! Solidarity against the imperialists!" They screamed as if at a soccer game, and there was no way we could sing, cheer, testify, or preach. All we could do was stand there while the uproar grew.

We could think of no counterattack, yet we did not want to run. We joined hands and knelt. "God, what would you have us do?" we prayed. I sensed He would have us do nothing. We would not have to battle this mighty force ourselves. The communists didn't know whom they were up against. They thought they were coming against men, some backwoods evangelists from America who had stolen some of their number.

But they were coming against God Himself. As we prayed, seeking Him, we wondered what would stop the chanting, what could drown out such hateful, boisterous noise. In an instant the answer came. Lightning flashed and thunder rolled and torrents of rain washed over Alexanderplatz. The chanters ran to escape showers we believed were meant just for them.

Keeping our hands joined, we Christians moved quickly under a shelter that had room for a couple of thousand people. It quickly filled with delegates, and suddenly we had a captive audience. As the rain continued, the communists had nothing to do but listen. We didn't want them to be bored, so we proclaimed the gospel the rest of the evening, our detractors having run for cover.

I preached five different times that night as we all testified to the love of Jesus Christ. We doubled our number, seeing the total of believers jump to about two hundred. I can't emphasize the magnitude of these young people responding to the claims of Christ and praying to receive Him right there in public in that setting. By making a public profession of their new faith in Christ they were saying, "I'm taking a stand for something that may cost me my freedom, my family, even my life because I believe that Jesus Christ is Lord." If these young people, in the prime of their lives, could risk everything for God, I can certainly trust Him fully and continue to obey.

We had moved into the realm of the authority of the resurrected Christ. Satan might have been able to come against us, but he could not come against the body of Jesus Christ. The Bible says the gates of hell shall not prevail against His church.

The Fest would officially end on Sunday at noon, so our last evening for witnessing at the plaza was Saturday. In spite of the inspiration the brave young people had been to me, if I had known what we would encounter that evening I probably wouldn't have gone.

We had spent some time at the home of an underground believer who could have been prosecuted just for entertaining foreigners. But by this time the believers were bold enough to sing choruses loudly, even with the windows open. As we were leaving for Alexanderplatz we were met at the door by the police, who demanded to see our passports. While most of us were East Germans registered for the Fest, a Czechoslovakian and I were foreigners and could be responsible for the imprisonment of the believer who owned the house.

I fully expected to be arrested, along with our host. I prayed that the Lord would intercede. The officer ignored my passport and studied my twenty-four-hour visa. "All right," he said, handing it back. I breathed a sigh of relief and a silent prayer of thanks. The same happened with the Czech.

At Alexanderplatz I met a young man who had read about our ministry and had come looking for me. He began to spread the word through occupied European countries that we had come to the World Fest to share Christ. He said it was an encouragement to the underground believers.

The Free German Youth were determined to stop us on this final night. They had been frustrated in every attempt during the week, and they came prepared. This time more than a thousand surrounded our two hundred, and when they began their incessant chanting again, we knelt again. As if on cue, God sent the rain again.

This time the FGY were ready for us. As we moved under cover, they stayed right with us. When we started to preach they started in again with "Peace! Friendship! Solidarity!" We could not be heard. I prayed and felt the Lord leading me to have a march.

"Let's march for Jesus!" I shouted, and the two hundred Christians rose as one and moved out into the rain. The FGY fell right in behind us and kept chanting. They followed us all the way around the plaza as we sang and praised God. To the thousands and thousands of other delegates it looked as if there were twelve hundred Christians marching for Jesus.

People seemed unable to believe it. They were running everywhere shouting, "The Jesus People are coming!" We kept changing direction, giving Jesus cheers, and then continuing. All over Alexanderplatz communists came running to see what this was all about. Eventually we were surrounded by about two thousand communists. Finally we were trapped in one corner of the plaza. We tried to keep moving, but the communists locked arms and shouted their slogans, holding us in.

As they jeered and screamed at us, thousands upon thousands of delegates came running to see what was going on. We found ourselves in a sea of shouting communists. An elderly German man, looking out of place among all these young people, held up a hand for silence. A few fell silent as he said, "We are all for peace, friendship, and solidarity," he said, and the place grew still. "But that comes only through Jesus Christ!"

Immediately he was drowned out by the snarling crowd, who shook their fists at us. One of the guys who had been leading the march caught my eye and pressed his palms together under his chin. I nodded and we knelt, two hundred Christians following our lead.

It was an incredible scene, and I felt vulnerable and exposed. I felt I might never again get the chance to preach to that many lost people. "Lord," I prayed, "Your strength and Your power will have to be with me. I can't do it on my own."

I stood and raised my hand, asking for silence. The crowd must have thought I was going to plead for my life or apologize or confess because they quieted. With that I cut loose with a rapid-fire tirade about how Jesus could change a person's life and how He had changed mine. The Lord quickened me to preach as fast as I could. I said more words in a few minutes than I thought possible.

The two thousand FGY burst forward, nearly trampling us as they swung their fists in my face and threatened me. I thought I had preached my last sermon. Party authorities tried to break up the crowd and keep the peace, but they could do nothing.

A convert from the Free German Youth shouted, "I'm a Christian, let me talk!" But they would have none of it. The communists grew louder and gritted their teeth, their eyes wild with hatred. I felt responsible for all these young Christians, and I feared a riot.

I shouted to the Christians to start a human train, and I led the way. Each person held the one in front of him with both hands, and we began to move out through the massive crowd. I broke through the locked arms of the communists and just kept walking, leading that huge train of believers from the center of the hostility.

As the communists shoved me and swung at me, I was overwhelmed with the joy of God. The words from the old lady's notebook from the night before came to me, and I rejoiced in the privilege of being persecuted for the name of Christ.

At the back of the huge crowd were delegates who still didn't know what was going on. All they knew was that the FGY had the Jesus People cornered and that trouble was brewing. They couldn't see us making our escape. It took about five minutes for us to pull free, and by that time I had gone all the way to the edge of the crowd and was circling around the back. To people at the edge I said, "Have you heard?"

They said, "No! What's going on?"

I said, "Jesus loves you."

"Oh, no!" some said. "They're everywhere!"

Our impossible mission had been accomplished. Jesus Christ

had become the major issue on the last night of the Communist Youth World Fest.

During our last two days in Berlin we spent several hours fellow-shipping with the believers and discipling them. Many of them rode the train back to the border with us, and my heart broke as I thought about leaving them. I wanted them to remain one in the Spirit so they would be able to stand in the evil day and hold fast the testimony of Christ. Twenty years later my heart still breaks as I think of that last ride with them.

As we passed Alexanderplatz I saw the sun reflecting from the huge TV tower. "There is our church," I said.

They nodded. "And there are the people who need Jesus."

When we got back to the Temple of Tears, the last night of the festival filled my mind. A brother from Czechoslovakia pleaded with me to come to his country some day.

And there was Ilse, who pronounced my name Sommy, the way all the German young people did. "Sommy," she said, "please come back. We need you."

Kids from the other countries gathered around, and we embraced and wept. "Sommy, please come back," they said.

"*Danke* [thank you], *Sommy*," each said in turn, tears running down their faces. "*Danke, Sommy.*"

"*Danke, Jesus,*" I said, smiling through my tears, my voice thick. "*Danke, danke, Jesus.*" It was He who had drawn them to Himself. They had met the resurrected Savior.

I did not know what their futures held, but I praised God for their boldness. All the way to West Berlin and then all the way to the States, all I could think about were the brothers and sisters we had left behind. I was grateful for the solid underground church I had heard about, and I encouraged the new believers to get involved and begin to grow in the Lord. I knew I would be returning soon to our new friends in Christ. I just had to.

CHAPTER SIXTEEN

NARROW ESCAPE

My burden for the lost and for the oppressed believers behind the Iron Curtain was in full bloom. For the next few years Tex and Davey and I lived in Europe, and I ventured behind the Curtain as frequently as I could. Not many people understood a young evangelist living on faith, living in danger, not serving under the auspices of any official mission board or agency but with the backing of only a single church.

Some thought I should get into a pastorate. To me that sounded as foreign as anything I was involved in. There was a comfort zone, such as it was, in what I was doing. I was learning to travel internationally, learning to negotiate with travel agencies and bureaucracies, to be unintimidated by gruff responses and seemingly shut doors. That would all serve me well in the years to come.

Prior to that—and even somewhat today—people saw me as maybe a little flaky. I knew our ministry was small-time. We didn't claim to be a well-oiled, sophisticated machine. I used to refer to myself as a "dingaling," because we sometimes appeared to just take advantage of whatever the Lord put in our paths. I can be a driven person, knowing exactly what I want to do and how I want to do it, but on the other hand, I can be forgetful, like an absent-minded professor. I don't know how those two traits go together, but the people who have worked with me and for me know it's true.

For instance, I am obsessive about local customs and protocol. I care about being on time, deferring to my hosts, dressing, speaking, carrying ourselves in a manner that will not offend. At the same time, I'm one who will get to the airport with a passel of luggage and travel companions, only to find I've left my passport at home or misplaced my wallet.

That's why, when I look back on some of the narrow escapes we endured after the Communist Youth World Fest, there will be some who will shake their heads and say, "Yeah, that sounds like something Sam would have done." But I'll spare you the ordeals brought on solely by my being young and naive and getting myself into situations I would avoid today.

Maybe there was some humor and even some foolishness in the following situation that can be attributed to my having been a dingaling. But also wonderful blessings came as a result of doing what I felt the Lord was driving me to do. There is a place in the kingdom for being a fool for Christ, not risking peoples' lives or just doing something for attention, but for stepping out on faith, against all odds, and doing something that someone else might have talked himself out of.

Fred Bishop and I visited Bratislava, Czechoslovakia, and looked up a born again priest we had met at the Communist Youth World Fest. What an eye opener this was for a kid raised as a Baptist! While I may not agree on certain doctrines and emphases, and while I believe that much of the Catholic Church has missed the most crucial doctrine of all—salvation by grace through faith alone —I will never again say that there are no true Christians among the Catholics.

This beloved brother had translated "The Four Spiritual Laws" into Slovakian and had personally typed several copies for us to use as we witnessed there. We could have argued about the pope, the virgin Mary, and praying to the saints, but when you find yourself in a society where Christianity is hated, you get back to the basics. You emphasize what you do agree on, and in our cases that was the death, burial, and resurrection of Jesus Christ, His work on the cross as the only basis for personal forgiveness of sin and salvation. There are people even within American evangelicalism I am less comfortable with than others, some with whom I disagree on emphasis and practice and teaching. I don't mean to imply that these things are not important, but again, when the rest of the world is at enmity with God, we who believe in Christ have to find common ground and work together to get out the most important message of all: the saving work of His death and resurrection.

The young priest showed us a hiding place where nuns studied and prayed, out of the view of communist authorities. I asked if I could spend some time there alone. As I browsed the tiny room it hit me that I was standing in a privileged, holy place. I represented freedom, plenty, ease, and comfort. I represented not just the West, but America, where we are so free to practice our faith that we have taken it for granted. Here people had to hide because they were sought after by their own government. It broke my heart and I felt privileged anew to be allowed to fellowship with and minister to suffering saints in the oppressed countries.

Our new friend introduced us to an older priest who had spent several years in prison for his faith. I say this man was imprisoned because of his faith, but of course the charges were couched in different terms. A Christian in a totalitarian state never knows what might be his downfall. I heard of a man who tried to bring Bibles across the border and wound up in prison for years, not for smuggling or preaching the gospel, but because he pulled away from a guard. He was charged with resisting arrest and attempted murder. The Christian was set up and spent years behind bars. For his faith? Of course. But the authorities would say, "We do not persecute people for their beliefs."

I learned to be very careful about everything I did in Eastern Europe.

The priest asked me about my background, and when I told him I was a Baptist a huge smile came to him. "I spent years in a cell with a Baptist pastor," he said. "We discovered we had much more in common than we thought. Jesus Christ was our common denominator."

I know that many Catholics use the same words we do, but often in different contexts and with different meanings. But in talking with this man and the younger priest we had met at the Youth Fest, there was no question that they were Bible-believing evangelicals.

Fred Bishop and I did not know either Czech or Slovakian, the two languages of the country, so when we went to a nearby university to pass out the tracts the priest had prepared for us, we hoped the educated people there understood either English or our rapidly improving German. Otherwise, we would be unable to communicate orally with anyone.

That would be frustrating, but it was also rewarding to pass out our leaflets. As was always the case behind the Iron Curtain, people were hungry to read anything new. I have found that if you pass out anything on the street, people will flock to receive it. In America most will ignore you or take one and let it fly away. But people in communist countries are eager for news and information and philosophy.

After passing out a few tracts, Fred suggested that we kneel in a great hallway at the university and commit our time to God, then sing the chorus "Alleluia," a word that seems to mean the same in every language in the world.

We earnestly and quietly asked God to move in the great university, and then, still with our heads bowed and eyes closed, we softly sang, "Alleluia, alleluia, alleluia, alleluia. Alleluia, alleluia, alleluia, alleluia."

> **As we sang we sensed and heard people gathering around us. I was afraid to look up.**

We knew that beautifully haunting little chorus would mean little except to those who might be underground believers. Yet as we sang we sensed and heard people gathering around us. I was afraid to look up, but eventually we had to. A couple of hundred students had gathered, just staring. We rose and began to speak to them, I in German and Fred in English. As if on cue, those who understood English moved toward Fred and those who understood German came toward me.

Two recent graduates, young women who had just received their teaching certificates, read over "The Four Spiritual Laws" and said, "This is wonderful. We've never seen anything like this. Would you be willing to tell us more? It would have to be a secret meeting, but we will make sure other students hear about it and come."

I told her we would come back the next day to meet with her and anyone she brought along. About that time an official of the university angrily told us to leave the campus, and the crowd quickly dispersed.

Fred and I were excited, but that night Fred lost his enthusiasm and couldn't sleep. "I'm worried," he said. "Something's wrong. I think we're in trouble and we need to get out of here."

He was my traveling partner, my mission companion. I knew enough not to travel alone, but I didn't know enough to realize that God might use him to speak to me. "You're just worried about that guy kicking us off the campus. We made a commitment to those girls, and we have to honor it." He reluctantly agreed.

When we arrived the next morning, only one of the girls was there. Her hands were red and raw from her nervously wringing them for hours. She pulled us off to the side and spoke quickly, her voice strained and apologetic. "You must get out of here. The authorities have been questioning everyone. They know there are two men from the West, and they don't know whether you're German or American or what, but they're going from hotel to hotel. They've already arrested people they know were here but who are not cooperating, and it's just a matter of time before they find you. You need to get out of the country as soon as possible."

We thanked her and ran back to our hotel, packed, and checked out. The last train from Bratislava to the West was leaving, and just like in the movies, we ran down the track with our luggage and hopped on. We wondered if our names might show up on some list at the border, but we got into Austria without incident. The only problem was that when we changed our money back from Czech currency we realized we had been ripped off and had only enough to get train tickets from Vienna to Salzburg and to spend one night in a youth hostel. Then we would be broke, with little idea how to get back to our families in Germany.

It was snowing when we got to the hostel in Salzburg, and I was discouraged. The last of our money went to cover that night, so in the morning we would have to leave. When I awoke I pulled the blanket up over my head and prayed, "O God, here we got chased out of Czechoslovakia, we're broke, we're stranded, it's cold, we're hungry. Help us."

Meanwhile, Fred got up and had his prayer and quiet time outside. He came in with the joy of the Lord. "Praise God, Sam!" he said.

Miserably I pulled the blanket from my head. "For what?"

"Because this is the day the Lord has made!"

Frankly, I wasn't in a mood to hear that. I turned over and sighed.

"C'mon, Sam," Fred said. "Get out of bed and get with God."

I was sullen as I started to dress, but what should I find on the floor but a wadded up bill, one hundred West German marks! It must have fallen from my clothes the night before, and I didn't even know I had it. Suddenly I felt ashamed, at the same time at peace again that God was in control. We enjoyed some time with the Lord in Salzburg until it was time for our train, then we got as far as Heidelberg where I connected with some friends who helped us get home.

If nothing else, I learned to be prepared for anything and not to despair when things looked bleakest. It was a lesson I needed for our continued forays behind the Iron Curtain. There were many people to follow up from the World Fest, and it seemed to be an encouragement to underground believers that people in the West were aware of them.

Fred Bishop and Fred Starkweather and I planned a trip into East Germany and got the word out that we would meet with underground believers—many of whom had been converted at the Fest—at a castle outside Dresden. The three of us preached and taught about forty young people who risked their freedom, their futures, and their lives by sneaking to the meeting.

At the end of the meeting a young girl came to me and said, "I'm a Christian, and I want to serve Jesus. But I have sin in my life and I don't know what to do about it."

I showed her from the Bible, "If we confess our sins, He is faithful and just to forgive us our sins and to cleanse us from all unrighteousness" (1 John 1:9). As she was a new believer, that was a revelation to her, and she wept as she confessed her sin and thanked God for forgiving her and empowering her to continue serving Him.

At the end of her prayer, as the rest of the room was hushed and listening, she added a poignant and powerful phrase that God used to grip us all. She asked God to make her willing to follow Him and to do His will, and in her own language she said, "No matter what it costs." The rest of the young people immediately went to their knees, many weeping, all praying and committing themselves to Christ. I prayed with each of them, and one after another they vowed to follow Jesus and live for Him, "no matter what it costs."

It struck Fred, Fred, and me that when these kids said that, they meant it. We can say that same phrase in our culture and in our country, and the cost may be no greater than a little embarrassment or poverty or ridicule. We may lose a few privileges or get laughed at, but we don't lose our educational opportunities. We don't lose our ability to earn a living. We don't lose our freedom. We don't see our families suffer or get set up for arrests on bogus charges. When they said they would follow Jesus no matter what it cost, they were putting their very lives on the line.

We had gone to minister to them, but we had been taught a lesson in real obedience. I wanted to be willing to do what James Robison counseled me to do the day I came to Christ. I wanted to be willing to pay whatever price was necessary. But I knew I always had the option of escaping to the West, to freedom, if things got too hot.

What I didn't know was that the day was coming when I would get my big break, my cherished opportunity to invade the very Soviet Union itself. There I would find it not so easy to escape, and my commitment would be tested to the extreme. Was I really ready to give up everything to do what God wanted? Or would the faith of these new believers in the underground church in East Germany put mine to shame?

CHAPTER SEVENTEEN

HOUSE ARREST

I t was thrilling to make a couple of trips into East Germany and find the Christian movement growing. In Leipzig one day we held a meeting with young people who were so enthusiastic that they boldly went into the streets, marching, singing, and inviting others in. They filled a cathedral with about 1,500 kids, and I shared my testimony, asking them to commit their lives to Christ. Many did.

Later we went to Dresden, where it was illegal for anyone to preach. But I was told in advance that the people would find a way for me to bring a "greeting," and my greeting could be a sermon as long as I wanted. At an open meeting of about two thousand young people, the speaker asked from the platform how many were from outside Dresden. Hundreds of us raised our hands.

"How many from outside Sachsen [the local district]?"

My hand was still up, along with dozens of others.

"How many from outside East Germany?" Now there were just two of us, a man from Hungary and me.

"How many from outside Europe?"

My hand was still raised.

"And where are you from, sir?"

"San Antonio, Texas, in America!"

The crowd applauded.

"Ah, as the one who came the farthest, you must bring us a greeting!"

I brought a three-minute greeting, expressing the best wishes of their brothers and sisters in Christ in America. "They know of you. They care about you. They love you. And they pray for you."

And then I spoke forty minutes on the cross of Christ.

During my long greeting in Dresden, I spoke of a conversation between Jesus and the apostle Peter. Rather than having Peter respond, *"Nein"* for "No," I used "Nay," which is more colloquial for that district. The people immediately broke into applause at that familiarity. I smiled. "Didn't you know Peter came from Sachsen?" I said, and they roared.

In our travels in and out of East Germany we found that about 90 percent of the young people who had prayed to receive Christ at the Communist Youth World Fest followed through with their commitment and were active in the underground church. How thrilling that was! I felt somewhat like their spiritual father, and it warmed me to see them growing in the faith.

All that time I continued to view the Soviet Union as the ultimate center of atheism. Back then it was still a land of mystery, an enigma wrapped in a puzzle, as Winston Churchill once said. We knew no one and had no contacts there, but Fred Starkweather and I were eager to go anyway. In my heart and mind, there could be no greater thrill, no greater privilege than to proclaim Christ in the Soviet Union. Even if that meant witnessing to only one person, it was worth every effort and risk.

At this point Davey was a preschooler, and Fred Starkweather and I were living with our families in Berlin in two camper vans. We helped serve in a church with a pastor named Herr Schoch, working with his young people. The entire church, and especially the young people, were excited about the plans Fred and I had to venture into the Soviet Union. The closer the time came to departure day, the more excited I became. I believed God had great things in store. Fred stuffed thousands of Russian language tracts into the lining of some ski clothes. We thought we were ready for any eventuality.

The day before we were to leave, I lost my passport. It could have been stolen. Berlin being a city of spies, an American passport is worth a lot of money. Now what was I going to do? I would have to get another passport from the American embassy and get another Russian visa, which would be next to impossible. The people at the American embassy told me they couldn't give me a new passport unless I brought a written statement from the German police saying that I'd lost mine. The German police told me, "It's not our business."

"It's not your business?" I repeated.

"That's right," I was told. "We don't care that you have lost your passport, and we don't have to give you anything."

In either youthful frustration or holy boldness I said, "Well, I'll tell you what: I'm going to sit right here at your desk, and I'm not going to leave until you give me a statement that says I reported losing my passport."

The officer said, "You can sit there till you starve to death."

I sat there for an hour until he finally got tired of me. "Okay, okay," he said, rolling a form into his typewriter. "Here's your statement. Now get out of here."

I raced back to the American embassy, where I was given a ninety-day passport. When I got to the Soviet embassy it was closed. I was frantic. I couldn't let the whole trip fall apart on this one turn of events. I banged on the gates until someone came.

"I need a visa to go to Leningrad," I said. "I lost my passport and had to get a statement from the police. I got it and got a new passport, but I still need the visa."

"Come in, come in," the man said.

I was stunned. When they issued me a new visa on the spot, I sensed that God was in it.

Our plan was to fly into Leningrad and witness, then get to Moscow by Easter 1974 and preach the gospel in Red Square near the Kremlin. On Easter morning, in the shadow of Lenin's tomb, I wanted to proclaim that Christ is risen. That was the desire of my heart.

We went as tourists, of course. You don't declare that you're going to the Soviet Union to win them to Christ. So when we arrived in Leningrad we were met by Intourist, the Soviet travel agency and national sightseeing host organization. We took a tour with them, checked into our hotel, then essentially prayed, "Now what, God?"

We slit open a tiny compartment in the ski jackets and produced a few tracts. Then we hit the street and asked someone to direct us to the university. The school was huge and covered several blocks, but we were pointed to the linguistics department, clearly an act of God. Nearly everyone there would understand English.

Partly out of fear, partly to calm ourselves, we just looked the place over at first. In many ways it looked like any other European university, perhaps a bit more somber. We found a small cafe down one of the hallways where students milled about, and as we sat having a bite, we noticed a young man sitting by himself. Fred and I looked at each other. I had memorized a few words of greeting, as well as my testimony in Russian.

We approached the young man. I greeted him and asked if we could talk with him. He smiled, and we sat down. I asked if he spoke English, which, fortunately for all of us, he did. I asked if I could share with him the truth of the Bible, about how God loves him and wants a relationship with him.

> **"All my life I have been taught there is no God. . . . But two weeks ago I was staring into the sky and looking at the stars, and I began thinking: *This could not be an accident. Could it be there is a God?"***

The young man's eyes grew wide with wonder, and he held up a hand. "I need to tell you something," he said, his accent thick. "All my life I have been taught there is no God. My parents taught me there was no God. My teachers have taught me there is no God. My government has taught me there is no God."

I waited for the right opportunity to jump back into the Scriptures and defend the faith, but he continued.

"But two weeks ago I was staring into the sky and looking at the stars, and I began thinking: *This could not be an accident. Could it be there is a God?* I prayed for the first time and I said, 'God, if You exist, if You are out there, would You reveal Yourself to me?' " He looked solemnly at Fred and me. "I believe He has just answered my prayer by sending you here to me."

I told him I agreed, and my heart nearly burst with joy. What a privilege! What a great God we serve! All that we had gone through was worth this conversation alone, to be used of God to answer the prayer of a young man seeking Him. He looked at our pamphlet and asked if we had any more. "If I brought my friends, would you give them some?"

"Sure! Go get them."

A few minutes later he returned with nearly two hundred people! The hallway was filled with students, clamoring for a pamphlet from Fred and me. We began to preach to two different groups, and more people gathered around. Four girls approached and called out, *"Habla Espanol?"*

The only Spanish I knew was "The Four Spiritual Laws," so I went through them quickly. All the while, I still passed out tracts as the crowd surged forward. I had just given away my last tract when several men in dark suits grabbed me. There were six of them, roughly the same age as most of the students but the only people there in coats and ties. They hauled us into a room and interrogated us for hours, two men at a time.

I assumed they were KGB, but someone told me later it was unlikely that the KGB would have jurisdiction over such an offense as ours. Whoever they were, they had authority and they were scary. Once, while two interrogators were switching with another pair, a university official asked for one of our tracts. We handed it to him and he thanked us, folded it, and put it in his pocket. We got the impression from the look on his face that he would read it later. We prayed that he would.

They kept demanding to know where we got our pamphlets and how many we had. Every time they asked us for some, we produced a batch. They wanted to know if we had more. We directed them to our suitcases. "More?" they wanted to know. Fred asked if they had any scissors. When he cut open our ski jackets and produced hundreds of more tracts, their eyes bulged with anger. They were convinced we were part of some international conspiracy against the Soviet state, that we had the backing of some huge organization, and that we were committing a crime.

After about eight hours of questioning and photographs (of us and our tracts), they asked us to write out our confession.

"Our confession to what?" I said.

"To your crime."

"What crime? I thought the Soviet constitution guarantees the freedom to practice religion. What is our crime?"

"The people have the freedom to believe in God, but they are considered sick. If they spread their sickness among the masses, that is a crime against the state. To bring this sickness in from the outside, as you and your organization have done, is even worse. You must write your confession."

So I wrote my confession. It went something like this:

"It began when a man told me about Jesus, that He is God come in human flesh . . . that He lived a sinless life, and that He died for the sins of the world. Three days later He arose . . . I gave my heart to Him. Whoever is reading this confession now can know Him too. . . ." I wrote out a prayer of repentance and faith in Christ.

Some time later they came back with what they said were our confessions translated into Russian. I studied the document carefully and knew enough to know that they were not what we had written. "You sign it," we were told.

"No," I said. "We won't sign unless we can speak with someone from the American consulate."

"No. You must sign."

"No."

"Ah, so you *are* spies."

"No."

"Charge them as American spies unless they sign the statement."

"Fred," I said, "what do we do?"

"I think we need to sign it," he said.

"I think so too."

And so we did. It was wrong, and I wouldn't do it today because we admitted to something that wasn't true.

We were then taken back to our hotel room and were told not to leave. There was someone at the end of the hall, but the door was not locked, so we were under house arrest. When we hadn't heard anything for several hours, and we were hungry, Fred ventured out and got on the elevator, hoping to go down and find us something to eat.

The elevator stopped between floors and the phone rang. "You will be taken back to your floor," a voice said. "Stay in the room."

So we were stuck there. For two days we heard nothing and ate nothing. If they were trying to work on our minds, they were succeeding. But it was also making me mad. We decided to call downstairs every so often and demand to be put through to the American consulate. I had learned in the German police office that authorities admire persistence and eventually get tired of resisting. Finally, they put us through.

I spilled our story, and a man told me in American English, "Listen, whatever happens, I'm coming straight over there. Don't leave with anybody. This is very serious and extremely dangerous. It will take me about a half hour, but I will be there. Stay there."

We weren't truly frightened until then. But now I started wondering, *How do we know they really put us through to the Americans?* We decided we would test the man when he arrived. We would ask him who won the most recent Super Bowl. Only a real American would know that. We waited nervously, wondering what was going to happen to us.

Finally a knock came on the door. "Who is it?"

"American consulate," he said.

"Before we open the door, tell us who won the Super Bowl in January."

There was a pause. Fred and I looked at each other. "I have no idea," the man said. "Who did?"

Fred and I thought. Then shrugged. We were Americans, and we didn't know either. (It was the Miami Dolphins.) So much for our safety measures.

"Look," the man said, "I have identification. Let me show you."

We cracked the door and saw his official-looking ID. He marched us downstairs and chewed out everybody involved. "You have no right to force them to sign anything about their presence at the university. We'll be filing an official protest. Now I'm getting these boys something to eat."

Our money and our plane tickets had been confiscated, and after some negotiating between him and the authorities, he gave us the news. "You're going to be deported to Helsinki, and then you'll be on your own."

After he left we were ushered into a fancy room where officials bawled us out for violating the Soviet state by trying to spread a disease among the people. Then we were taken back up to our room where we waited—for what, we didn't know. We had no idea who would come for us or when.

Finally, at about ten that night, two tall men in plainclothes came and said in English, "Come with us."

We didn't know what was going on, but we didn't feel we had a choice. By then I wondered even about the man who claimed to be from the American consulate. He could have been in a plot to get rid of us, for all we knew. We were driven in a limousine to a train station and were put on a train. When we asked where the train was going, no one answered.

The farther the train got from Leningrad, the harder it snowed. I remember that today as vividly as if it were yesterday. I became convinced that we had been banished to Siberia. We stopped briefly in a little village where a guard with a machine gun paced the platform.

I began to weep, wondering if I would ever see my wife and son again, wondering if I had gotten Fred Starkweather into a situation from which there was no escape. I asked myself, "Sammy, was this all a result of your own stupidity? Was God not in this at all? Was it just a crazy, foolish thing?"

In my heart I told God, "If we end up in Siberia, it was worth it. That one young man coming to Christ was worth it all. Thank You for letting us be part of the answer to his prayer."

Meanwhile, the clock moved well past midnight, and in the faint light of the train I saw the huge, thick flakes fall. I had no idea where we were going, but it sure didn't look like Helsinki.

PART 2

THE
BREAKING

CHAPTER EIGHTEEN

A RESTLESS SPIRIT

As that drafty train clacked into the desolate Soviet night, I searched my soul. Even in my fear and remorse over perhaps being banished to a wintry wilderness, I came to the conclusion that God works in the context of situations and history. In other words, at that time the Soviets would not allow anyone to come in and preach the gospel. It took a couple of brash young people, almost blindly knocking around the corridors of a university, to find the one young man God sent us there to minister to. One person coming to Christ back then was as great as the thousands who come forward at outdoor crusades in the same nation today.

People say we were foolish. I say we were young and naive, but that we were obedient and went with a purpose, God's purpose— one we didn't even fully understand until it was over. I also came away from that visit to the Soviet Union with a knowledge of the hunger of the people. Just as at the Communist Youth World Fest, these people didn't mob us just because we were foreigners, just because we spoke English, just because we espoused some radical new philosophy.

No, they knew immediately what we were about because in that setting you don't have time to explain or apologize for what you're about to say. You get the floor, you have the attention of a crowd, and you preach Christ. That's all we knew to do. Sure, their curiosity over these two dingalings kneeling and praying and singing may have drawn them to us, but what made them stay and ask questions and clamor for tracts? Our speaking of God, of Jesus, of forgiveness, of life.

Fred and I breathed huge sighs of relief when that train did arrive in Helsinki, Finland. We thanked God for everything that had happened—even the scary parts—but especially for the privilege of talking about Christ where few have been allowed to.

Getting all the way back to our families in Berlin without money, tickets, or passports was typical of what I went through for years. Traveling internationally is an ordeal and an adventure. You can either cave in and give up or be creative and trust God.

Without a penny to our names, we walked to the American embassy, made one collect call to God's Love in Action board member Morris Todd, asked him to get hold of Herr Schoch in Berlin and have Tex wire us airline tickets to get us from Helsinki to Berlin via Oslo and Hamburg. We waited all day, and when the tickets arrived, we didn't have even the two dollars required to get us to the airport. A kind woman somehow arranged to get us to the airport.

I was nearly thirty, and restless about my future.

On the flight to Oslo we enjoyed steak. On the flight to Hamburg we were given a sack lunch, which we saved. We arrived in Hamburg too late for the last flight to Berlin and, since we had no money for a taxi or a hotel, we talked the authorities into letting us sleep in the airport overnight. The next morning we were grateful we had hoarded our lunches. Finally we were reunited with our families.

After a couple of years of traveling and speaking in Europe and making occasional forays behind the Iron Curtain, Tex and I settled in San Antonio. We briefly spent eight months in Switzerland, where Renee was born in 1976, when Davey was about four and a half. The next year, while on a brief speaking tour in the States, I met Dr. Sam Friend, a pastor in the Seattle area. God began to burden his heart for ministering in Eastern Europe, and he later became a key factor in my ministry plans.

Perhaps because our second child had come along and I was

nearly thirty, I sensed something happening within me. There was a certain maturity that made me more reflective, introspective, and restless about my future. There were needs in my personal life and in my family life. I sensed an uneasiness in my spiritual life and for the first time began evaluating whether it was time for a shift in my ministry emphasis.

An evangelist travels and preaches the same types of sermons numerous times. In many ways, unless you are very careful and mature, you don't stay on the growing edge of life. As a pastor, I knew I would be forced to study the Word, to feast on it and live on it. The more I thought about considering a pastorate, the more I realized that my character development had stopped—somewhere along the line. I was still active, still burdened, still enthusiastic, but something was wrong. And that something was me.

Whatever my blind spots were—and they were revealed to me over the next few years—I desperately and sincerely wanted to serve God. I began to read voraciously, and several books made tremendous impacts on me. Two things struck me when I read *The Life and Diary of David Brainerd* by Jonathan Edwards. First, Brainerd was a deep man of prayer. Second, he was a man of deep humility.

I prayed a lot, but I was aware that I knew nothing of the kind of prayer life Brainerd had. I also knew I was a long way from the type of humility that characterized his life. I wanted to glory only in the cross, but I discovered within me a tendency to glory more in the success God had given our ministry. I knew deep in my heart that grace would be planted only in the soil of humility, and that humility was found only in Jesus and what He did on the cross:

> Let this mind be in you which was also in Christ Jesus, who, being in the form of God, did not consider it robbery to be equal with God, but made Himself of no reputation, taking the form of a servant, and coming in the likeness of men. And being found in appearance as a man, He humbled Himself and became obedient to the point of death, even the death of the cross. (Phil. 2:5-8)

I decided to read biographies of the great saints—like Wesley and Whitefield—and also make an in-depth study of the life of Moses. I saw qualities of character of which I knew little. Moses was eighty years old before his ministry began. For forty years he was proud and strong. The next forty he was devastated and broken in the wilderness. The last forty was when God used him most mightily.

I was troubled in my spirit and knew that God needed to do a deep work in my heart, maybe even breaking me and reshaping me so He could use me most fully. Only by grace could I become a man of godly character, and I knew that was a worthy goal—something God Himself desired for me.

As I delved deeper into the Word and did some fresh, independent study, I began to pray, "Lord, give me a wilderness. Put me where nobody knows me, where it's just me and You and You can do in me whatever You want to do."

I told Tex, "I'd like God to put us where no one knows us and He can teach us simply how to be like Him." Little did I know that this was an answer to her prayers, and that I needed it much more than she did.

Some might fear a deeper work of God in their hearts, but in truth I longed for it. I still didn't know my weakest areas, and because I was blind to them, I didn't know where God would start. I just sensed a general spiritual need and knew I had to get more serious about prayer and the Word.

I prayed about it daily and talked with Tex about it as often as I could. Where might God put us? Where might I land? In the States? In Europe? In a pastorate?

God works in mysterious ways. I was preaching in the Atlanta area, eager to get back to my family, when I ran into an old friend in the airport, a preacher named Manley Beasley. I approached him and said, "Manley, how are you doing?"

The man turned white as a sheet. "Sammy!" he said.

He was nearly speechless, but he quickly pulled me off to the side. "I just returned from Europe," he said, "and I spoke with a missionary who's familiar with you. He told me, 'Manley, I feel like God has his hand on Sammy for Europe. Sammy needs to be in Europe.' "

"Really?" I said.

"That's not all. Another pastor came to me and said the same thing. Then, when I was in Stuttgart, I saw a bunch of young people in a McDonald's, and I could just see you telling them about Jesus."

"Wow."

"But listen, these people who mentioned you to me, I told them, 'Well, I'm not going to talk to Sammy. No way I'm going to try to tell a man what God's will is for his life.' Well, they were pretty persistent, so I decided, and I told them, 'I'll tell you what, if God brings Sammy across my path, then I'll tell him what you told me.' Sammy, I just told you, and I've got to catch my plane."

He walked away, and I somehow found my gate. I sat on that plane and I wept. People may call that a coincidence, but to me it was a divine appointment. God was telling me it was time to get out of my traveling evangelism, at least for a season, and to take a pastorate in Europe, away from where I was known.

Within a month I received the first two calls to churches I'd ever had in my ministry. One was from a church in Stuttgart, and one was from the Hahn Baptist Church in Hahn, West Germany. I preached there once during my travels. The word *Hahn* is short for the German word for chicken, so I was asked to consider becoming pastor of the Chicken Baptist Church in Chicken, Germany! It mostly served a nearby American military base, but was otherwise on the backside of nowhere. It sounded perfect, and I accepted a three-year call beginning in 1978.

Many friends and advisers told me I would make a mistake to take that church. "You need to stay in evangelism," they told me. But I felt certain this was what God wanted me to do.

After the first month, I was no longer so sure. To go from the exciting world of traveling evangelism—where every few days or weeks you're in a new place, seeing people come to Christ, seeing the saints revived—and enjoying all that goes with that, to the middle of very typical church problems and hassles, well . . .

I was discouraged. It hadn't entered my mind that every church has similar problems. When I came to town and preached in a church or held a crusade with a few congregations cooperating, I wasn't there long enough to get involved in the politics and personal skirmishes. People were either on their best behavior or felt bad talking about each other to a stranger who was supposed to be a man above such things. But when you're their pastor, people tend to want to immediately get you on their side and let you know what's really going on in the church.

The first Sunday I was there someone wanted to call a business meeting after the morning service, and I was dumb enough to let him do it. All of a sudden there was petty charge after petty charge, all kinds of things. I didn't know how to handle it. I had seen the big picture, had a burden for souls, and was praying for nations to turn to Christ. Now here was my first pastorate, and the people were not getting along. If I hadn't needed just this kind of wilderness experience, my friends would have been right: I should have stayed in evangelism.

From somewhere—obviously the Lord—I got the insight to put the focus on Christ and call the people to action-oriented holy living. I knew if they could get their eyes off each other and onto God and the lost, they would get past some of the personal problems that seemed so important. The key was spiritual leadership in each home—which ironically was one of the blind spots in my own character—so after a month I started discipling men. The Lord gave me a deep love and hunger for His Word at the same time. I believed He wanted me to "preach the Word," and so I started in Genesis. Over the next two-and-a-half years, I preached from that great Old Testament book.

We set a goal for every member of our church to develop a quiet time, and we began to build the church on prayer. That started a thrust in my whole ministry that has stayed with me to this day: the prayer factor, trying to build a prayer team around our efforts. From that point on, prayer became foundational to that church in all areas: discipleship, teaching, preaching, and outreach. Based on that, a church can take off by leaps and bounds, and Hahn did.

I also began to develop deep friendships with a group of guys who were committed to one another. We had fun together, won people to the Lord together, grew together. I had put a difficult challenge before the men. I agreed to meet and study and pray with those men who were willing to get up at a ridiculously early hour like 6 A.M. That's how I knew they meant business. That small group grew in number and in maturity, and as they affected their homes and families, the church became healthier and began to grow too.

Two guys in particular, with whom I became prayer partners, were Don Shelton and Ken Leeburg. When Don first came to the church he merely took up the offering. I asked him to teach Sunday school after a while, and after he had taught twice he came to me. "Sam, I'm just not a public speaker."

But he got into the discipleship group, grew in the Lord, became a key leader, a teacher, a deacon, then chairman of the deacons. Eventually he entered the ministry and became the pastor of the Hahn Baptist Church!

Ken Leeburg was an attorney who became my best friend. We became jogging and prayer partners, our families grew close, and our friendship became a very special thing in my life.

Soon the church was exploding. We had to take out the pews and hold multiple services. Eventually we moved out of the church and into a local high school for Sunday evenings. People came to Christ and attendance soared. Some of us went to the European Baptist Convention meetings in Interlaken, Switzerland, where I was voted program chairman.

I loved the opportunity to line up exciting speakers from the United States, and I knew the English-speaking churches in the European Baptist Convention would be thrilled to hear them and motivated to live out their faith.

The Wednesday night I was elected program chairman of the convention, Tex nudged me and nodded toward Davey, now a third-grader, who had dozed off between us during the meeting. His eye had begun to twitch uncontrollably, which worried Tex and me. I put my hand on him and prayed for him, but it kept twitching. It didn't wake him up, and it eventually stopped, so we didn't think any more about it. I looked forward to getting home and finishing my study of the Genesis passage where Abraham is asked to sacrifice his son to God. I'd been studying it all week.

We returned to Hahn on Friday. Late that night in bed, I heard noise coming from Davey's room. I went to check on him and found his eyes had rolled back in his head and he was in the grip of a grand mal seizure. Frantic, I yelled for Tex, who came running. We prayed over him, pleading with God to give him relief, but he continued to convulse. We rushed him to the hospital, scared to death.

CHAPTER NINETEEN

DEEP WATERS

The doctor on duty, in God's providence, was Chuck Patterson, a member of my discipleship group. Chuck and I sat up all night with Davey, whose entire right side was paralyzed. Only if you've been there can you imagine the deep pain of watching your own young flesh and blood suffer like that. It was so hard. I wept nearly the whole time.

A day later, with Davey's condition still a mystery, I was expected to preach on Abraham offering his own son as a sacrifice. It was one of the hardest things I have ever done, and I cried through the whole message. I knew God was trying to do something in my life, but I didn't understand it, and I didn't know what it was.

We were civilians, so we could use the military hospital only on a one-time emergency basis. Yet we were salaried by Americans, so we did not have access to the German social medicine either. We had to take Davey to a hospital in Wiesbaden. There a neurologist asked him to walk, and it broke my heart to see my normally rambunctious little guy move in a horribly spastic way.

The neurologist said, "I'm afraid he will never again have full use of his limbs. This will only get worse."

The doctor could not pinpoint a reason for Davey's condition, but I have always suspected that a choking incident when he was younger caused some hidden problem that surfaced this way. Davey had lodged a tiny plastic toy in his throat and was without breath for several minutes while we rushed him to the hospital. He seemed to come out of it all right when the doctors were finally able to dislodge the toy and treat him, but now this strange seizure years later made me wonder.

The neurologist in Wiesbaden put Davey on medication that had to be carefully monitored. There were days—and especially nights—when we thought the cure was worse than the symptoms. He would wake up in the middle of the night screaming with excruciating headaches. One Christmas Eve he ran a fever of 105 degrees.

For a year and a half we went through hell on earth with him sick almost all the time. We had to hold him down every time they took blood, and his little veins couldn't take it. It was hard on Tex and me. We would have given anything to trade places with him, as any loving parent would.

Meanwhile, I tried to concentrate on my Bible study and discipleship, and the church was growing. I was invited to speak in lots of places in Europe, and it was difficult to balance all the demands. We still maintained our family devotions every evening, and one night after our devotions, Davey asked if he could talk to Tex and me.

He began to cry and said, "I want Jesus in my heart." We prayed with him, and that is one of the sweetest memories of my life as a father.

At about that time in 1979, Sam Friend came over from Bothell, Washington, to hold a church growth conference at Hahn Baptist. He checked things out in Eastern Europe and, after talking with Josif Tson, asked if I would go in with a five-member singing group to try to reach the nation's youth. I had always wanted to minister in Romania, so we set a date for June of 1980 for me to go into the country for the first time. Of course, I didn't know what a significant relationship I would begin with that country and its church.

In February of 1980 my friend Manley Beasley held a international congress on revival in Interlaken, Switzerland, where I also spoke. Britain's Roy Hession, author of the classic *Calvary Road*, was one of the keynote speakers, and he enthralled me.

At one point, when I shared all the wonderful ways God was blessing our church, I added, "But I have to be honest with you; I don't understand why God seems silent concerning our son." I asked the people to pray for us. Later, when we were checking out of the hotel to return to Hahn, Roy Hession approached me. I was honored to chat with him, but that's not what he had in mind.

He said simply, "Young man, God is not only calling you to give back your son to Him, but he's also calling you to give back your self-righteousness."

I had no idea what he was talking about, and I was speechless. Here was this great man whose preaching I loved, and I couldn't imagine what he had seen or sensed in me to make him say that. I tried to maintain my composure as we parted, but as soon as he turned away, my face fell. I was hurt. More than that, I was offended. Most of all, I feared he was getting at the root of something God wanted to do in my life. It was a devastating blow.

I went to Don Shelton, Ken Leeburg, and John Labash, another friend and key man in our church (from the military). I said, "If what he's saying is true, I don't know if I can even preach." They encouraged me to just take it at face value but to not let it discourage me. That wasn't easy. God was quietly working in my heart, nudging me to be as receptive to the Spirit as possible.

In June the five young singers from Bothell flew to Europe. I met them, and we squeezed into a rented van with their sound equipment and headed toward Romania. After the long drive through Austria and Hungary (including an overnight in Budapest), we reached the Romanian border at 10 A.M. and spent eight hours there. I got my first lesson in Romanian bureaucracy. They required a $2,000 deposit to ensure we would bring all the sound equipment out with us when we left.

They confiscated our personal Bibles and three Romanian language Bibles we had hoped to bring in, which caused one of the girls in the group to start crying, pleading with me to get her Bible back. I smiled. "The man has a machine gun," I said. But she was nearly hysterical. I saw the guards put the Bibles into a small shipping container, so when they weren't looking I dug out three of the Bibles and put them back in suitcases that had already been searched. When we got into the country we discovered that the guards had given us all our Bibles back anyway, probably because of the girl's crying!

As soon as we crossed the border, we headed for Josif Tson's house before the first service. We had been instructed to park down the street so the secret police wouldn't know whom we were visiting. It was also my first time to play cloak-and-dagger games. At that time Romanian citizens were required to report in writing their entire conversations with any foreigners or risk prison.

Josif's wife, Elizabeth, gave us our itinerary and advice on how to deal with officials and authorities.

I knew something major had taken place in Romania when I noticed the crowd where Josif pastored at the Second Baptist Church of Oradea, one of the largest Protestant churches in Europe. The place was nearly full an hour before the service, and even as we set up our sound equipment, people sat in the pews—men on one side, women on the other—praying and weeping.

I preached on suffering, how God builds our character by allowing hardships in our lives. I openly shared our terrible experiences with Davey's illness. I found out years later that Elizabeth Tson thought it was the best sermon she had ever heard on the subject and that it had deeply ministered to her.

After the service I met a young man Josif was discipling, a sharp, dynamic young man named Paul Negrut. At the restaurant in the Hotel Dachia, he pointed out two secret policemen at the other end of the table. "If they're secret police," I asked him, "how do you know who they are?"

"Because they call me into their offices every day and interrogate me for two hours before I go to work." I found it hard to believe how much intimidation the Christians endured in Romania. In later years Paul would put a transistor radio in the window and play it loud when we spoke, to throw off any bugging devices of the Securitate. Once, even with that in place, he was summoned to their headquarters to explain why he had foreigners in his home.

On our travels across the country to various meetings we picked up an interpreter and a relative, so now there were eight of us in the van, two sitting on laps. In spite of the discomfort we found Romania a beautiful fifty-year throwback to a culture with rudimentary farm implements, horse-drawn hay wagons, and livestock herds at the side of the road.

We arrived at one church half an hour before the meeting and began unloading the equipment. People from the church stood watching us, then pitched in to help. After the musicians sang and played, I preached with our interpreter, and then—as is their custom—the church fed us. As we sat talking we found out that they had never gotten the word that we were coming. They had scheduled another man to preach, and here we had taken over their whole service! I was so embarrassed.

"That's awful!" I said. "We're so sorry! We were just following our itinerary and we never thought to ask if you knew we were coming."

But they insisted, "No, no, no! No problem!"

I learned on that trip that if you don't present hotel clerks with small gifts (like coffee), you may not get rooms. We also learned that we couldn't leave the van parked just anywhere. Once I had to talk a policeman into settling down and returning our driver's passport.

At several stops I had to sleep on the floor. Once I had to sleep in the van to protect it, and I nearly froze to death. After one meeting people gathered around to ask questions until someone whispered "secret police" and everybody disappeared.

One church backed out at the last minute so we were scheduled for an alternate church on a Monday night. I asked our hosts, "How are they going to get people out on a Monday night?"

He answered, "Don't worry."

I shouldn't have worried. When we arrived, the church was so full that they removed the doors so people could see from the outside.

The next night we were joined by Radu Gheorghita, a recent high school graduate and the son of Dr. Nick (who later became one of the pastors of the Second Baptist Church of Oradea and is today executive secretary of the Baptist Union of Romania). Radu traveled all the way from Deva to Bucharest to join us, and I found him a most enthusiastic and warm believer. He was eager and hungry for the Lord.

I took to him right away, and it angered me when one of the young men in the singing group said there was no room for him in the van. I told him, "If there's no room for Radu, then you can take the train." It was one of the best decisions I had ever made. Radu has become a dear brother in the Lord over the years.

At one of our meetings the huge crowd was so enthralled with the fellowship that they kept asking for more music and more preaching. I had never experienced anything like it. It had to be what heaven will be like. Soon we enjoyed our first meeting in Timisoara, where I fell in love with the Timisoara Christians, just as with all the Romanian believers. When it was finally time to leave, I knew I would be back. We had tearful goodbyes all around before heading to the border. The last thing I told Radu was that I would be back to minister again soon.

I make it a point not to engage in situational ethics, such as lying to border guards. As we had left three of our Bibles with believers inside the country, the Bibles we brought out didn't match the number listed for us when we entered. When the guard asked us about the discrepancy, we said nothing. He probably assumed we didn't understand.

All the way back to Hahn I was excited. It had been a wonderful experience to counsel and disciple the kids in the singing group, even in our cramped van as we rolled across Romania from meeting to meeting. But more than that, I knew I had been in a country during the flowering of revival. The crowds, the hunger and thirst for God, the intensity among the young people was like nothing I had ever seen. I wanted to get to Luxembourg soon to get visas for Tex and me so we could go straight back.

I was on cloud nine, realizing that I had walked into what I had read about in church history books. This revival was the real thing, and as I shared my excitement with the church in Hahn, the people urged me to go back and take Tex with me, so we started making plans.

One of the men in the church there who was excited about what I had encountered in Romania was Ken Leeburg, who had fast become my best friend. We prayed together, talked together, jogged together, and dreamed of winning the world for Christ. He was an attorney in the military, and I used to kid him and say that I had planned to be attorney before I got saved. He said he was going to be a minister before he got right with the Lord.

Ken challenged me physically, spiritually, and intellectually. He pushed me to be all I could be in those areas. He might have been a threat to another preacher, demanding to be shown from Scripture if he disagreed with a point. There was a basic doctrine we disagreed on, but instead of trying to ram it down his throat, I challenged him to memorize Scripture as we ran. Then I chose several verses that drove home my point. Before long, with no input from me other than Scripture, he began to espouse the same doctrine.

One of the things I learned best from Ken was persistence. He pushed me harder and farther physically than I had ever dared push myself. I got to where I was running six and seven miles a day fairly regularly. We dreamed of running in races and marathons. Running me up a huge hill we called "Difficulty," he would shout, "C'mon, Sam! You can do it! Up the hill! Over the hill! Through the hill! Conquer the hill!"

Ken often shared with me the cases he was defending. I encouraged the guys in the discipleship group to use the four-point outline from Campus Crusade on how to share your faith. It basically recommends telling (1) about your life before you became a Christian, (2) the events leading up to your becoming a Christian, (3) your actual conversion experience, and (4) the change Christ has made in your life since. Ken used it on a man who was being discharged from the military due to alcohol abuse, and the man broke down and wanted to receive Christ. Ken hadn't learned how to actually help the man make the transaction, so he called and asked if I could come over. I had the joy of leading the man to the Lord and showing Ken how he could lead others.

The commander at the base was so impressed with the change in the man that he told Ken he would be sending more guys to him. He did, and one Sunday we had six new families in church due to Ken's witnessing in his office. He sent people to me for counseling, and I sent people to him for legal assistance. He really knew my heart.

One of the men from the base became a Christian through our witness as we ran. He started inviting his other running friends, and we shared Christ with them every day. Besides having a ministry to them, I was getting into good shape.

Ken and I ran in a half marathon and dreamed of running in the Athens Marathon, which follows the path of the original marathon. I met a man at the Hahn Air Force base who had once won that marathon, and I peppered him with questions. His answer to almost every one was, "Run hills, man. Run hills."

I was so inspired by that counsel that I decided to run from my home to the church, which was all uphill. I had already finished my workout and had enjoyed a sauna, and even though it was the dead of winter with deep snow all around, I was pumped. I hurried home and took off jogging on the little country roads, heading uphill toward the church.

I heard something and spun around just in time to see a car sliding right into me.

I heard something and spun around just in time to see a car sliding right into me. I jumped, and it hit me and knocked me thirty feet into a field, where I sank into four feet of snow. As I lay lodged there with my head sticking out, I saw a young, terrified boy at the wheel of the car. He took off.

I was afraid to move for fear that every bone was broken, and people drove by looking at me. I tried to wave for help, and I wondered why they couldn't notice that there were no footprints between the road and the crazy guy lying in the snow.

Finally a couple drove by, and the wife recognized me. She was a member of our church, though her husband—a policeman—was not. She had him stop and she called out, "Brother Sammy! What are you doing out there?"

I told her and asked that she notify Tex and call an ambulance. Half an hour later I was taken to the base hospital, where I found the couple and Tex and the young man who hit me. I was cut up and bruised but had no broken bones, and the boy looked worse than I did. He was frightened and remorseful, and I wound up comforting him. I assured him that it was all right, that I knew it was an accident and not to worry about me. The husband of the woman from our church was so impressed that I had not chewed out the boy for his carelessness that he started coming to church, committed his life to the Lord, and became one of the key men in our discipleship group. He's living for God to this day. I hadn't done it on purpose and wouldn't have volunteered, but in a strange way God had brought me low to bring someone else to Himself. As I look back on it, I can say it was worth the pain.

God brought me low for my own benefit too. Davey was not getting better, and Tex and I were desperate. We were exhausted from being up with him in the night, trying to comfort him as he screamed with the headaches caused by the medication. It tore my heart out every time he had to have blood taken, always wishing I could promise him it would be the last time.

Almost imperceptibly, God humbled me through Davey's illness. Here was something I had no control over, and it took me to the edge emotionally. In my fatigue and worry, I still tried to stay in the Word and preach. For some reason God saw fit to bless my ministry, and the church continued to grow. But, hardly realizing it, I grew more vulnerable, maybe more sensitive. My nerves were raw, and God somehow made it possible for me to be more reflective, more introspective.

I had long been impressed by Tex's dedication to Jesus. She read her Bible and prayed every day, and she heard and studied my sermons right along with the rest of the congregation. She had mentioned something about wanting to be fully right spiritually before we went into Romania, where the fires of revival were sweeping. She sensed, as I did, that a lukewarm Christian would not be comfortable where God was truly at work, searching people's hearts.

One evening as we sat down to dinner with Davey and Renee, Tex was unusually quiet. Usually I was the one whose feelings were on his sleeve, right out there for everyone to know. Tex was more often steady, hardly showing a difference in her behavior unless she was very upset. She was also a quiet person anyway. But now I could tell something was troubling her. It wasn't that she was stony. She was hurting.

After I prayed and we began to eat, I noticed she began to tear up. "I was having my quiet time today and I was studying the holiness of God," she said. "Sammy, I need to talk to you."

In her subdued way, she had gotten my attention.

CHAPTER TWENTY

THE BREAKING BEGINS

I n His way, God had prepared me for this ominous moment, but still I didn't see it coming. After dinner Tex and I sat together in the living room and she told me that she had some things to say and that she didn't want me to say anything until she was finished.

The very fact that she felt she had to say that might have offended me. Here I was, the pastor of a growing church, sought after to speak many places, becoming known in Europe and behind the Iron Curtain as a man of the Word and a man of prayer. I didn't go as far as to think my wife should feel privileged to live under the same roof as a man of God who would likely be able to counsel her through any difficulty, but if I had probed the depths of my heart, that attitude might have been there.

> **But my wife didn't want my wisdom or my counsel. She didn't want me to serve as her pastor just now. She had something to tell me.**

But my wife didn't want my wisdom or my counsel. She didn't want me to serve as her pastor just now. She had something to tell me. And so I listened.

"Sammy," she began, her voice thick with emotion, "I've come to realize that there are things in my heart that are not pleasing to God. In studying the holiness of God I've been led to see myself in light

165

of that, and now I'm broken over what's been in my heart, and I need to confess it to you."

I was more puzzled than anything. I thought I knew this woman, this love of my life. What could it be? Surely she couldn't have committed some major sin without my knowing.

"Okay," I said as gently as I could. "What is it?"

She looked down and the tears came again. "The last few years, I have misplaced priorities. I've drifted from the unity we used to know. I've not been the wife God wants me to be. And I have had bitterness in my heart toward you since early in our marriage."

I wanted to interrupt, to say, "Toward *me*? What could *I* have done to cause *anyone* to harbor bitterness toward me?" But I was supposed to just listen.

"I was deeply offended by the way you acted, by things you said, by your attitude when we disagreed, by the way you treated me. I've harbored bitterness toward you for that, and I want you to forgive me."

Of course I would forgive her, but what had I done? I didn't remember having said or done anything to hurt her. I loved her, believed her to be a great spiritual wife and mother, and I thought we had a good marriage. In fact, compared to most marriages, I believed ours was great.

I stared at her, begging with my eyes for her to be specific. She sighed, tears streaming down her face. "When we have an argument, whenever we disagree, you always win. I never win. Have you ever noticed that?"

Noticed it? If she hadn't put it that way and forced me to think back on our disagreements, I probably would have said that most of the time I *was* right. Unconsciously I no doubt thought I was smarter, quicker, more knowledgeable in the ways of the world, all that. Being skilled in debate and public speaking, I could win any argument whether I was right or wrong. Worse, I could convince *myself* I was always right.

What I had seldom thought of—except in those rare occasions when I was so obviously wrong and boorish and had bullied her to the point where she cried and I had to apologize—was how all that must have made her feel. Now I was finding out. Tex was a quiet, inward person. Instead of expressing her feelings and believing that her opinions were worth something, she believed it senseless to even express herself. She let me win, and I usually went on believing I was right.

Had it not been for my reading about humility, my preaching in Genesis, and my vulnerability because of what we were going through with Davey, I'm sure I would have leaped to some defense. Ashamed as I am to say it, I might have turned the spotlight on her and tried to make her feel badly for bottling this up over the years. I could have demanded to know why she hadn't told me, made her see how I couldn't do anything about a problem I was unaware of, or asked her if she was implying that I didn't truly love her.

But God was working on me through her. I sought a ministry in a remote area so He could do a work in my life, but I had no idea that work would begin through my son and my wife. Somehow I knew enough to keep my mouth shut and take this. Tex had already tried to take some of the blame by saying that her biggest concern was the bitterness she had harbored against me. But now I was exposed, and I didn't like the harsh glare of the light of truth. What she said gave me a glimpse of myself, and I wanted to turn away from that image.

I thought my marriage was so good because my wife was so easy to live with. I was this macho, driving, successful guy with a wife who knew he was always right. Make no mistake: I wanted to serve God with all my heart, but my tranquil home life was a house of cards. I had been living in a fantasy world, leading a fairy-tale life.

I was dazed and humiliated. I held Tex's hands and tried to tell her that I had heard her, really heard her maybe for the first time. I told her that I wanted to hear more so I could make it right. I loved her and wanted to treat her the way I should, the way God would have me treat her. We asked the deacons for a few days off, found someone to take the kids, and spent three days in Luxembourg in a hotel room, just to get everything on the table.

I had a sense there was more, that I had not been given the whole dose at first. She had merely awakened me to the problem. Now it was time to face the day of reckoning. Deep in my heart I wanted to please God and be the kind of husband and father He wanted me to be. All of a sudden I realized what a miserable failure I had been at home.

Change didn't happen overnight, but God began a deep work in my heart immediately. Once we got to Luxembourg I realized how much Tex could never talk to me about because I won all the arguments. After having included her in the ministry itself in the beginning, with the witnessing in the French Quarter, the walks to Washington and to Miami, and the street work in Chicago, as soon as Davey came along, I began to cut her out.

I had bought into a lie that you can't risk your family in the ministry. I believed it would be poor stewardship if I subjected my family to the same dangers and pressures of international travel and ministry. I came back with stories of excitement and success and the blessing of God, insensitive to the truth that she used to be right there on the front lines with me. If, in her resentment, she accused me of not spending enough time with her and Davey, I lashed out with an unanswerable, logical argument and shut her down.

I realized that my rationalization for protecting my family was, in truth, a lack of faith and trust in God. I was the macho protector, rather than really relying on God to protect my loved ones.

When I realized how deeply I had hurt Tex and how I had sinned against God with my attitudes, I cried for hours. The Lord showed me that because my life and my ministry have always been intertwined and I don't see ministering as a separate job, by cutting Tex out of that, I shut off a major part of our life together. My motive was not love; it was fear for her and the kids' safety. But I had kept her from serving God and being used of Him. Our communication had broken down, and I hadn't even known it. We were drifting apart, and who knows what might have happened to our marriage if I had continued on that destructive path.

I was truly broken now in that area, and Tex could sense it. I asked her to hold nothing back, to give me both barrels so I could prove my love for her. That was one thing she says she never doubted, but she had sure become aware that I didn't know how to express it. She forgave me, and I believe she knows I was simply blind to my excesses. From that point on, however, I had no excuses.

One of the most important things that came from our three days away was that I rearranged my priorities. I knew I was in no shape to go back to Romania with Tex. I had to get my life in order. It had to be God first, family second, and ministry third.

Putting God first meant that I had to get to the root of my problem as a husband. I also knew I needed a deep work in my heart as it related to motives for ministry. I could not identify with the humility of David Brainerd, who said he was humbled to speak to pastors, worrying that they had to hear such a poor speaker. When I was asked to speak to pastors, I reveled in the opportunity, and I didn't understand why.

I also knew that after two and a half years in Hahn, I had to take my family back to the United States to get proper medical treatment for Davey. Because we were not part of the military, we could not take advantage of U.S. military hospitals. Not being German, we couldn't afford German health care. We simply couldn't go on this way any longer.

It was hard and heartbreaking to leave our friends in Hahn, where the church had grown from about 150 to more than 500. Friends there said, "Within six months you'll see a church in America grow to 5,000." I actually believed that.

I hated to postpone a second trip to Romania, but I knew God would allow me back there one day. I left my best friend, Ken Leeburg, with the dream that I would take a church in the U.S. and from there we would thrust out and win the world for Jesus. We just knew that at some point we would be involved in the effort together.

Back in the States we were finally able to get Davey's medication regulated and have him monitored carefully, and his condition began to improve. What a relief that was to all of us! It was a slow process, but we hoped and prayed for a full recovery, which came within a couple of years.

Meanwhile, God worked in our marriage. I had been brought low, and while I still need to change habitual responses, Tex and I began to really communicate for the first time in years. This was no phony, first-aid solution. I wanted her input, and I needed her disagreement and correction. As she slowly gained the confidence to speak forthrightly to me, I eventually got to where I not only accepted it, but also longed for it. I knew because of her love for me and the Lord that she would not abuse her right to bring me up short when necessary. I would be a better man for it and a better servant of God. It also served to soften my heart for one more deep work of the Spirit that was necessary for God to prepare me for further service.

I accepted the pastorate of a small church near Portland, Oregon, Mt. Hood Baptist in Gresham, which was in many ways similar to Hahn Baptist. It was filled with people close to the age of those in our military church. They seemed to be growing through discipleship, which struck a chord with me. Interestingly, the church was founded by the first man who had ever witnessed to me, when I was in seventh grade in Baton Rouge, Louisiana.

We moved to Oregon in January of 1981, and it wasn't long before I was miserable. It wasn't the church or the people. They were good. If they had been a bunch of rebels who weren't committed to evangelism or godliness, I could have understood why the church didn't grow. But nothing I tried worked. What had turned to gold at Hahn turned to dust in Portland.

I still had a heart for winning the world, and I'm sure the people did too. But the chemistry or something wasn't right. I tried the same discipleship techniques, but except for a few encouraging signs, little succeeded except the building program. The church was involved in raising a new building, and because they were committed to doing it debt free, it went very slowly. I agreed with not going into debt to build, but for some reason it also drove me batty to have anything to do with the construction. It was important, sure, but it wasn't nearly as important as the spiritual work of the church in the community and the world. I wanted to see people grow in Christ and reach out to others.

Not long after we arrived, the assistant pastor's baby daughter died. Renee, then five, was deeply moved by that and got a sense of her own mortality. Soon she came to us, as Davey had done, and asked Jesus into her heart.

Of course I was thrilled about that, but everyone knew I was unhappy in my work. I couldn't hide it. I called Ken Leeburg, and he tried to encourage me, telling me to hang in there. Sam Friend was in nearby Washington state, and he too encouraged me to stay and slug it out. What I finally realized was that God was still taking care of some unfinished business in my life.

Slowly I came to realize that my value, my own personal worth and identity, had to come from who I was in Christ, not from the results of my ministry. I had to redefine success. Success is not found in the size of your congregation or the number of people who receive Christ in your meetings. In asking myself if I had missed God's will by going to Oregon, I was forced back to the mirror of the Word to re-examine my motives. I knew because of the improvement in Davey's physical condition that it had been the right move to return to the States. But with no success, no fruit, no church growth, what was happening there?

As I struggled with these issues day after day, seeking God through His Word and in prayer, He finally began to reveal to me the source of my problem. It was me. It was my ego. Roy Hession had been right. Tex had touched on it. God had to teach me that true success, His kind of success, was in obedience, not in results. I had to examine my motives and realize that my self-worth could not revolve around the size of the ministry, not even in how many people came to Christ. I had enjoyed being known and respected and in demand. I had enjoyed pastoring a church that was exploding with growth. Flying in the face of church growth principles, I believed we were doing the same things in Oregon as we had done in Germany, but the church was stagnant.

The question was, Had I obeyed God? I came to see that what He was interested in my life was neither my ministry nor the results of it. Those were His responsibility, not mine. My job was to be conformed to the image of His Son, and He would bring the increase. All I could do was obey.

I knew God was revealing this to me, and that He had allowed circumstances in my life to show me these truths. My marriage was better and I was becoming the husband God wanted me to be, but the price had been a humiliating blow that brought me low. Davey's illness had exacted a huge emotional price, though he was now on the mend. Both the kids had prayed to receive Christ, and I was profoundly grateful for that. Then God showed me that I was egotistical and self-centered, even while wanting to please Him. It was a lesson I desperately needed, and I was glad deep down I was learning it. But I was discouraged. I was whipped. When I asked God to humble me and teach me and do a deep work in my life and character, I didn't know how much work He had to do. I didn't know how painful and comprehensive it would be.

In revealing myself to me, God allowed me to see a picture I didn't find so pretty. One requirement for true humility is the ability to see yourself honestly for what you are. I didn't like what I saw, and for the first time in my ministry, I felt like giving up. Totally discouraged, I actually began looking into secular work. I believed that other than seeing a building go up, I was doing nothing of any spiritual worth and that I would see more people come to Christ if I was out in the world.

After about a year and a half, when I got as low as I thought I could go, I knew it was time to move on. I needed to get out of the situation. I had learned that success is in obedience rather than in fruit, but if I had stayed there it would have been psychologically and emotionally unhealthy.

When friends in San Antonio told me that University Baptist Church there needed a pastor, I thought that might be the answer. I needed a change, and when I accepted the call in mid-1982, we looked forward to returning to Texas. I would learn that this was just another small step in a long journey.

CHAPTER TWENTY-ONE

BROKEN

Good and bad things happened at University Baptist. The best was that several people from Hahn transferred to San Antonio. John Labash, Ken Leeburg, and Jerry Anderson were among them, and Jerry became my assistant pastor.

Two things I wasn't happy about were that the church started to grow and the people began looking to build. I knew it was good we were growing and that building was the only option, but I didn't want to get involved in another building program. The idea of raising money for a building really got me down.

I was restless. The death of the assistant pastor's baby daughter in Oregon planted a seed of urgency in me, and my burden for the world had not lessened a bit. It came through in my preaching, and people noticed.

I felt flaky. Here I was, a guy fast approaching his mid-thirties, and I wasn't finding my niche. I wasn't happy. I wasn't comfortable. I felt like a square peg trying to fit into a round hole. Ken Leeburg still was an encourager. He believed in me and would tell me that God had His hand on my life and that I was destined to serve Him in a mighty way. I knew by now that mere obedience was what God wanted from me, but I wasn't even sure I was doing that anymore. It seemed there would be more joy if I was in His will.

━━━

"Where is the young man who was afraid of nothing? What's happened to you?"

Late in 1982 Josif Tson came to speak at our church. At lunch one day he looked at me soberly. "Sammy, what has happened to you? Where is the young man who came to Romania and shook cities across the country for the glory of God? Where is the young man who was afraid of nothing? What's happened to you?"

I hung my head. What could I say? "I don't know."

But deep down inside I knew. I was like Jonah, hiding from God. I wanted to go to Romania. I wanted to go to all the countries behind the Iron Curtain. And though I had allowed the Lord to work on my ego and on my failure as a husband, I still had not released from my grasp my own family. How could I go and take them? How could I risk Davey's health? How could I take a young daughter so far away? What kind of a husband subjects his wife to such an ordeal?

Again, my motive was not love and protection. My motive was fear. Truth be known, I didn't want to trust God with the safety of my family. I felt more secure trying to handle it myself. I was not conscious enough of it to admit it to Josif that day, and I'm not sure I would have, if I had been. Yet Josif's words stung. The urgency for the world task that had been ignited by the death of the baby girl in Oregon was kindled by Josif's admonition. I felt torn by the call of God and the love of and fear for my family. What was I going to do?

The next month I went to the Texas Baptist State Evangelism Conference where 15,000 pastors, staff people, and lay leaders go each year for spiritual refreshment and training. I asked Tex to pray earnestly that I would get a word from God. "We've gone to Portland, we've come here, and nothing satisfies me. I need God to do a work in my life."

When I arrived at the conference in January of 1983, I was still pierced by what Josif had said to me the month before. Silently I prayed, "God, I need You to direct me." One of the first people I ran into was Manley Beasley, who was warm and affectionate as usual. Unaware of my inner struggle, he merely said, "Sammy, God has uniquely gifted you. There's a call of God on your life. I don't know what it is, but I believe God still has something for you in Europe."

In one of the sessions Arthur Blessitt spoke about people he had known on the front lines who were now on the shelf somewhere. After that session I ran into another old friend, a kind of smart-alecky guy who thought he was funny. He said, "Why, Sammy Tippit! Now, talk about a has-been who's been on the front lines and is now on the shelf! Man, that's you! You used to be out there on the streets witnessing for Jesus, and you're on the sidelines pastoring now."

It made me sick, and I moved on. I was so agitated I was about to burst. But it wasn't just because of the insult from a wiseguy. I sensed I was on the verge of a serious decision. What was standing in my way? Should I resign my pastorate and get back out where I belonged? I revere the office of pastor, but I also believe a man has to be called and anointed for it. I'd like to believe that the churches I've pastored have benefited from something I've given them from the Lord, but I fear they basically had to endure the deep water I was treading in my own life at the time.

I made my way up to the empty balcony of the huge civic center auditorium so I could be alone with God. My heart was heavy, and I felt a lump in my throat. I needed something, anything, some word from God. As I sat there, deep in thought, who should walk in front of me and sit down with his back to me but Arthur Blessitt. I hadn't seen him in years. "Arthur," I said quietly.

He turned and looked. "Sammy!" He quickly came to sit with me. "How are you doing, brother?"

"Not so well," I admitted, and I quickly brought him up to date, including our struggles and fears over Davey.

He thought for a while and then looked me in the eye. "Sammy, I can count on the fingers of one hand the guys who have been courageous enough to go where you and I have gone. There are lots of pastors and lots of men called to the pastorate, but not many can do what you've done. That's where you belong. I hear what you're saying about your son, but you know you need to give him to God."

Soon we knelt and prayed, and Arthur asked the Lord to make clear to me His direction and that I would have the courage to make the right decision, no matter how hard it was.

I sat thinking and praying until the great hall filled and Dr. Stephen Olford spoke. It was a message specifically aimed at me. It was on God asking Isaiah, "Whom shall I send?" and Isaiah replying, "Here am I, Lord; send me."

During the invitation I went forward and knelt. I prayed, "Here am I, Lord; send me."

I believe God answered my prayer and worked in my heart. I knew what I needed to do, and there was no need to stay for the rest of the conference. I headed home to be with my family. At the airport I changed my ticket to an earlier flight and had a little time on my hands, so I strolled to the gate. On the way I glanced into a restaurant and there was another face from the past: Leo Humphrey of the New Orleans French Quarter.

I hurried in and embraced him. "What are you doing here?" I asked.

"I was at the conference," he said. "I just brought Arthur to the airport." Never one to hesitate to get to the point, he said, "Arthur told me what you're going through, Sam. You know you've got to give your son to God, and you know I know what I'm talking about."

I sure did. Leo's own son, Kelly, was dying of cancer in his early twenties. "Leo," I said, "how do you deal with that? How can you travel and all that with Kelly in the hospital?"

He told me that one day he was pacing the hospital corridor when his son called him in and asked him why he wasn't following the Lord's leading to preach in Honduras. "I told him I was afraid. He asked me what I was afraid of, that he was going to die? I said of course.

"You know what he told me, Sam? He said, 'Dad, you've got to give me back to God and trust Him to take care of me.' Sam, it was the hardest thing I've ever had to do, but I gave Kelly back to God." He looked at his watch. "Brother, my flight's about to leave, and I've got to go. You've got to give Dave back to God." And he left.

I still had an hour before my flight, so I found a secluded corner and just sat crying. On the plane I was still crying, and I'm sure people wondered about me. As soon as I got home, I called the family together and told them everything. "I've got to give you all back to God," I said. "We all need to go to Eastern Europe together. I've been afraid to subject you to it, but I need to trust the Lord and do it." We knelt and prayed as a family and committed each other to God. I didn't know when, but I knew I had to go back behind the Iron Curtain, not alone, but with my family.

A few weeks later I got a call from a friend who told me that Leo Humphrey's son, Kelly, had died. I flew to New Orleans for the funeral, which was a beautiful experience where several people were saved. I came away with an even deeper sense of urgency. I had no premonitions about the historic changes on the horizon in Europe, but these confrontations with death made me realize how unpredictable life is.

I re-established the board of God's Love in Action, putting layman Frank Corte on it with Morris Todd, John Labash, and Ken Leeburg. We began dreaming about getting back into Eastern Europe and especially Romania.

That summer (1983) I got a call from Sam Friend in Bothell, Washington, at a time when I was about as ready as I could be to move on. He said, "Sammy, I know what you're going through because I'm going through the same thing." He suggested I become co-pastor of his church and preach Sunday evenings and that we cover for each other, one taking the church when the other traveled in Europe.

It sounded good to me, but I worried about being the second man. "I'm not saying I couldn't adjust," I said, "but you need to know that I've never been in that position, and I don't know how I'd function."

"Sammy, that's going to have to be your call," he said. "But in my opinion, if you can't be the associate pastor of a church, you have no business being senior pastor either."

That was the last nail in the coffin of my ego, though I know when Paul wrote of dying to self, he meant dying daily—being in the process of continually dying. I told Sam I was willing and ready but that it would have to be only temporary. "I know this restlessness in me will make me want to get back into traveling and speaking full time."

We agreed. I joined the church in November of 1983 and stayed two and a half years. It was a good experience for me to be in a situation where I sometimes disagreed but kept my mouth shut. I handled Sunday evenings, counseling, and young marrieds, and I administered the church when Sam traveled. I was allowed a couple of weeks of preaching in the States each year, and I scheduled a four-week trip to Eastern Europe.

Our first major trip was set for the summer of 1984. We planned to go to East Germany, Poland, and then the beloved Romania. We would start by going to the Hahn Baptist Church in West Germany, where Tex and Renee would stay until it was time for all of us to go to Romania. It was a major step for me to commit to taking Dave for the first time.

Now almost fourteen, he would go with me into East Germany and Poland with a young student, Brent Saathoff; my former assistant pastor at Mt. Hood, Cork Erickson; and Don Shelton, who was by then pastor of Hahn Baptist.

Our first stop was West Berlin, where we crossed the border to the East. We enjoyed reuniting with Pastor Schoch, but for me the Berlin stopover was important for another reason. God seemed to burn into my mind two words: *availability* and *adaptability*. I sensed He was telling me to make that a hallmark of our ministry. It's so easy to have one without the other, but both are important, especially in a foreign culture. In the ensuing years I have tried to maintain those traits, and I believe God has helped us avoid unnecessary conflict because of it.

In Berlin I noticed that a family watched us while we quietly witnessed to young people at a restaurant. The family finally introduced themselves as Christians from Karl Marx Stadt. We enjoyed fellowshipping with them, and I asked if they could confirm a rumor for me. "I heard years ago that there were two thousand Christian young people meeting in this city. Is that true?"

"No, that is not true," they said. "There are five thousand!"

After we enjoyed fellowship with them, they urged us to call them from the autobahn if we passed through their area. We promised we would. We visited some of the believers we had met in Dresden after the Communist Youth World Fest and ministered in several places in Poland. On our way back through on the autobahn, we called the family we had met and said we had time only to say hi. They pleaded with us not to leave, and the father and daughter drove out to see us. They brought with them two angels carved in that area and presented them to us "because we believe angels sent you to us. We are praying that you come back someday too."

We picked up Tex and Renee and headed back into Romania, where I hadn't been in three long years. I had served in four different churches and had been through deep waters. I believed God had done a profound work in my life, breaking me so I could be molded and used for just such a ministry as this. I trusted Him to be the protector of my family, but that trust would be sorely tested before it was over.

CHAPTER TWENTY-TWO

DANGER

The three questions we were always asked at the Romanian border during our five- to ten-hour stops were: "Do you have Bibles?" "Do you have weapons?" and "Do you have pornography?"

The first time I was there with my family seemed the easiest. Apparently the guards were less suspicious. They were the stereotypical 'movie' guards—formal, pompous, strutting, and grim. Eventually, we were allowed through.

Sam Friend arranged with Dr. Nick Gheorghita and Paul Negrut to meet us just outside Oradea. You don't simply go and expect people to know where you are. It all has to be arranged carefully in advance. We quickly transferred some foodstuffs and gifts from our cars to theirs, wary of the Securitate. Nick and Paul told us of our schedule to preach in various churches and meeting with believers secretly in the woods for discipleship. That was the most dangerous of all because nationals were not supposed to interact with foreigners without reporting it.

The first three nights I preached at the Second Baptist Church of Oradea, including performing a wedding ceremony on a Saturday that lasted into the wee hours of the morning. Renee began playing with a little girl from the family of Nelu Dronca, a lay leader from the First Baptist Church of Timisoara. He asked if I would preach in his church before the end of our trip, and that started a relationship that knit our hearts together over the years. I found it interesting that because I was obedient and trusted God to allow me to bring my family, this contact came through my own daughter. Who knows if I would even have met this family, had it not been for Renee?

On Monday morning we left Oradea by car, headed toward a little village in the mountains where Radu would meet us after arriving there by train. His father, Dr. Nick, had a shack in the woods where we were to meet with several college-age new believers who were friends of Radu. Of course it was illegal for them to get Christian training, especially from a foreigner, so this would be the most dangerous part of our trip.

Once we arrived we couldn't find a hotel room. I finally realized that maybe I'd do better if I took Renee in with me. The people of Romania love children, especially little blonde girls, and if they took pity on us, that would be all right with me. So I brought my eight-year-old, blue-eyed, pig-tailed girl in, and out of sympathy for her, they gave us rooms.

At a prearranged time, we met Radu in the village, but we could not speak to him or appear to be with him. When we spotted him, we passed him going the other way, and he said quietly, without looking at us, "Follow me to the edge of the village." We watched where he went and followed him into the foothills to the shack.

The college kids came by train and made their way through the trails in pairs to the cabin. We had to go by twos as well, so we wouldn't be noticed. If we were caught together and the authorities figured out what was going on, we would have been deported, and the students would likely lose their educations. Of course, with the Securitate, you never knew what might happen. We all could just as easily have gone to prison.

What a wonderful time we had in the mountains with those kids! Normally we ate at churches or in the homes of believers who had saved their meager rations for months and months and fed us like royalty. They hardly ever ate with us, but hovered over us, eager to meet our every need. They would not accept any refusal to eat more, but just kept piling it on. In the U.S. we would have appeared to be taking advantage, but in Romania anything short of letting them stuff us offended them.

In the mountains we ate the way the people did, mostly onions and potatoes for every meal. It broke our hearts to see their meager rations and poor diet. We did, however, feast on the Word of God, and they couldn't get enough. With Radu interpreting, then teaching the others how to do the same, we sat far from the rest of civilization. We talked hour upon hour about how to witness, how to pray, how to argue for the faith. The fellowship was sweet.

One day one of the girls had a high fever, and we suggested that she go to a doctor and not climb the mountain for the secret meeting.

> **"I may never have the chance to get this information again. I wouldn't miss it." It touched me to see her struggle to the meeting place and drink in the Word.**

"No," she said, urgently, "I may never have the chance to get this information again. I wouldn't miss it." It touched me to see her struggle to the meeting place and drink in the Word.

One day we insisted on making an American lunch, but the only thing truly American about it was a little peanut butter. They got a kick out of it. The day before we were to leave we were having some fun, tossing a Frisbee with the kids and goofing around, when someone spotted men coming from the village.

Radu rushed to us and whispered, "Say nothing in English. Don't let them hear your accents. I'll handle it."

Davey was excited about all the cloak-and-dagger stuff. I knew how important it was but had never really had a close call. Seeing these kids freeze in fear told me this was the real thing. Education, freedom, lives were at stake.

When the men arrived, I was inside the shack. Dave was out in the yard, prompted to be quiet. Radu told the authorities he was with a group of friends and families, most of them young university students. Apparently the authorities were satisfied because they didn't ask to see passports or visas and they didn't lecture anyone. When they left the group was subdued by the brush with trouble.

That night we visited Pastor Peter Dugalescu in a small town called Hateg. He eventually moved to a church in Timisoara and became a major player in the Romanian revolution, but when we met him he was a struggling pastor in Hateg. About 150 people jammed into a church so small that the balcony seemed to sag and looked as if it would fall any time. Peter had petitioned for years for permission to knock out some walls and add on to the church, but the local authorities considered him a troublemaker and continually denied his requests. Yet we found him a stocky, jovial man, full of humor and the joy of the Lord.

The next morning found us back in our little mountain shack with the students, and Radu wanted to have communion. We wedged ourselves into the place that had no electricity or running water, but it was one of the most beautiful communion services I had ever enjoyed. The Securitate, walking in on that scene, would have had all the evidence they needed to put us away.

We felt like the early church, meeting in secret and singing songs, enjoying the Lord. We wept as we sang, "You Are My Hiding Place"—we in English, they in Romanian—softly so as not to attract attention.

After we ate, we left for Timisoara. I had advised everybody in our party not to drink anything but bottled or boiled water because our Western systems were intolerant and would develop diarrhea and get dehydrated. Everyone followed that advice, but Dave must have eaten or drunk something contaminated because he began feeling sick in the car on the way to Timisoara.

By the time we covered the three-hour drive, he was in the full throes of diarrhea, upset stomach, and high fever. Nelu Dronca directed us to a Christian doctor, who happened to be the husband of the woman who had interpreted for me in 1980 when I first preached in Timisoara. The doctor told us what to feed Davey and to keep an eye on him for dehydration.

At about two in the morning Dave was worse, his temperature rising to about 105. We rushed him to the hospital, such as it was, and I was heartsick. Only Tex was allowed in the room with him, and I chastised myself for not following my original hunches and fears. Why had I brought my family? What was wrong with me? What kind of a father was I to subject a young boy, one who had already suffered seizures and related problems for years, to the dangers of a strange culture?

All my fears had come home to roost. Everything I had struggled with and worked through was coming to pass right before my eyes. My son was suffering and had been admitted to a pathetic facility in a town where years later parents would see their wounded children die from gunshot wounds at the hands of the Securitate. I didn't know in 1984 that God was allowing me a foretaste of their grief and suffering. All I knew was that I was to blame.

I got back to the hotel at about three in the morning and I stayed awake all night, weeping and pleading with God to give my son some relief. I thought I had given him to God, but I didn't want him to suffer like this. At six I went to the hospital and found that he was not much better. I headed to the First Baptist Church where I had committed to preach that morning. The pastor was so afraid of what the authorities would think about our being there that he did not show up.

The Lord laid it on my heart to preach a message from Philippians on joy in the midst of suffering. It was something I had studied and preached on in Bothell, but I sure didn't feel like talking about it just then.

Before the service I noticed that most of the people were crying. They would pray and they would cry, pray and cry. "Radu," I said, "what is this?"

"Sammy, to the people of this church, your coming is a miracle. They need revival. They have not seen anyone come to the Lord or be baptized for years. They haven't wept like this. They are deeply moved that you would bring your family and enter into their sufferings with them. They are praying for your son and weeping for him."

That touched my heart. God was making me confront every fear I'd had for my family. Had I not been willing to bring Dave, this never would have happened, and their hearts would not have been softened by what had come over him. They were ready for that message that morning, and God moved in a mighty way. He knit with ours the hearts of the people of that church.

I listened to the sermon myself! I went back to the promises of God and stood on them. Was I going to trust the Word or live under my circumstances? What would happen? I knew God had led me to that point. I had to trust Him.

The service became a turning point for that church. Going from the risk of having an illegal outside speaker in a morning service to the audacity to hold evangelistic crusades, the First Baptist Church became a major force in Timisoara and key in the revolution years later. I had to realize that none of it would have happened had it not been for Renee and Dave coming with me. She had struck up the friendship with the daughter of the lay leader, and Dave's illness had melted the hearts of the people. I had not been just another American preacher passing through, but someone who risked bringing his family, suffered for it, and thus truly identified with them.

After the service we went to the home of an opera singer for lunch. Davey had been released from the hospital and was waiting for us. He had improved and progressively grew better from then on.

Before I left, we went back through Oradea and I spent some time debriefing with Radu. Though he was still only in his early twenties, I considered him a mature brother in the Lord. "You've been with me the whole time," I said. "Give me a critique. What should I do to be more effective?"

He thought it over, and in the direct Romanian way—which I wanted and knew I would receive—he said, "I have seen you teach, disciple, and preach, and though I believe you do them all well, you are gifted and anointed in preaching. Bring someone else in and let them do the other things. You come in and preach."

He wasn't saying I was bad or weak at the other disciplines, just that I should minister from the place of my strength. I found it very important counsel and followed it. I believe in discipleship, and I don't shirk it. But I do emphasize the gift God has given me, and our ministry has been more effective for it.

Once again I felt I had bonded with the believers in Romania, and I couldn't wait to get back. A few months after our return to the States, I got a call from John Labash in San Antonio. It was October 5, 1984.

I hadn't talked to John for several months. Now he had news about Ken Leeburg, my best friend. Ken had been super-excited. He had just a couple of weeks left in the military, and he and his wife, Lyn, and their daughters were moving. He had bought a horse ranch and was going to have time to travel with me, so we had begun laying plans for him to go with me on the next international trip.

"Sam," John Labash said, "you'd better sit down. I don't know how to say this, Sammy. Ken's dead. He was killed in a wreck."

"What?" I couldn't comprehend it. My best friend, my encourager, the man who really knew my heart, was gone. And how? In a wreck?

John explained that Ken had been on his way back from his last responsibility for the Air Force, training defense attorneys in New Mexico. He was coming back to start his private practice and live on his new horse ranch. An amateur artist, he had recently painted a picture of a horse. Ironically, he had been killed when he struck a horse with his car.

Our families had been close. His oldest and youngest of four daughters had been the same ages as Dave and Renee. It was hard to grasp, but if I thought I was in shock, Lyn, of course, felt worse. Tex and I told her we would get there as soon as we could. We flew all night and got in the next day.

After a few hours' sleep at John's house, we went to see Lyn. She asked if I would identify the body. She couldn't bring herself to do it. We all went to the funeral home and I identified him for her, which was also therapeutic for me.

I wish I could have been of more comfort to her, but what could I say in my own grief? I knew we were not to grieve as the heathen do, and I knew God was sovereign and in control. But what can you say when a man is cut down in the prime of his life, a man who loved the Lord and served Him? He was the healthiest and strongest person I knew, a man with a vision for the world and for his family.

Lyn asked me to preach the funeral service, and it was the hardest thing I had ever done. But if his daughters could sing "Our God Reigns," I knew I could manage to labor through a brief message. I told of Ken's urging me up and over and through the hill called Difficulty.

We held the service in a tiny military chapel, packed with his colleagues. One of the pall bearers told me later he had never seen such faith and love in his life.

The urgency of the task had been driven home to me again. From the baby girl in Portland to Leo Humphrey's son, and now my best friend—whom I had been convinced would long outlive me—I couldn't ignore the harsh truth. People are here one day and gone the next. It is the way of life. I had long ago accepted the task of trying to reach my generation with the claims of Christ. If I had never felt the urgency of the need before, I felt it now.

Every day was important. I may not have tomorrow to tell a lost person about Christ. Today is the day; now is the accepted time. I had always had a head knowledge of eternity, but now I had really come to grips with it for the first time.

Three months later Sam Friend and two associates were detained several hours as they left Romania. Names and addresses of believers were found among their things, along with a note to someone in the West from a Romanian citizen. Though they had done nothing illegal and no charges could be officially pressed against them, they had fraternized with nationals and had been active in the churches. They were interrogated and then informed that they had been blacklisted and would not be allowed back into the country.

Sam was devastated. He loved the Romanian people, and the thought of never seeing them again broke his heart. I ached for him. I also worried about the trip I had planned for the summer of 1985. My family, two other guys, and the daughter of an evangelist who had been kicked out with Sam planned to go with me. The question was whether we would be allowed in.

THE USING

TITUS

In the summer of 1985 we put together a singing group from our church, First Baptist in Bothell, Washington, and planned to take them overseas in June. Besides my family and the singing group, I was taking Mike Mahan, who had been my associate pastor at Hahn, and Gary Maroney, a local Portland pastor and long-time friend. Gary is a big guy who looks like a group leader and was always treated that way at the borders. That took a lot of the pressure off me. We would rent two vans once we got there, start in Hahn again, go to East Germany and Poland, and then go into Romania.

We had no idea whether we'd get in after what had happened to Sam Friend and his two companions, Jon Randles and evangelist Barry Wood. Barry had a college-age daughter, Collynn, whom he and Sam decided should go with us. Frankly I was a little bent out of shape at having to accommodate Barry Wood's daughter. I didn't know the girl, and I wasn't excited about her going along, but I didn't say anything to Sam or Barry about it. Of course it turned out to be God's will.

After preaching and singing in free Europe, in Poland we ministered in a town that didn't seem to have more than fifty people in it. Yet some 250 showed up for our service in a tiny, wooden Baptist church.

We were so close to the Soviet Union that before the service we drove to the border just to look across the field at that huge nation. I walked out into the night, praying, "O God, somehow one day, let me bring the message of Christ to the masses there. Somehow let me reach those people."

We ministered in a town that didn't seem to have more than fifty people in it. Yet some 250 showed up for our service.

For some reason the people in this Polish village were especially sweet and seemed to take to us. None of us knew Polish and only one interpreter knew English, so it was almost impossible to communicate with the people after the meeting. Yet they crowded around and wanted to express their love to us in some way.

They embraced us and shook our hands, murmuring words of peace and love in their own tongue. We did the same in ours, trying to communicate with our eyes and our smiles. Suddenly one of them got an idea and began to sing an old hymn of the faith in Polish. We joined in English. What sweet fellowship we enjoyed, finally realizing what the other was saying because we were singing the great hymns of the faith together.

In East Germany I got to speak to a great crowd of young people, the thousands who met regularly to worship. There I learned that two pastors had prayed for a solid year before the Communist Youth World Fest that someone would come and preach there. Young people had been turning away from the church en masse, and these pastors had pleaded with God for movement of His Spirit. I felt as if I had been a small part of the answer to that prayer, and speaking to the young people was a great thrill.

Preaching to two huge crowds of young people in a great old cathedral was one of the highlights of the trip. It was like stepping back into the Jesus movement, seeing the kids with long hair and casual clothes, singing and playing guitars and talking about the Lord. Rather than applaud, they knocked on the pews when they heard something they liked. When I was introduced I was greeted by all this loud knocking, and they interrupted my message often with the same.

I had been worried about Dave for some time, fretting over his spiritual temperature, wondering if he was really on fire for Jesus. Now that I had given him back to God, God gave him back to me.

At evangelistic services in Karl Marx Stadt some of the kids recognized him from the previous year. Since some in our group understood German, they translated for him as he renewed acquaintances. He got involved praying with the kids and sharing their enthusiasm for the Lord. I could see the love of Jesus growing in him. I believe it was a turning point in his spiritual life, as was the whole trip.

Finally it was time to drive across Hungary and into Romania. The two vans split up, heading to separate borders in case there was any trouble. We hoped at least one van would make it through. Gary Maroney, Mike Mahan, Tex, and I were with Collynn Wood and some of the others in a van that would try to get through a southern border. The music group and the rest of our party would cross the border in Oradea and head directly to the Second Baptist Church.

I had been doing most of the driving and, with all the preaching and diplomacy, I was exhausted. I got someone else to drive and fell asleep. In the wee hours of the morning I was awakened by the sound of a cassette tape someone had given to Mike Mahan to enjoy on the way. One of the people he was discipling had created a comedy skit about his being arrested at the border and sent to prison for being a Christian. Everyone in the van was laughing except me. It may have been funny, but it was also dangerous.

"We're going to stop before we get to the border crossing," I said, "and you're going to get rid of that thing. Can you imagine what would happen if they confiscated it and listened to it? Do you think they would think it was funny?"

When we finally got to the border in midmorning, we must have looked suspicious. The guards went through all our luggage, and when they found Bibles and Christian literature, they intensified their search. They confiscated all our twenty or so tapes and began listening to them. Sometimes people put messages in the middle of music tapes, so the guards would just play all the tapes all the way through.

The guards found a birthday card I had translated into Romanian for Cork Erickson's daughter and was bringing in for Paul Negrut's daughter. That made them very suspicious, demanding to know who we were going to see. Collynn Wood had stuffed up her shirt a bunch of Jesus stickers with her dad's name and address on them. He had been kicked out the country a little more than half year before.

As we sat there for hours, the guards literally tearing apart our van, I learned a lesson in how to pack, what to bring and not bring, and vowed I would never attempt a border crossing without checking all the suitcases first myself.

Everything that could be unscrewed or unsnapped in the van was removed. It's a good thing it was rented and fully insured because, by the time they got finished with it, it could not be reassembled correctly. While the guards removed the quarter panels, tore out the gear shift, and unfastened the ceiling and floor panels, several of our people were stripsearched. I paced the small guard booth, hearing the familiar Christian songs coming from the tape player where guards were checking all our tapes. I walked past Mike, who looked glum.

"I'm sure glad you got rid of that one tape," I said. He said nothing and looked away. "Mike!" I said.

"Sam, I'm sorry. I forgot."

"They've got it?"

He nodded.

"Mike, do you understand what's going on here? We're in so deep now with the birthday card and the Barry Wood stickers there's no chance we're going to get in."

"Sammy, I'm so sorry."

It looked disastrous. Here I was with my wife and kids and this great team, scheduled to minister all over Romania, and now this. Hour after hour we watched as our van was turned inside out. From the little Romanian I could understand, it was obvious the authorities thought Gary Maroney was in charge. He was stripsearched and interrogated, and they kept referring to him as a preacher.

The team grew more solemn as the day passed and we quit looking at our watches and wondering if we would make it to the service at Second Baptist. Mostly we tried to imagine where we would go when they turned us away.

Suddenly, I got an idea. When I was sure no guards could hear us, I told the others, "Let's act as natural as possible and pretend that getting across the border doesn't mean a thing to us. Let's play and have fun and look casual. In fact, let's go scrub down the van. It's filthy."

We found a bucket and a faucet and soon we were out there washing the van down. The guards looked at us like we were crazy. When we were finished they put the vehicle up on a rack and began taking apart the oil pans and everything underneath. I don't know what they thought they were going to find, but I believed they had enough on us already to justify turning us away.

Inside we started inventing games like football with a wad of paper. We were whooping and hollering and laughing, and even the guards seemed amused. It was party time. We acted as if we didn't care to get in any more than the guards did.

We'd waited at the border for about eight hours until they finally determined that I was in charge. They asked me to come out to the van because they had it almost completely torn apart. I watched as they tried to reassemble it. By this time they knew who we were, what we were, and what we were about. I figured the whole exercise was a lost cause and that it couldn't get any worse, so I decided I might as well witness to them. I asked them in broken Romanian if they liked the Christian music tape they were listening to.

They said yes and asked what it was. I told them it was a song about Jesus, how He was God's Son who had died for their sins and would come to live in their hearts if they asked Him to. They were very interested and full of questions.

A few weeks later, when we got back to Bothell, Sharon Arrington (one of Tex's praying ladies) came directly to me and said, "God burdened me while you were over there to pray for a border guard. Did you happen to have a chance to witness to any guards at the border?" Needless to say, she rejoiced at my report.

As the hours dragged on, I knew the service at Second Baptist had long since ended. Finally I was summoned to the guard house. "Mr. Tippit," one said, sliding our passports across the desk, "we are going to keep all of your materials, but you will be allowed to enter the country."

I was shocked and thrilled but tried to hide both emotions. I thanked them and hurried to tell the others, determined to never again bring anything to the border that would remotely make anyone suspicious. Our aim, our mission was evangelism and revival, not smuggling. I'm not against anyone who does that and I praise God for those who obey Him by doing it. But that was not our calling, and we had risked our ministry by flirting with smuggling. From then on we would never bring in anything with obvious Christian connotations. We would enter the country to preach and sing, nothing else.

When we finally reached the church in Oradea, we expected to see the van with the singing group because Oradea was where they had crossed the border two days before. Nick and Paul were scared, wondering all day what had happened to us. Now we were scared too because nothing had been heard from the other van. All we could do was wait. There was no way to check on the others without drawing suspicion from the Securitate.

That Sunday morning I spoke at Second Baptist on the subject of revival. After the service I was approached by a striking and intense young man who spoke earnestly and softly. He introduced himself as Titus Coltea, a medical doctor who had been vacationing with his wife, Gabriela, and their baby daughter at the Black Sea.

"We were having a good time," he said in heavily accented English, "but the Lord gave me a deep impression that I was to return to Oradea to meet someone who would be very important in my life. That is why we are here. Sammy, my heart burns to see revival in Romania. I have been praying for it for fifteen years. Please, can I travel with you and learn more about revival? I can interpret for you."

If there was one thing I needed, it was a bright and articulate translator who was mobile and available. "I'd love that," I said, not knowing that Titus would soon become one of my dearest brothers in the world. "Let's talk to Nick and see what he says."

Dr. Nick was enthusiastic and encouraged us. Titus immediately got on the phone and called pastors of churches in the hinterlands, setting up speaking engagements. In the South and in the East, he set up meetings where outside speakers had never been heard. He told me of all the places he thought would be ripe for revival because they were off the beaten path. He was speaking my language. I had been called to the hard places, not just the big cities and the successful churches where revival had already taken place.

From the moment we hit the road, I recognized in Titus a heart for God. He was dedicated to the task, willing to sacrifice all for the sake of the gospel. He was so excited about the chance to be involved in a ministry to his countrymen that he asked question after question and made many good suggestions. He told me that Romanians are committed people and commitment-oriented. "If you preach about something today, when you come back a year later, they will still be doing what you said."

We decided that I should speak to these small congregations about prayer. We would call them to be people of prayer for the sake of reviving their country for God. Our pattern was to get the church praying and to come back a year later and preach evangelistic crusades built on that prayer.

We preached around the country, and I found Titus to be like a twin. He shared my speech patterns, shouted when I shouted, whispered when I whispered, gestured the same. Occasionally, when I needed a small correction or made a little mistake, he would cover for me without making it obvious. After each meeting he critiqued my message and made helpful suggestions. He was direct and blunt in the Romanian way, and over the years we have not always agreed on everything. Like me, he is human and has his weaknesses, but I have never questioned his heart, his motives, or his commitment. (I've questioned his breakneck driving at times, but never his heart!)

Sometimes during an invitation, Titus would simply take over and plead with his countrymen on their own terms, beckoning them to receive Christ. That never bothered me. It seemed right for the situation and the occasion. Titus risked everything to become a minister of the gospel, and he was an evangelist in his own right. How I grew to love him!

After preaching in several small towns around the country, we gravitated to Cluj, the university town. Who should we meet up with there but the music group! They told me the story of how they had been turned away at the border because of all their sound equipment. The guards had not believed they were going to use it, but assumed they were trying to sell it for profit. "You told us to never give up, Sammy," they said, "so we drove back out to the west, stored our equipment, rented another van, and tried another border. And here we are!"

After Cluj we had a four-day meeting lined up in Timisoara with our dear friends at First Baptist. I had looked forward to that for a year, as had the rest of my family. What memories flooded us as we pulled into that town! The people had rallied around us and bonded with us because of Renee and her new friend and because of Dave's illness. He was glad to be going in healthy this time. I was thrilled to have Titus with me.

On the first night the pastor was again absent. He was negative and fearful. Dave gave his testimony, and the people just wept. It was great to fellowship with the Dronca family again, and we looked forward to the rest of the time. The pastor attended the second night, but the next day he invited us to a picnic lunch way out in the woods where no one would see us.

He told me that we shouldn't be doing what we were doing. It was clear he was filled with fear. "It's dangerous and there will be problems from this," he said.

We had a good time of sharing anyway, and I told him how I had been paralyzed with fear for my family, but that when I trusted God to take care of them, he blessed our ministry even more. I didn't try to correct him, even though I politely disagreed. I was just there to listen.

One day in Timisoara I was invited into a small room in the church and was introduced to a man named Buni Cocar. He had been a pastor in Bucharest who had defied the authorities by knocking out a wall and expanding his church. Now he had been threatened by the government and was on the run. He hadn't seen his family for some time, and he was desperate for help. "I have been living in hiding from one place to the other. Sammy, could you help me?"

I promised him I would do what I could. I was aware that many Americans make such promises and promptly forget them. I had decided that if I said I would try to help, I would follow through. I didn't know how successful I would be, but I would try.

In Romania the crowds tend to get bigger every night as more and more people hear about what's going on. Wednesday night about 1,500 people crowded the church, the balcony, the court-yard, and the street. But that night nothing was clicking. I didn't feel freedom in my speaking. Titus noticed it, but he couldn't help either. We weren't flowing. It was frustrating. Here was a big, en-thusiastic, sympathetic crowd. We had a message for them, but apparently I didn't know precisely what it was. I would speak a line and pray while Titus translated it. He would pray while listening to the next line, but nothing was working.

Finally I stopped and said, "Folks, for some reason I don't feel God wants me to finish this message. I feel led to just share with you the Word of God. I'm going to quote Scripture."

I began to recite verses and passages that God brought to mind. With no commentary, I just pronounced them. It was then that I knew what kind of a man of the Word Titus really was. Here was a man who had to be in the Bible consistently. As soon as I would announce a reference or just start a verse, he would begin translating it. Suddenly we were clicking, humming like a well-oiled machine. I would step forward and shout out a verse, he would translate it and be ready for the next. I had the feeling that he knew exactly where I was going and what was coming.

God promises that His Word will not return unto Him void. There is nothing so powerful as the Word of God itself. No preaching, no matter how anointed, can match the sheer energy of Scripture. We need more of that: allowing the Bible to speak for itself.

I had never seen anything like it. For the rest of the evening Titus and I simply quoted the Word, back and forth, back and forth, rapid fire and with conviction as the Lord led. The people were thrilled, lifted emotionally by God as they basked in His truth. The Spirit of God fell heavy on that place and people began to weep. I felt emotion rise in my throat as we continued, mirrored by Titus.

The message had been entirely made up of Scripture, closing with the passages on the need for salvation and how to receive Christ. It was as if the glory of God had come down. We were in His presence, bathed by His power. All over the church people wept, and then hundreds came forward to receive Christ.

I had never in my life been in a service like that, and I'll never forget it. Titus and I were bound by that experience, and it remains one of our sweetest memories.

When it was all over, the pastor pulled me into his office and stood there in tears. "Tonight was for me," he said over and over. "Tonight was for me. My life will never be the same. I've been fearful, but the fear is gone."

We were to leave that night and head directly back to the West, but we almost could not get to our vehicles. The people lined the street and shouted to the glory of God. They prayed and wept and sang as we tried to move out. It took about a half hour just to get our van down the block from there. One of the teenage girls handed Collynn a sheet of paper that read: "Jesus is coming soon."

We drove back to a little village outside Arad where we dropped off Titus, who had to change clothes in the dark. We put him on a train back to Oradea. Our hearts were one. That was the beginning of God's taking us and thrusting us throughout the nation of Romania in a mighty way.

CHAPTER TWENTY-FOUR

CLOAK AND DAGGER

Not long after we returned to the States, I got a call from an old high school classmate, Woody Jenkins, who was a member of the Louisiana House of Representatives. He was a Christian, active in evangelical concerns, and after reading some of my earlier books had re-established contact with me. Now, he said, he had someone on the other line he thought it would be important for me to meet. He introduced me to David Funderbirk, recently resigned U.S. Ambassador to Romania.

Funderbirk had resigned after a vain attempt to end the U.S.'s favored-nation trade status with Romania. He had tried to communicate to the White House, to Congress, and to the State Department that atrocities by the Ceausescu regime must not be ignored. Eventually his efforts would be rewarded by a lifting of the favored-nation status from Romania, but at the time we spoke by phone, he was still lobbying.

I told him of the problems with Buni Cocar and asked for any help he might be able to give. In return he encouraged me to go to the U.S. embassy in Bucharest and meet the people there. "It's important that they know you and that they are aware of it when you are in the country. What you are doing is dangerous."

I tried to tell him that I had always tried to stay away from the political arena. I was in Romania as an ambassador of Jesus Christ, not of the United States. The former ambassador insisted that it was still a good idea to stay in close touch with U.S. representatives over there and assured me I would in no way compromise my own mission. He warned me that if I was not protected that way and was arrested for any reason, I would likely be charged as a spy and could disappear, possibly never to be heard from again. That got my attention.

I assured him that I wanted to leave no doubt that I was there on a mission for Christ. One of the policies of our ministry was that we would not exchange money on the black market. If we got into trouble, we wanted to make sure it was for preaching the gospel, not for breaking the law.

In January of 1986 I coordinated my return to Romania with trips by both Barry Wood, the evangelist, and Jon Randles, a pastor from Graham, Texas. Barry and Jon had been blacklisted with Sam Friend the year before. The three of us each had different traveling companions and different arrival dates for our flights into Bucharest because we wanted to be sure we didn't all get deported at the same time.

What I didn't realize was that Randles had not made it in. Sure enough, his blacklisting made it onto the computers.

Randles tried to enter the country through the Bucharest airport on January 1. I came in on the second, and Wood would try to come in a few days later. What I didn't realize was that Randles had not made it in. Sure enough, his blacklisting made it onto the computers, and as the authorities had warned him before, he was not allowed in. Fred Gough, a former professional football player, traveled with Randles, and since they didn't go through the line together and Gough's name was not on the blacklist, he was allowed in. The problem was, it was his first time in the country. He knew no one, didn't know the language, and would just try to make contact with the names he had heard from Randles and Wood.

Frank Corte of our board and Don Shelton, by then pastor of Hahn Baptist, went in with me January 2 without incident. We rented a car and checked into the Hotel Parc, a downscale hotel compared to the Hotel Intercontinental where Fred Gough was registered. We were still unaware of him at this point, of course.

We got in touch with Pastor Vasile Talos of the church where I was to preach, and he led us there. Meanwhile, Fred Gough had found the church and was mistaken for me. They knew an American was coming to preach, so they began talking to him about his message.

"No," he said, "I'm not the speaker. I don't have a message."

"Praise the Lord! He will give you one," they told him, and began trying to tell him the order of service. Fred panicked, not knowing what to say, afraid and alone in a strange country, knowing he was probably being watched by the Securitate, and fearing for his freedom.

Just then the door flew open and in I walked with my long, black, wool coat that looked to Fred like CIA or KGB or Securitate. He breathed a huge sigh of relief when he heard me speak and knew I was an American. When he found out who I was and that he didn't have to speak, he was *really* relieved!

Fred bragged about how he had lost a taxi driver who spoke English and had taken him on a tour. "I knew he had to be connected to the Securitate, so I didn't have him take me to the church. I waited till someone got out of a taxi at the hotel and jumped into that one."

The pastor smiled. "And did your new driver understand English?"

"Yes!"

"Then you went from one Securitate driver to another."

Fred was a great guy and we hit it off right away. I admired that he had come in on his own when many others would have given up and left immediately. He kidded me about my insistence on staying in a hotel that was "only twenty or thirty dollars a night cheaper than the Intercontinental when the difference in comfort is like night and day." Still, I didn't want to spend money where we didn't have to, and I certainly didn't want a reputation as a wealthy American preacher—especially when it wasn't true.

Fred gave his testimony that night, after I had given him tips on local customs, advising him to take off his rings and not put his hands in his pockets while speaking. Westerners appear to be showing off their wealth even with simple jewelry, and putting your hands in your pockets is a sign of dishonesty. Those tips served only to make Fred more nervous, but he did fine. (He eventually became a member of the board of God's Love in Action.)

The next morning Fred wanted to go to the U.S. embassy, across the street from his hotel, and check on Jon Randles. I agreed to meet him at eleven to see how it went. He reported that they got word that Randles had been deported to Budapest and had checked in with the U.S. embassy there. Fred was virtually communicating with him through the embassies. Our embassy in Bucharest had already heard about Fred from Jon, and now Fred said he had told them about me. They wanted to meet me. Had it not been for my phone conversation with former Ambassador Funderbirk, I would not have been happy about that. As it was, I planned to be extremely careful.

I was escorted to Funderbirk's former office and the U.S. operatives began asking a lot of questions. I interrupted them. "Let me ask you something before we go any further. Is it safe to talk here?" I didn't want them asking me pertinent questions about key people in the country if they couldn't assure me that our conversations weren't being bugged.

"This is as safe as any place in Romania," they said, eyebrows raised. That was all I needed to hear. That meant it wasn't safe at all because few places in Romania weren't susceptible to bugging.

"Well," I said quietly, "the conversation basically ends here." I wasn't about to compromise my friends.

"Just a moment," one said, rising. "Come with us."

I followed them to another area where they punched a button and an entire fake wall slid open to reveal a state-of-the-art soundproof room. I wondered what in the world I had gotten myself into. We sat at a table and they said with confidence, "It's safe to talk here."

We traded a lot of information. They told me all that had happened with Randles, and they also told me how dangerous it was for me. They repeated what Funderbirk had said: that I could disappear and never be heard from again.

I asked them what was bugged and what wasn't, and they told me that the Romanians are as sophisticated as the Soviets in their communications devices. They warned me not to trust any public place, any hotel room, any restaurant. "The woods are the safest places."

I asked where the microphone would be in a hotel room. They told me in the ash tray, the TV, the phone, behind a picture. "It could be anywhere. If they know there are Americans in a room they might sit outside in a car with a directional microphone discreetly pointed at the window. The phones are all bugged, of course, and you'd be amazed what they pick up."

We learned to talk about our friends in code, by their initials, whenever we were indoors.

The embassy officials asked us to keep them informed of our itinerary so they could keep track of us, and they also offered to help if we knew of any overt acts of oppression or persecution. I left wondering if I had done the right thing and worrying about Barry Wood. This was the day he would arrive.

I drove to the airport to see if he made it through all right. He would notice me, but we could not be seen together. I saw him in the line and watched as he approached passport control, where his name would be in the computer. While others were admitted and took their luggage off the conveyor belts, Barry was asked to step off to the side. I caught his eye and he looked away. I knew then it was bad news. He was not going to get in.

I preached that night and visited the U.S. embassy again in the morning to report what I had seen at the airport. They traced Barry to Budapest and I realized that with all the calling and checking around, Tex had to have heard about Jon and Barry not making it in. I knew she would be worried about me, so I called her from the Hotel Intercontinental. We have a code we use to not give away too much information. I told her I had arrived safely in Bucharest and that the weather was beautiful. "We're enjoying the scenery and meeting a lot of new friends." That meant that I had been to the churches and gotten reacquainted with our friends. "Everything is going very well."

"Is there anything else you need to tell me?" she asked.

"No, I just wanted to tell you I love you and that I had a good trip."

I about had a heart attack when I went down and got the seventy-dollar phone bill for two minutes to the U.S.! From that point on Fred kidded me about "staying in a rat hotel to save a few bucks, but spending seventy dollars on a two-minute phone call."

That night after I preached in Bucharest, Nelu Dronca arrived to talk to me. He had taken off work and made the eight-hour trip from Timisoara just to talk with me for a few minutes before heading back. "Sammy," he said, "it was worth the trip because I knew if I came all this way in person you would not be able to say no to me. I've come to ask you to come to Timisoara on this trip. You must come and see us and preach to us."

I smiled and nodded. How could I turn him down? "You're right, brother," I said. "I couldn't tell you no. I'll work it out somehow, and I will be there."

We embraced and he hurried out to catch the train back so he could be home by morning.

Back in Oradea I was admonished by Dr. Nick and Paul for having spent too much time in small churches in the dangerous areas the last time I was in Romania. They believed I risked too much by going to those places in the southeast where the churches were small and the work difficult.

I told them, "Look, there's something you have to understand about me. I'm not a rich American. I'm just one little guy. The people who support me know I'm not going to sit around in the big cities and wait for the big events at the large churches. When I come, I come to minister. There are too many cities here that have never had an evangelist come and preach the gospel. I would violate the trust of the people behind me if I didn't do that."

"But your ministry is so valuable," they said. "Do you want to risk that?"

"My ministry is nothing. Obedience is everything. You have to understand, I'm a risk-oriented person. For me, it's faith. My whole life has been going where no one else goes."

When I had been at a small church in Galati the year before, one of the men asked why I was the first preacher from the West to visit his town. I didn't know what to say. "Why haven't you ever been here before?" he asked.

I accepted the rebuke. Oradea is a great city with a wonderful church that is also close to my heart. But there are needier places, places just as important, struggling and persecuted. Many of the most well-known preachers in the world had spoken in Oradea. Who would go to the hard places?

One of the challenges was that there are not many interpreters available in the small, out-of-the-way places. That was why it was so important that Titus be willing to go with me. Paul and Nick implied that I should minister in Oradea and let them take the message to the rest of the country. But when I asked the people elsewhere, "Do ministers from Oradea come here?" they answered, "No."

By the end of our discussion, I felt Paul and I had come to some basic agreements. I apologized for having been insensitive to him, and I believe he understood that I could not be restricted from preaching to the small churches in difficult areas.

After we had cleared the air, I felt much more freedom to preach out the rest of the campaign in Oradea. On Thursday night the daughter of a local Securitate commander received Christ, risking everything. Paul told me it would be very difficult and dangerous for her now and that she needed our prayers.

Afterward one of the church leaders came to me and asked if the Lord had worked that night. Why, the place had been full to overflowing. Many were saved. Many more rededicated their lives. The daughter of the Securitate official came to Christ. "Didn't you see what happened?" I asked him.

"Oh, no. While you were preaching, I was with a hundred other men in a prayer room. In another room were a hundred women. We just came out to see if the Lord had worked."

I was happy to tell him that the Lord had indeed worked, and after hearing where he had been, I knew why.

During that time in Romania, I enjoyed many hours of good discussion and debate with Titus and Radu. I loved discussing strategy with them. Radu was intrigued by the concept of humility being a base for revival, according to 2 Chronicles 7:14. "I find it elusive," he said. "Once you know you have it, you have lost it." To him, true humility was really seeing God for who He was and seeing yourself in comparison. Titus challenged me to preach on hell. I had a lot of namby-pamby excuses for not preaching on it, but he persuaded me that it was a needed topic, even among the persecuted. He challenged me to be the best I could be, to make the best presentation of the gospel. I went back and studied so I could preach on it.

Taking such input all boils down to relationships. If someone I wasn't sure loved me and had my ministry at heart said that to me, I might have been defensive and reacted in the flesh. But Titus, a man of deep prayer and commitment to the revival and evangelization of his people, could not offend me with his input, even when we disagreed.

I loved preaching and being with the Romanian believers, but boy, those trips were draining. Don Shelton, Frank Corte, and I preached twenty-seven times in twelve days, sometimes four sermons in one day. They don't allow you to get to bed at a reasonable hour because feeding you is part of their spiritual gift of hospitality, and the biggest meal of the day comes late at night, after the services. Then because of our schedule, we had to be up early for prayer and quiet time and then hitting the road.

There were times I felt I was spending myself, but what better, more fulfilling way was there to be used up than for Jesus Christ?

CHAPTER TWENTY-FIVE

MAKING THE BREAK

W hen I got back to the United States I told Tex, "There's no doubt in my mind that it's time to leave the church. I've got to go full time."

Despite all I've said and all I had learned about faith and trust, I have to admit my biggest hesitation was finances. I had lived by faith before, but now I was used to eight years in pastorates where the salary may not have been lucrative, but was secure. My family was getting older and had more needs, and I wondered whether there would be enough income.

By this time all the people who had supported me regularly before I took my first church gradually slipped from our list. We still kept in touch with about five hundred of them through an occasional newsletter, but we didn't want, need, or seek outside support. If I needed extra money for an international trip, I applied some of the love offerings from my ministry in the United States. Then one day, in response to the news that we were planning another trip overseas, an old acquaintance sent us a note and a pledge of fifty dollars a month. Tex said that with that check, the Lord breathed faith into her heart for our future. I said, "Honey, I don't think you understand. Fifty dollars is not going to do it."

She said, "Sammy, God is going to touch other people's hearts just like this."

She was right.

Sam Friend was great about our decision. That church and those people have been behind us all the way. We moved back to San Antonio June 20, 1986, and ten days later we left for Europe. Collynn Wood, whom I had reluctantly taken with us the first time, was an important member of the traveling team now, as were several others. Joe Davis, a newcomer from Jon Randles's church in Graham, Texas, became a frequent companion overseas.

One of the highlights of the trip was returning to Bratislava, Czechoslovakia, where I had visited following the Communist Youth World Fest years before. Now I was given the name of a godly old man from the Brethren Church, a man who had been imprisoned for five years for trying to share his faith publicly.

What a blessed time of fellowship we enjoyed with this deep man of prayer! I didn't understand Czech or Slovakian, so he spoke to me in German. He pointed to a huge soccer stadium across from where he lived and said, "I am praying that one day we will preach the gospel in that stadium."

I smiled and nodded, but inside I thought, *Oh, man, not likely in your lifetime. Or mine.* I had so little faith. I knew it was an honorable thing to wish and hope and pray for, but practically, realistically, it wasn't going to happen without a miracle from God.

"You know," the old man continued, "many people come to my country and want to make a big fire for God. I don't want to make a big fire for God. I want to be consumed by God's fire until I am ashes. And when I am ashes, then I will see His glory. Do you understand me?"

I thought he was asking if I understood his German. I told him I did.

"No, no," he said, "do you understand what I am telling you? When I am so much nothing that God is everything, then I will see His glory."

I was so deeply moved I could not speak. I just nodded and bowed my head.

"Now let me leave you with a promise from the Word of God," he said. Slowly, and with great dignity, he quoted the 121st Psalm. I'll never forget it. Though we had no other business in Czechoslovakia, the meeting with the old man of faith was worth every minute. Especially to hear from him the Word of God:

I will lift up my eyes to the hills—
From whence comes my help?
My help comes from the LORD,
Who made heaven and earth.
He will not allow your foot to be moved;
He who keeps you will not slumber.
Behold, He who keeps Israel
Shall neither slumber nor sleep.
The LORD is your keeper;
The LORD is your shade at your right hand.
The sun shall not strike you by day,
Nor the moon by night.
The LORD shall preserve you from all evil;
He shall preserve your soul.
The LORD shall preserve your going out and your coming in
From this time forth, and even forevermore.

Titus and Radu organized a Romanian singing group to travel with us so we wouldn't have the expense and hassle of bringing more people from the States. To qualify for this group, the singers were required to memorize the entire book of James. When they performed they sang a song, quoted a chapter, and so forth. It was a thrill to be involved with kids who were so committed to the Lord and to the task.

Meanwhile, we were ministering in the town of Constanza when Radu told us that some local young people wanted to play Dave and me in basketball. It seemed like a good witnessing opportunity, and we both loved to play anyway, so I told Tex that after the game we would meet her and Renee on the beach at noon. That way we would get in some basketball, time with the family, and still have time to prepare for that evening's meetings.

After we played basketball and shared the Lord with our opponents, I drove to the prearranged spot to meet Tex and Renee. There was a huge crowd out on the boulevard, but I couldn't see why. After we parked, a young Romanian came running. "Sammy! Sammy! It's Renee!"

Dave and I took off running and found Tex in the middle of the crowd, huddled over Renee, comforting her and praying for her. Renee had stepped around a parked bus into the path of an oncoming car and was hit. Her head was bleeding and had a huge bump. Tex would not let anyone put her in an ambulance because we had heard stories that Christians mysteriously die in Romanian hospitals. The doctors blame it on complications.

I lifted her into the ambulance and climbed in with her. I told Tex to meet me at the hospital. Renee kept sobbing, "Daddy, I don't want to die. I don't want to die." As if to be sure she wasn't losing her mind or even her memory, she repeated, "My name is Renee Tippit and I'm ten years old and I have Jesus in my heart. Daddy, I don't want to die. I want to grow up and be a singer and come back to Romania and sing about Jesus."

It was all I could do to fight back my own panic and tears and try to tell her she would be all right. Even after X-rays and an examination, Tex had not arrived at the hospital. I was told that Renee would have to stay there a few days, which made me nervous. I knew Tex would insist on staying with her, but where was she? Renee and I sang, prayed, and quoted Scripture together until Tex and the rest of the team finally arrived.

Tex was upset. A local policeman had impounded our car—though it had nothing to do with the accident—had confiscated Tex's passport, and was threatening to imprison her for six months for being a neglectful parent! When Renee seemed stable, we asked Collynn Wood to stay with her while Tex and I went to the police station. I admit I reacted in the flesh. I told our interpreter, a girl from the singing group, to tell the policeman that if he didn't return our car and Tex's passport and stop threatening ridiculous punishment for what was clearly an accident, I would complain to the U.S. embassy and have his job.

The girl told me she wouldn't translate that, so Tex had to take over. She was really in the Spirit and shared her faith with the man while pleading for her passport. Things were much calmer, but still he held her passport. And the threat of imprisonment still hung over her head.

I hurried to the hotel for a quick shower before taking Tex back to the hospital and heading to the church. While in the shower I dropped the soap, and after picking it up I banged my head hard on the metal soap dish sticking out of the wall. I slid to the floor crying. I don't know when I've been so discouraged. I had lost all hope. "God, I came here for You," I said. "Why are You letting this happen? I can't take it! Renee's in the hospital, Tex has no passport, and we may go to prison! Lord, what's going on?"

> **"God, I came here for You," I said. "Renee's in the hospital, Tex has no passport, and we may go to prison! Lord, what's going on?"**

After I dropped Tex off at the hospital I went to the church and found Titus and Radu waiting for me in the pastor's study. They had just heard about Renee. As they reached out to comfort me and pray for me, I broke down. "Guys, I can't preach. I'm in too much turmoil. There's no way."

Radu and Titus said, "Sammy, we're going to find a place to pray for you," and they left the room. Sitting there, alone with God, knowing that my two dear brothers were praying that He would raise me up to continue serving Him, I got some small understanding of the Fatherhood of God. My heart was hurting so much for Renee that I would have traded places with her in a second. But I realized that God had given His own Son, knowing He would die. And God cared more about Renee than I did. He cared about me too. I'd needed to give Dave back to the Lord when he had to go to the hospital during a previous trip. I thought I had given Tex and Renee back to him too, but here was the real test. What would happen if Tex went to prison and Renee did not survive? I knew I had to come to the place where I was really willing to entrust them to Him alone. This was beyond my control.

"God, they're Yours," I said, sobbing. "You're our only hope."

I felt God's supernatural peace wash over me, and I sensed He wanted me to speak that evening on how to stand under pressure. Anything I said on that subject would have to come from God, and I knew I had to be totally honest and vulnerable. I preached the message and told of my own struggles with everything from my ten year old lying in the street to banging my head on the soap dish. The people wept and prayed for Renee. Many came to Christ that day, and many more recommitted their lives to Him.

Near the end of the service I was handed a note from Tex, which I joyfully read to the people. It said, "Sammy, Renee is okay. She's out of the hospital and we're back at the hotel." We praised God together. On my way out of the service a woman professor met me, her daughters in tow. "At noon my family and I were having lunch," she said, "and we were deeply burdened to pray for your family because something was wrong." That gave me great reassurance because that was right about the time Renee was struck.

When I got back to the hotel I found that the passport had been returned and the car released. Glory to God!

It seemed that on every trip I learned hard lessons about myself and great lessons about the faithfulness of God. In November, when we went back, the believers were stunned to see me because they had heard about how hard it was for people from the West to get in, especially as many times as I had.

We went to see Titus and Gabi at their humble apartment, tiny even by Romanian standards but minuscule when compared with where doctors in the West live. We had to be careful not to speak English outside. If anyone reported that Westerners were in the Colteas' place, Titus and Gabi would be in trouble. When Gabi opened the door and realized it was me, she looked like she had seen a ghost and threw her arms around my neck. How great it was to see her and Titus!

During that trip we spoke to three thousand at Second Baptist in Oradea, though the power was out and the place was lit by candles. In Bucharest we held a secret training session for area pastors in the basement of a church. Every time someone walked by we fell silent and the pastors looked at each other in fear. Yet every day they took copious notes and enjoyed warm fellowship in the Lord. These poor men each wore their only suit of clothes, day after day. They were grateful for training in the Word, which they hadn't had in years.

I met again with officials at the American embassy, and when we were finished one of them volunteered to walk me back over to the Hotel Intercontinental to meet others from the team for a meal. "Keep your eyes straight ahead and don't make any expression while I talk to you," he said. "I am a Christian too, and I have a safe, guaranteed way of getting books into the country. If you want to do it, here's how." He handed me a paper with the instructions.

I asked, "How many can we ship in? The pastors need commentaries and Bible study aids."

"All you want."

"Boxes?"

"Sure."

Later we took advantage of that, shipping in box after box of books for the Christian leaders through that contact in the embassy.

When we went to Galati to minister, we ran into an interesting situation. Two deacons stood at the entrance to the church, turning away any they knew to be Christians. The Christians were to stand and listen outside. The church was full of unbelievers and seekers. Josef Stephanuti, the pastor, arrived a little late one evening and couldn't get in himself! He had to stand in the bitter cold with the rest of the Christians.

Stephanuti is one of the sweetest men you'll ever meet. He's soft-spoken and godly and has a beautiful, warm smile. He and his family lived in a tiny apartment above a church in a neighboring town, and his church's application to build him new living quarters languished for years. They were crammed into three tiny rooms with an outside kitchen and no indoor plumbing.

After we ministered at his church he was informed that he would never receive permission to enlarge his living area. I was devastated. "Brother Stephanuti," I said, "I'm so sorry we caused you trouble. Had I known I would not have come."

"Oh, Sammy, no, no," he said. "If just one person had come to Jesus Christ, it would have been worth it. And look at all who came! I can live like this the rest of my life."

Titus was very careful in every city. He was not able to stay at any hotels and could not appear to be with us, other than in the churches. One day it became clear to him that he was being followed. He did not want the ruthless Securitate to know what he was translating, whom he was with, or where he was staying. He was afraid. If he continued to be followed, they would learn everything and we could all be in trouble. He prayed and prayed about what to do and felt the Lord saying to him, "Turn around and face your fear." So Titus turned around and looked directly at his follower. The man was disconcerted and looked away. When he looked back, Titus was still looking him full in the face. The man turned and walked away, so Titus followed him. He followed him all over town until the man eluded him, and Titus was not followed again.

Galati overlooks the Danube, across from the Soviet Union, so after we ministered each night, the team and Titus and I bundled up and walked down by the river. I looked across and wept and pleaded with the Lord for the opportunity to "one day go there and proclaim Your gospel."

Titus too had a burden for the Soviet Union because it had long been the center for atheism and socialist dogma. All the Eastern European communist countries fell under its domain, and he longed to see God do a mighty work there. But his main focus and burden was for his own country. One night as we walked and prayed, he fell prostrate on the frozen ground, his face in the dirt, and prayed a prayer that pierced me.

"O, God," he said, "if it takes the blood of the martyrs to bring my people to Jesus, let me be the first to offer my blood."

That commitment shook me to my core. I never heard a man pray like that before. Eventually, of course, it did take the blood of martyrs in Timisoara when the great revolution against the dictator began.

My dream of re-entering the Soviet Union came closer to reality when Pastor Stephanuti gave me the name and number of his friends in Kishinev, capital of the Soviet Republic of Moldavia. "You need to preach there," he said.

There was nothing I wanted to do more.

CHAPTER TWENTY-SIX

MY GLIMPSE OF MORTALITY

With the natural limitations of communication between Eastern Europe and the United States, I got the word late in 1986 that Pastor Stephanuti had made contact with a key person in the church in Kishinev and that I could arrange to meet with him there. Actually setting something up in the Soviet Union, after having been deported from there as a young evangelist, was the realization of a dream.

Fred Gough and a man named Jerry Cadenhead and I flew into Kishinev in Soviet Moldavia in February of 1987. Everything that happened there convinced us that the authorities were well aware of our mission from the beginning.

First of all, we were met at the plane by Intourist and were assigned a guide who led us on a tour of the area. We endured that, but as soon as we could politely shake the guy, I wanted to make contact with the man whose name and number Stephanuti gave me. In the hotel room, Fred and Jerry and I spoke in code and decided that I would go outside to make my call from a pay phone.

I ventured out into a raging, frigid blizzard and made my way to a nearby bank where I changed some bills into coins. I came back to a pay phone at the edge of the courtyard in front of the hotel and dialed the number. I needed to know I was talking to the right person, a Christian, so when he answered, I said "*Pace* (pah-chay) [Peace]."

Only Christians greet each other that way, and I listened intently for the only appropriate response: *"Pace Domnului Isus Kristos* [The peace of the Lord Jesus Christ]," he said.

I immediately began speaking to him in Romanian. "Good to talk with you, brother. Stephanuti gave me your name and said I should get in touch with you."

With that the phone went dead, and I knew we were being hassled by the secret police. I dialed back immediately. The man picked up the receiver and said, "I will meet you in front of the hotel in one hour. Wait out by the street." And he hung up.

Fred and Jerry and I waited outside in the snow much longer than an hour, and Fred finally said, "I have to go in and get warm."

While he was inside, he told me later, the lobby began to fill with what looked to be plainclothes secret policemen. None of them approached the desk clerk; in fact, none seemed to have anything to do there but watch. Fred grew nervous and tried to decide what to do. A man walked past him and spoke in English. "I'm here but I cannot talk to you now."

The cold was getting to me too, so I asked Jerry to continue waiting while I went inside. I sat next to Fred, and without looking at me he said, "Our guy is here. He's standing right over there. I can't point to him, but look around. What do you see?"

"Police," I said.

"They weren't here when I got here. Something's wrong here. We need to get out of here."

"Let's take a walk then," I said. And so, in the middle of a blizzard, we strolled out, met up with Jerry, and took a walk through the city. Forty-five minutes later we returned to an empty lobby. The woman at the desk said, "Your friend was here."

I said, "What friend?"

"Your friend who was to meet you. He said he was late but that he would be back at seven."

It didn't make sense that the man would say he couldn't talk to us now, and then identify himself to the woman at the desk. That's when we knew for sure that the first guy was secret police. The second one might have been, but we would have to see who showed up at seven.

When we came down later, Fred didn't recognize either of the two elderly men in the lobby. One of them kept looking at me. "Maybe that's him," I whispered.

I walked past him and murmured, *"Pace."*

"Pace Domnului," he said.

I hurried back to Fred. "That's not the guy who said he was here to see us?"

"Nope."

The man approached us. "I'm here, and I have nothing to hide," he said. "Let's go sit down, and I'll talk in front of anyone." He seemed both nervous and bold. We enjoyed an hour of fellowship, ending in his inviting me to preach in his church.

I did, and though the response was good, the translation was not, and I left frustrated, wondering what had happened. I believe we were being set up and might have been arrested if we had made contact with the wrong person. I still wanted to come back to the Soviet Union and preach under better circumstances. Native Moldavians are of Romanian heritage, and there were many Romanian-speaking people. So we would need two interpreters. Still, that remained my dream.

When we returned to the States, my book *Fire in Your Heart* was released. I took a couple of boxes with me to Singapore '87, a conference for young emerging Christian leaders, and that resulted in my networking with other evangelicals all over the world. My ministry began to broaden and expand, and it would never be the same.

I was just as excited about an opportunity Dave, then sixteen, had to go to Kenya and share his faith while playing basketball. I counseled him on how to use "The Four Spiritual Laws" and told him I was praying that he would be able to lead someone to Christ. He said, "Dad, I'm only 16. That's kind of unlikely."

After the trip, he met us in Europe to go into Romania, and we were thrilled to hear that Dave had indeed had the opportunity to lead his first soul to Christ. In fact, he led twelve!

In Bucharest Titus told me we had been invited to a tiny church in an out-of-the-way town. I told him it was impossible because I was committed in Bucharest. He told me the pastor in Bucharest had released me because Titus pleaded for this small church that had never had a Western preacher before. "It's your decision to make, Sammy," Titus said.

We stopped along the road and prayed about it. We both felt peace that we should go. I had long since learned not to question the leading of the Lord in these matters. If I had passed this up, I would have missed out on a huge blessing. We drove to the town, but the pastor wasn't there. I wondered how he could plead with us to come and then not show up himself. But we got word that he wanted us to come to another of his churches in a nearby village. (The typical pastor serves between five and seven churches.)

We found the church housed in a place no bigger than a typical American bedroom, and it looked as if it had a hundred people jammed in it. Others stood outside. I preached and the people responded. Several came to Christ. Up to then, the meeting had been fairly typical of our ministry in Eastern Europe, and I was grateful for the opportunity. But after the service I found out it had not been typical at all. An elderly lady ran up to me and began speaking so quickly in Romanian that I needed Titus to sort it out for me.

> **"I have not been inside a church for twenty-five years. But last night I had a dream that at this church there would be two strangers that I must come and see. . . . This morning my son and I gave our hearts to Jesus."**

She said, "I have not been inside a church for twenty-five years. But last night I had a dream that at this church there would be two strangers that I must come and see. When I woke up I told my son that we had to go to the church and see these two strangers. When I came in, there you were [Titus and I], the same ones from my dream. This morning my son and I gave our hearts to Jesus."

At another small church that Sunday night I asked the people to pray about whom God would have them bring to the services. The next night one of the deacons told me this story: "I did what you said, and I felt led to invite a neighbor who had never been to church. When I went to invite him, he was sitting there all cleaned up and dressed and ready to go. He told me he had come home from work and felt like he should get ready to go somewhere, but he didn't know where. But the feeling was so strong, he did it.

Then I showed up and brought him to church. He became a Christian tonight."

I had never seen God work in such mysterious ways, but you never knew what might happen when you're really on the front lines. When we were invited to yet another tiny church in Comanesti, I couldn't refuse. Again the building was more like a small room, and there were four times as many people outside than inside. The pastor said it would make more sense to have the meeting outside, so I said sure. Titus pulled me off to the side.

"Sammy, it's against the law to preach outside. We could all go to prison. It's very dangerous. I'm not saying we shouldn't do it, but we need to know if it's God's will."

So we prayed about it. Again, both of us felt peace. Titus and I can be pretty loud when we're preaching, and as soon as we began, people began coming from the highrise apartment buildings near the church. They filled the courtyard and the street. People climbed trees and sat atop garages so they could see and hear. This was something totally new to them, and they were fascinated. About two thousand people gathered for the service, and a couple of hundred prayed to receive Christ.

We stayed and did the same thing the next night, and the pastor told us that more people had come to Christ in those two nights than in the previous ten years. The church tripled in size overnight, and they were forced to build. Just before the Romanian revolution, that pastor and his four deacons were arrested and sentenced to eight years in prison (later reduced to house arrest).

When we got back to Bucharest we transported from the embassy the books we had shipped in through our secret contact there. Three of us entered the embassy with huge, empty sports bags and left with them weighed down with books. Our bags were checked on the way in, but not on the way out.

Our contact person told us, "If you get caught with these, I'll deny ever having had contact with you. You'll be in great trouble, and I'll not be able to help you."

We kept those books with us everywhere we went, and one night we had them stored safely in a church when the van was broken into. We would have lost them for sure. Eventually a set went to Titus, another to Radu, and another to a man in Arad. It was a thrill to be able to provide these ministry tools.

During 1987 the Lord encouraged me by letting me hear from people who had come to Him over the years through my ministry. Though some of them talked about events that happened twenty years before and could have made me feel old, I simply felt grateful that God had sent them back my way. Coming up on my fortieth birthday, it was wonderful it was to know that I had had a small part in someone coming to Christ.

When I spoke at a church in Oklahoma, the minister of music introduced me, in tears, saying, "Twenty years ago a young man came to the city where I was raised. I gave my heart to Christ through his preaching. I have not seen that man since that day. But he is on the platform, and he will come and speak to us now."

On a radio talk show in Chicago a man called in to say, "I was saved under your ministry fifteen years ago, and I wanted to say thank you. My life has never been the same."

A letter to the editor of *Moody Monthly* magazine referred to an article about me and said, "In 1970, I was a seventeen-year-old girl from Monroe, Louisiana, when I met Sammy and Tex on their way to Washington. Their freedom to love and worship God changed my life."

A thirty year old from New Orleans wrote to say that both he and his wife were saved in different meetings and in different towns as children, before they met, both under my preaching.

I pray that twenty years from now people from all over the world will have that same testimony. To me it's a glimpse of heaven to learn of the children God the Father has allowed me to help bring to Jesus.

When one of my mentor-encouragers, Mike Gilchrist, asked if I would be willing to minister with him in South Africa in August of 1987, I put it on my schedule immediately. Besides being eager to work alongside Mike, I was curious about what God was doing in other parts of the world. I saw this as a rare opportunity.

Meanwhile, Tex had a surprise party for me on my fortieth birthday, July 27, 1987. Like anyone else who hits such a milestone (which was not nearly as traumatic to me as my thirtieth birthday), I had plenty of friends who enjoyed telling me I was over the hill, that I should rest in peace, or that I had one foot in the grave and the other on a banana peel. I got the typical gloom and doom cards and gifts. Frankly, with all the traveling and working out and jogging I did, I thought I was in unusually good shape for my age. With the Africa trip looming, however, I thought it would be a good idea to get a complete check up.

I went to the doctor's office not only confident of a clean bill of health, but also fully expecting a pat on the back for being one of the few men my age in such good shape. The doctor drew some blood, looked me over, asked some questions, and left the room. When he returned he looked worried, which worried me.

"Sammy," he said, "I'm very concerned about a couple of things. You've got high cholesterol." The last time I'd had it checked, my cholesterol was low. Now it was well over 250. "Further," he added, "are you aware of the mole in the middle of your back?"

"No."

"It's large, and of the four signs that a mole is developing into melanoma, you have three. Two of them are a darkening or that it's multi-colored, so you couldn't have four signs anyway. From every appearance, without a biopsy, it appears to be melanoma."

He was moving too fast. Melanoma sounded like cancer to me. "Whoa," I said. "What does that mean?"

"There's no cure and no therapy for melanoma. It cannot be treated with radiation." So it *was* cancer. "The only hope is surgery."

"What kind of surgery?"

"First we have to do a biopsy to determine what we're dealing with. If it is cancerous, we will remove a large area to be sure we got all the seedlings so it can't spread."

"And if it spreads?"

"You could be dead in two years."

I told him I was leaving the next day for a speaking engagement in Kansas City, then two weeks later flying to South Africa.

"We can do the biopsy immediately, and if the results indicate the need for removal, you would not be comfortable flying to Africa. We would have to perform the operation as soon as possible, and it will require a skin graft to cover the opening."

I needed time to process this. I needed to pray about it and, of course, talk to Tex about it. But there was one thing I knew for sure, and I told the doctor: "I will go to Africa anyway. I can put up with a little pain and discomfort for a two-day flight."

"That's a hard trip."

"I know, but if it won't make things worse, I still want to go."

He performed the biopsy and told me he would get the results in five days. In the meantime, Tex went with me to Kansas City, not knowing what the future held. We had the afternoons free, and of course every spare minute was spent walking and talking and praying.

"I'm having a rough time with this," she admitted. "I have to think you could handle this better if you risked losing me."

We talked about everything. What would happen with insurance, the kids, the house, whether she should remarry. It was morbid, but it had to be discussed. For me the biggest problem was not knowing. I thought I could accept it and resign myself to it, and I was determined to change nothing. I had always said I was willing to give my life in service of the Lord, so I would not slow down until I had to. I would continue to preach the gospel, and if I was gone in a couple of years, Tex should continue with her ministry.

She said she couldn't imagine remarrying. She also felt strongly that if I needed more extensive surgery, I should not go to Africa. I determined in my heart that unless it hampered my recovery, I would not let discomfort stand in my way.

I know I was still in a state of shock and didn't know what to say or do, but the exercise of evaluating our lives and our priorities was a good thing. We wanted to always live as if we were going to die soon. When we called for the results we learned that the mole was in a pre-melanoma state, so it could be removed with relatively minor surgery. I also had one removed from behind my ear, just to be safe, and of course I get regular checkups to keep an eye on other developing problems.

As scary and sobering as that uncertainty was, it was also a time of deep reflection and introspection, and I believe our lives, our marriage, and our ministries are better for it.

In South Africa I was one of three speakers at the big pastors' conference. Mike and a South African evangelist took the morning and the evening, so I spoke in the afternoons.

I was not known and not in demand there, which allowed me time to get alone with God. While we were in Cape Town I went out to a rock overlooking the Indian Ocean every evening to enjoy the sunset and to simply listen to God. I had long been teaching and preaching that true prayer is not necessarily talking to God, but being with Him, enjoying intimacy with Him. On those precious days and in those wonderful hours I simply adored the Lord and let Him speak to my spirit in His quiet way. He did not-impress anything specific on my heart, but I cherished the time alone with Him. Here I was at the southern tip of Africa, knowing that the same God who had been with me in Eastern Europe was with me there. I meditated on His greatness, and I know now that He was preparing me for a most unusual encounter with Him.

When I spoke on a Wednesday afternoon in August of 1987, I addressed pastors and church leaders of all races who had come from all over the nation of South Africa, hungering for a touch from God. I preached on prayer and emphasized what prayer was and what it wasn't. This was not an unusual service at first. It was as much teaching as preaching; in fact, Mike had to leave to help an ailing pastor, and he was surprised when he returned to see what had taken place.

I didn't give any type of an invitation or altar call. I simply asked the conferees to sing the chorus "We Exalt Thee" as we closed. When they began, all I can say is that the Spirit of the Lord fell on the place. Some people stood, some knelt, some lay on the floor. Most were weeping as they sang and prayed. People confessed sin and were restored to God and to each other. This went on for at least forty-five minutes. One of the hosts announced that it was time to stop and go in to dinner, but no one left. Husbands and wives reconciled, people prayed together; it was a special, holy time.

Thirty minutes later he again tried to dismiss the group, insisting that we must move on, but it was much, much later before the meeting finally broke up. I felt privileged to have been a part of it.

One of the best experiences in South Africa was meeting national evangelist Malvory Peffer. This precious brother has become a member of our staff, heading up our efforts in that nation.

I never doubted that God was just as much at work in other areas of the world as He was in Europe, but it was great to see it firsthand. I believe God wanted me to experience that because He was getting ready to send me out to other continents as well. I didn't know my schedule would allow such far-flung efforts, but of course God did.

CHAPTER TWENTY-SEVEN

BLACKLISTED

I should have known things were moving toward a breaking point in Romania. For our January 1988 trip I took board member Chuck Hollimon and his wife, Nancy; my new associate evangelist, Brent Saathoff; and Tex. We stuffed our van with food and supplies for the believers, but when it broke down outside Budapest, we had to leave it and most of the stuff and rent a car.

That worked out for the best because when we got into Romania we found that the border guards were either heavily taxing or turning away people bringing in supplies.

However, during our last night in Timisoara, someone broke into the car and stole only the rental papers. We concluded that it must have been the work of the Securitate because those papers were worth nothing to anyone. We needed them to get out of the country at the end of our trip, so the question now was what we could do. By that time I was going on very little sleep, and with all the complications, teaching during the day, preaching every evening, and staying up to be sociable with our hosts, I was exhausted.

Brent was off preaching somewhere else with Titus, and Chuck and Nancy and Tex were scheduled to go back to Budapest the next morning before dawn. It was well after midnight before we finished eating. Nelu Dronca and Peter Dugalescu decided it would be best for me to report the stolen papers to the police, so we would have something official to help us get out of the country later. The only problem was that I needed an interpreter, and they were not supposed to be with me. Nelu shakily volunteered to go with me anyway, and we drove to the police station.

By two A.M., when still nothing had been resolved, I said I'd be back. I drove Chuck and Nancy and Tex to Arad, and we rented a hotel room so we could sleep for just forty-five minutes. When we said good-bye, Tex told me to be careful because a man had come to her after the service and said he'd had a dream in which he saw me dying in a small room. Normally we don't put much stock in such things. I put the three of them on the train to Budapest, feeling as lonely as I ever had in the ministry, and drove to Nelu's house. After breakfast we went to the police station again. I was like a zombie, trying to get along on hardly any sleep.

After spending the morning in the police station and finally getting the documents we needed, I drove to Arad and had lunch with Pastor Titi Bulzan in his home. I was to preach in his church that night. At about two in the afternoon I felt queasy and went to take a nap. When they tried to rouse me to go to the meetings, I got up and then collapsed. I had no strength in my hands or fingers, and my legs and feet felt like lead.

They lifted me back into the bed and let me rest a while longer, but when they came to see if I was able to go, I couldn't move. I couldn't even lift my head from the pillow. Titi volunteered to stay with me. While I tried to sleep, he summoned a doctor, who found my pulse dangerously weak. The diagnosis was total exhaustion.

By eleven that night I knew I had to get up and get dressed to try to get to the hotel. It was illegal for me to stay in a private home, and I didn't want either of us to get in trouble. He could be sent to prison, and I could be deported. I told Titi I was going to try to make it if I could just get out of bed.

"You have to be able to walk into the hotel, Sammy," he said. "If they see us helping you they will take you to a hospital, and eventually they will kill you."

I told him I thought I could make it. He helped me out of bed and left the room when I started toward the bathroom. Titi sensed something wasn't right, so he rushed back in and caught me as I passed out in the bathroom. He carried me back to bed like a baby. *Is this it?* I wondered. *Was the guy's dream right? Am I going to die right here in this little room?* "Sammy, you can't go to the hotel," Titi said. "It's too dangerous. We'll have to take our chances here."

> **"You have to be able to walk into the hotel, Sammy,"** he said. **"If they see us helping you they will take you to a hospital, and eventually they will kill you."**

As with most intestinal viruses, even those complicated by such acute fatigue, I slowly recovered enough to be able to get out and preach the next night and Sunday morning—against the advice of my host. When Brent and Titus came to get me, they were shocked by my sickly appearance. Before we moved on, I thanked Titi for saving my life.

We had a thrilling time of ministry from that point on, but we were also followed everywhere we went. At one point Titus counted six Securitate following the four of us. We decided to confuse them by splitting up four different ways and meeting back at Titus's place. It worked temporarily, but we noticed Securitate agents at every meeting. This was the worst I'd seen it in all my years of ministry.

The crowds were the largest I had ever seen in Romania, so there was no hiding what we were doing. In the town of Alba Iulia the people were so hungry for the Word of God that they came even to the youth services and "small group" discipleship meetings in the afternoons. Later, when we asked new converts to meet with us in the sanctuary after the rest of the crowd left the regular evening meeting, people began filing back in and filling the place so they could hear what we were telling the new believers. Titus referred to that time in Alba Iulia as "days of heaven, when people lost all concept of time. Eternity became their focus."

Brent and I were followed on our way out of the country. When we stopped at the border we happened to pull up behind another car with a Hungarian license plate that also happened to have two Americans in it. The guards assumed we were together, and as they had apparently seen a professional photographer in the lead car shooting pictures throughout the country, they confiscated all the film from both vehicles.

At first I chatted with the photographer, but as soon as he realized that I was in trouble too, he wanted nothing to do with me.

The guards wouldn't believe we were not together. When they discovered a videotape of one of my messages and played it, it became clear what I was all about. The photographer asked if I was a religious dissident. I hadn't thought of that, but it was a fair description.

A plainclothes Securitate agent showed up and angrily informed me through an interpreter that I would not be allowed back into the country again.

I told the girl to ask him why.

"You know why," he spat.

"No, I don't. What have I done?"

The interpreter was clearly terrified. Apparently she was not used to anyone challenging a Securitate officer. "I can't tell him you said that. You'll be in trouble if you talk to him that way."

"Please go ahead and tell him. I want to know what I've done."

When she did, he was really hot. "You have broken our laws."

"No, if I have committed a crime, you tell me what crime I've committed. I have done nothing illegal." If I was going to be kicked out of the country for preaching Christ, I wanted to hear it from his lips.

"One more minute and you're in very serious trouble. Now get out of here!"

I had never been told quite that directly before that I was blacklisted, yet it had been suggested and threatened before. People had been turned away for having been with me, but every time I tried to get back in, I made it. How serious this threat was, I didn't know.

We sent Brent by train into Romania in June to see whether he had been blacklisted (as they told me I was). He got into the country without a hitch, which made me confident I could get in the same way.

As I look back on it, I had scheduled myself too ambitiously, even if everything had worked out as planned. I was to speak at Brent's ordination service in San Antonio, then fly to Dallas for the International Christian Booksellers Association convention. From there I would leave directly for Eastern Europe for three weeks before heading to Africa for four and half more weeks. It was a killer schedule, but I didn't feel I could say no to any of these open doors.

In my prayer letter I didn't even list Romania as the country I was heading to because I didn't want word to get to the authorities there that I was going to test their prohibition.

All the way overseas the song "Great Is Thy Faithfulness" kept coming to mind. I sang it over and over as I gazed out the window during the long hours on the jet. Sam Friend, who was ministering in Europe, met us during our stopover in Munich.

"Sammy," he said, "what happens if they don't let you in?"

"They issued me a visa," I said. "If I was blacklisted they wouldn't have done that."

"But what if they don't let you in?"

"Sam, I believe I'm going to get in. I really do."

"But what if they don't?"

I smiled. "I can't imagine it, Sam."

"Look," he said, "let me give you Bryan's phone number." (I use only Bryan's first name here because this is a man near Austria who houses Christians traveling in and out of Eastern Europe. I had stayed with him before.) "I'll be there, so call if you have any problems."

I put the number in my wallet, but I assured Sam again that we would make it in. I sensed a peace from the Lord about it.

When Scott and I met Darryl Gardiner in Budapest we decided to split up on the train, just in case. If any of us were detained, maybe the others would make it in. We were in three separate cars when the train arrived at the Romanian border, just outside Oradea, at 10 P.M., Thursday, July 21, 1988.

Normally this is a one-hour stop where passports are checked and the train continues into the country. When two hours passed it was clear something was wrong. I was in a compartment with a German-speaking gentleman. I spoke to him in his language: "Somebody must be in trouble."

"Yes," he said, nodding solemnly. "I don't know what it is all about."

When the guards finally got to our car, they came directly to my compartment, and one flipped open my passport. He pocketed it and spoke in English, "Mr. Tippit, get your luggage and come with us."

The man next to me demanded, "What are you doing? Where are you taking him?" I was touched by his concern after we had spent so little time together.

"Don't worry," I told him. "Thank you. Don't worry."

Six soldiers escorted me off the train and surrounded me next to the tracks as the rest of the passengers' passports were checked. When the train slowly began to pull out, I knew I would not be seeing my beloved Romanian brothers and sisters this time. I wondered whether I would ever see them again.

Scott and Darryl were still on the train, near the back, and I needed to catch their eyes so they would know I was not with them. I watched carefully as car after car rolled past. I didn't want the guards to see whom I was looking at. When Scott and Darryl saw me standing outside with my luggage, surrounded by guards, their mouths dropped. Looking away, I raised one finger to the sky, indicating that they must trust in God now. They had depended on me for this trip, but they were on their own with Him now.

As the train disappeared slowly in the distance I was reminded of how lonely I felt after putting the Hollimons and Tex on board in Arad the trip before. I was so exhausted and had gone through so much that I felt as lonely as I ever had. But this was even worse. This was more than soreness and fatigue after a car accident and getting the bad news of the death of a friend's father. This was more than missing your wife in a foreign country. Besides fatigue and disappointment, there was fear and the frustration of having no information.

Sure, I had been blacklisted, but shouldn't they have told me why I was being taken off the train? Shouldn't they tell me what would happen now? One guard was assigned to stay with me while the others moved fifteen or twenty feet away. It was summer time and I was wearing light clothes, but in the middle of the night it was chilly. I stood, I walked in place, I sat on my luggage, and for a while I simply felt sorry for myself.

Would they put me in prison? How could a government keep me from seeing my best friend? I felt God had provided Titus as a sort of replacement for Ken Leeburg, who had been such an encourager and a challenger. Would I ever see my wife and my kids again?

I knew that within ten minutes Titus would meet the train in Oradea and learn that I had been detained. Would I be put on a later train? Would they wait for me? The only thing I knew was that my brothers and sisters in Christ would pray for me and try to get word out to my loved ones that I had not made it in. I was glad I had Bryan's number in my wallet. Sam Friend had been right after all.

By about three A.M. I was chilled to the bone and depressed. Then the Lord visited me. He brought to mind again the words to that great old hymn of the faith, and I began singing "Great Is Thy Faithfulness." Then I sang all the verses I could remember to "How Great Thou Art" and "Holy, Holy, Holy." I put my focus on God and sang all the great hymns about His character. Frankly I'm not much of a singer, and some have accused me of deciding to torture those guards with my voice before they did whatever they planned to do to me!

I was singing 'Amazing Grace' when I realized I had been singing in English. I knew enough Romanian to be able to communicate, so I started making up songs and singing sermons the guards would understand. I knew they couldn't leave. I was the captive, but they were a captive audience. By morning, they would know the gospel.

When I got through singing, I preached to them for about twenty minutes, which was the extent of my Romanian. I said, "Jesus loves you and He died for you. He wants to forgive your sin and live in your heart." They wouldn't look at me or respond. They hadn't answered any questions about what would happen to me or why I was being detained, so I didn't expect any dialogue about God.

Just before dawn it was as chilly as it was going to get, and no one had offered me anything more to wear. I dug a sport coat out of my luggage, but I was still freezing. The guards wore big, heavy coats, and one by one they found places to lean and then crouch and then sit. By 5:30 or so, I was the only one left awake.

Behind me were two small buildings, one with people in it, one empty, with a hallway in between. That hallway would be warm, and I could still see the guards in case they woke up and panicked. I tiptoed in there and felt a lot better. About half an hour later a bus pulled up on its way to Oradea, and several people got on. My mind was racing.

None of the guards had stirred because apparently this was a regular stop, nothing out of the ordinary. The passports of the people getting on the bus were checked when they got off the train, and it didn't appear the bus driver was checking anything. I could grab my luggage and be on that bus and into Oradea before the guards knew I was gone. For an instant I seriously considered it.

What a miracle Titus would think that was! I realized I would be in deep trouble and would risk prison. I thought of Titus's brothers, who had escaped to the West by swimming the Danube. Was I up to that? I knew it would be foolhardy. I have to admit, though, there were moments there when I was seconds from making a run for that bus. When it pulled away I still could have walked the ten kilometers or so into Oradea.

I had gone two nights without sleep and had nothing to eat since the flight over. I was scared, tired, hungry, and frustrated. When a factory whistle blew, the guards awoke and spun around to see where I had gone. I casually walked out and sat by my luggage again. Still, none of them had said a word to me since we left the train. None scolded me for having moved either because they would have had to admit that they had been asleep and didn't know how long I'd been gone.

I knew I looked pretty haggard as the morning dragged on. Still nothing happened. At ten o'clock a train from Oradea headed for Hungary stopped at the station. I was moved into a holding area with waiting passengers, glad that something was happening, even though I wasn't sure what. I didn't want to go to Hungary, but that was better than standing outside all day. I wanted to go to Romania, but I had the feeling that if they didn't put me on that train to the West, I would go to prison. Hungary was better than that. The waiting passengers were ushered onto the train, and still I stood alone in the holding area. The steam began to build in the engine, and I knew the train was about to move. At the last instant, just as it began to slowly roll, a guard approached and handed me my passport without a word and nodded toward the train.

The train was full, and I had to stand all the way to Budapest. There wasn't even room to lean anywhere for a little nap. When I changed trains in Budapest to go to Vienna, only one seat was available, and it was in a compartment full of punk rockers. By now it was evening, and I still hadn't eaten, slept, or shaved. I couldn't have looked much different from them.

"Hey, man," one of them said with a British accent, "what happened to you?"

His hair was spiked high and multi-colored. I told him I had been arrested and deported.

"Hey, cool!" They thought that was really something, so they asked more questions. I got a chance to witness to them for the next several hours. Though they were professed atheists, I sensed they listened with respect because of what I had been through.

On the train God gave me this promise from His Word: "We are hard pressed on every side, yet not crushed; we are perplexed, but not in despair; persecuted, but not forsaken; struck down, but not destroyed" (2 Cor. 4:8-9).

I was also led to this passage:

Do not fret because of evildoers,
Nor be envious of the workers of iniquity.
For they shall soon be cut down like the grass. . . .
Trust in the LORD, and do good;
Dwell in the land, and feed on His faithfulness. . . .
Commit your way to the LORD . . .
The steps of a good man are ordered by the LORD,
And He delights in his way.
Though he fall, he shall not be utterly cast down;
For the LORD upholds him with His hand." (Ps. 37:1-5, 23-25)

In Vienna I called Sam Friend and told him what had happened. I caught a train to where he was staying with Bryan, and they met me at the depot. Finally I was able to call Tex and get some sleep.

The next day they were going on a ten-kilometer fun walk and asked if I wanted to join them. It was on that walk that the reality of what had happened finally hit me. I let them get farther and farther ahead as I wept over Titus and Nelu and Stephanuti. I thanked God for the beautiful times we spent together in ministry and fellowship, and I prayed that one day I might see them again. My love for them and for all the believers in Romania would never cease.

I didn't know where Scott or Darryl might be, but I knew they were performing the ministry I had been denied. Sammy Tippit could be turned away at the border, but the Spirit of God could not be contained.

CHAPTER TWENTY-EIGHT

THE WORLD AS A PARISH

Encouraging words were smuggled out of Romania to me by friends and acquaintances. Titus asked someone to tell me simply, "The glory of God comes only through much suffering."

That fall (1988) I went to the Frankfurt Book Fair for Moody Press and made a strategic contact with Yugoslavian publisher Branko Lovrec. Expanding my international ministry through the translation of my books was an exciting proposition. God also allowed me to still have an influence with Romania by speaking at the Romanian Baptist Church in Chicago, where Titus's brother, Lucian, and his family attend.

A new friend, evangelist Steve Wingfield, asked if there was any way he could help out in Romania in my absence, and I helped arrange for him to speak in Timisoara the following January (1989). He came back with a message from Nelu Dronca: "Tell Sammy that I have all the assurance in my heart that one day he will sit again at my table and eat in my house." I knew he believed that sincerely. My faith was small. I longed for his prediction to be true, and it broke my heart to have to stay away.

I also received a letter from a minister that told roughly the following story:

I recently returned from my first trip to Romania. It was a thrilling experience for me as I met some wonderful people. One young lady told me she was saved under your ministry and asked me to tell you her story.

After her conversion she wanted to be baptized. Her parents, with whom she lived, opposed this as they are Orthodox; her brother is in the secret police and is afraid for his job because of his sister becoming a believer. Her father whipped her 39 times to the point that she was unconscious. The doctor who examined her said he had never seen such deep wounds.

She was encouraged to leave her hometown, which she did. She was baptized recently. She also wanted me to express to you that she was disappointed she wasn't able to see you again this summer.

The next month word came out of Romania in a carefully coded phone call from Darryl Gardiner that they desperately needed preachers to come in and fulfill speaking obligations. Apparently more meetings had been lined up than speakers, and Darryl wanted the word to get to me so I could suggest some possibilities. I called throughout the U.S. but found no one willing to sacrifice for the Romanian people. I felt terrible. I knew the believers in Romania would feel neglected, as if we in the West didn't care.

I also knew that I had very little chance of getting in, but I had to try. If word got to the Romanians that at least someone tried to get to them, it would encourage them. Fred Gough agreed to go with me on hardly any advance notice, so we left immediately. We flew into Belgrade, Yugoslavia, where we would try to get through a border we had never attempted before.

When we changed our money to Romanian currency and we appeared to receive our visas, I praised God despite my nervousness. But all of a sudden I sensed a change in the atmosphere. There was a lot of scurrying about, impromptu meetings, and looks of concern.

Sure enough, my name had turned up on the computers as an undesirable. They had nothing on Fred, but clearly I was a problem. They knew I was not welcome in their country, but they didn't know why. They interrogated us about drugs and tore apart our vehicle and all our belongings. In the end, we were deported, but I knew word got to our brothers and sisters that we had made every attempt to get in.

So as not to make the trip a total waste, we visited Branko Lovrec and finalized plans on yet another book translation.

In the summer of 1989 I went to Manila for the Lausanne II Conference, where I made friends with leading believers from other areas of the world. I saw the day coming when I could say with John Wesley, "The world is my parish." In 1989 alone I preached in Africa, India, Yugoslavia, Ireland, Peru, and Brazil, many times in areas where there were few Christians.

One of the highlights at Manila, besides making all those contacts for future world ministry, was meeting a lady who stood at the edge of a crowd after I spoke. Finally she made her way to me and asked if I was the Sammy Tippit who had been arrested in Chicago years ago.

When I told her I was, she said, "Today is the day God has answered my prayer. I have prayed that God would let me meet you again someday and just say thank you. When you were passing out tracts on Rush Street, I was a go-go dancer in one of those clubs. I received one of your tracts and actually went out and heard you speak. I ended up giving my heart to Christ, and my husband and I are now on the mission field serving the Lord."

She shook my hand and walked away, and I was left dumbfounded. I thanked God and prayed that I would never get hung up looking at numbers and always remember that people like her are what evangelism is all about.

My schedule filled with speaking engagements, evangelistic crusades, and revival conferences all over the world. I felt humbled by all the opportunities, still wondering how our little organization could do it all. My board was supportive of my selectively accepting strategic invitations on various continents, while still trying to help me decide where our emphasis should lie. They were, naturally, concerned about my health, given my age and the age of my family, my cancer scare, and the grueling travel schedule.

Despite enough ministry activity to seemingly keep me fully scheduled the rest of my life, come September of 1989 I felt myself so burdened for Romania that I found it hard to concentrate on anything else. I had to do something. I called Josif Tson, head of the Romanian Missionary Society in Wheaton, Illinois. I said, "Josif, my heart is burdened for Romania, and if I can't get in, I want to do the next best thing. I want to go next door. I've been to Kishinev [in Soviet Moldavia]. You know all about that debacle. If you have any solid, concrete contacts there, I'd like to go and know whom I'm dealing with."

The only time open on my schedule was May of 1990, and Josif liked the idea. He knew many Romanians in Kishinev and helped me arrange some meetings. I secretly hoped that somehow Titus could get to Kishinev, if it wasn't too dangerous for him.

While all that was being worked out, I had a commitment in Nigeria in November and Peru in December. It was while I was in Nigeria and feeling deathly ill that I got the word from Tex that the Berlin Wall was coming down. My life and ministry would never be the same. A month later, after returning from Peru and seeing on the news what was happening in Timisoara, I was like a mother hen who couldn't get to her suffering chicks.

When word came that Titus wanted me to come immediately, I couldn't get to Romania soon enough. My suitcase never arrived, and so I was there with only one set of clothes in the dead of winter. I have to say that the way those people of God received me warmed my heart. Being welcomed to the pulpit and asked to preach at the Second Baptist Church of Oradea, even though the service was about to close, remains one of the highlights of my life. I began the last decade of this century and this millennium preaching to a people who had just been freed from a godless dictatorship. You can't imagine the looks on the faces of people who had seen a miracle take place.

These people had not heard the details of my arrest and deportation. They knew I had not gotten in, and they knew I had tried once to return, but they knew little of the story. Before that, it would have been impossible for anyone to tell the story in public without risk.

Titus and I and, it seemed, the nearly three thousand in the pews were in tears when I concluded: "I can now say publicly that no dictator, no Ceausescu, no communist, no atheist, no anyone could keep me out if God wanted me here!" The people's beautiful, beaming smiles and their heartfelt *amens* (which they pronounce *ahmeen*) were glorious.

For the first time ever I was allowed to stay with Titus in his home. Though it was small and they really didn't have room for a guest, he said, "Sammy, you must stay. We have waited for this day."

We talked until the wee hours about what Titus should do with his newfound freedom. In the past he always thought he served the Lord best as a layman, a physician who also had a ministry. Now he wondered whether he should take a role in the transitional government, stay with his medical practice, preach full-time, or what? "I'm free to do what I want to do, but I don't know what I want to do."

> **Everywhere Romanian flags flew, the communist hammer and sickle had been cut from its center.**

The next day we went through Oradea and saw an amazing sight. Everywhere Romanian flags flew, the communist hammer and sickle had been cut from its center. God spoke deeply to my heart that the hole in the flag represented the vacuum in the hearts of the people. The symbol and ideology had been removed from the flag and from their minds, and something someday would replace it. What would fill the hole in their hearts? I knew well the answer to that. The time was now to take advantage of the window of opportunity. No one knew how long the nation would be free. No one knew whether Romania would become democratic and free or simply fall under another type of socialism or dictatorship.

That night, when I spoke again at Second Baptist, my message was on the hole in the flag. Later, Dr. Nick Gheorghita told me, "No evangelist knows Eastern Europe like you do. You must go, not just to Romania, but to the other countries here, and you must call the people to God. He has uniquely qualified you for this." That word touched my heart.

In the next few days I went back to many of the places in Romania where I had preached in the past. In every city every church was packed, and with more non-Christians than I had seen before. The people were hungry to hear the Word of God. What a thrill it was in Alba Iulia, the last place I preached before being blacklisted, to hear dozens of people tell me they became Christians at those meetings, were baptized, and were now members of the church.

We had great fellowship with Steve Wingfield, who was preaching in Cluj. I spoke three times in Resita where we saw many saved and, again, a great hunger on the part of the people. By now Nelu Dronca of Timisoara had heard that I was in the country and sent word that "you must come and sit at my table."

It was so good to see Nelu and to indeed eat with him in his home, as he had predicted I would. He reminded me that I had come and suffered with the people, and now it was time to rejoice with them. Pastor Peter Dugalescu agreed to meet me in the great plaza where the revolution had taken place and where he had preached to 200,000 people.

I can't describe the emotion of standing in that plaza and having Peter tell me the thrilling story of how the tens of thousands of people knelt with him and recited the Lord's Prayer, how he preached the gospel to them, and taught them a song about the return of Christ that became the theme song of the revolution. I would have given anything to be there when that great mass of people began to shout, *"Exista Dumnezeu!* [God exists! or There is a God!] *Exista Dumnezeu! Exista Dumnezeu!"*

As Peter told me the story, people in the plaza began to gather around us. Others who saw the crowd joined it, and soon hundreds were gathered. I was so full of the joy of the Lord, I said, "Peter, can I preach?"

He said, "Brother Sammy, this is the new Romania." And he motioned to the crowd.

As soon as I began to speak, they began to shout, *"Exista Dumnezeu! Exista Dumnezeu!"* You have to understand, these were not church people. For the most part, these people had lived under atheistic communism their whole lives. A cloud of fear and godlessness hung over that country for so long that never in my wildest imagination would I have dreamed I would ever speak in a public square in Timisoara and hear the masses cry out, "There is a God!" I found myself speaking on the miraculous, mighty hand of God that could not be held down by any human, any ideology, any regime. And the people shouted, *"Exista Dumnezeu!"*

Titus was encouraged to get into politics, but before I left the country he told me that he felt led not to do that. "I don't know why," he said, "because it seems sensible. I am one of very few who has read enough about democracy to have some idea what it should be like. But the great need of our country is not political. It is not ideological. It's not even just moral. It's spiritual. Our people are searching for something, and I want to give myself to that."

We decided between ourselves that we should talk to the God's Love in Action board about his coming on full-time as director in Eastern Europe. He would come to our board meeting in San Antonio, and we would see if the board wanted to go out on this financial limb. I had felt nervous about hiring Bill Smyth just the month before, and now I wanted to bring on Titus. But the board was enthusiastic and remained committed to not going public about our need for increased funds. The month Titus began, our income increased enough to cover both new men, and we have had sufficient income ever since. If God is in something, He will provide. We were able to provide Titus a computer and an automobile to put Titus on the cutting edge of ministry in Romania.

One of the best things that happened as a result of the revolution was that the arrest of the pastor in Comanesti (the one whose church had tripled after our meetings) was lifted and he was allowed to pastor once again. After his church grew, he came to the United States, and we had helped him build a larger facility. The Ceausescu regime was angered by that, and when they came to bulldoze it down, the congregation tried to interfere. That resulted in the arrest of the pastor and his four elders, and the church was leveled. Now, since the revolution, they were building again.

Before I left Romania, Titus urged me to come back again soon, but I told him how full my schedule was on so many continents. I told him I might be able to squeeze in something in September because another arrangement had fallen through in Zambia.

"That's too late," he urged me. "You must come sooner."

"I'm scheduled for Kishinev in May," I told him, "so maybe we can work in a few days in Romania at that time." He immediately went to work arranging sites and cities, and he planned on doing the Romanian translating in Soviet Moldavia. That would be a unique experience, being translated first into Romanian and then into Russian.

I ministered in Indonesia, Peru, and Brazil before getting back to Romania in May. When I arrived to preach in a stadium following a soccer game in Baia Mare, Titus asked me how it felt to walk into history.

"What do you mean?"

"This is the first stadium crusade in the history of Romania. Next week Luis Palau will come and preach in a stadium here, but tonight is a first." And then Titus told me a most unusual and inspiring story. One of the early pastors of the Second Baptist Church of Oradea was a man of prayer who called the people to pray for revival. He taught them to pray that one day God would allow His people to stand in the great stadiums of the nation and proclaim the gospel. He also taught them to pray for the miracle of being able to preach through the media, broadcast and print. "Sammy," Titus said, "today is the beginning of the answer to that prayer. You will stand for the first time in the history of this nation and proclaim the gospel outdoors in a great stadium. A host of others will follow, but this is the beginning of a new era of evangelism."

I was overwhelmed.

When I stood that night and faced ten thousand people for the first time in my ministry, I felt so at home that it was almost disconcerting. God gave me a sense that this was what I was created to do. His having gifted me in public speaking and the ability to minister cross-culturally and to be willing to go to the hard places all led to this point. I felt as if I was doing what He created me to do, had saved me to do, had called me to do. I felt at home. I sensed, "This is it. This is my purpose in life." You know when something fits, and this fit.

When I gave the invitation that first night and saw hundreds and hundreds and hundreds stream forward, I fell to my face and wept. This was a day of which I had dreamt and for which I had longed, to stand and proclaim the gospel publicly in Romania. In three days four thousand people prayed to receive Christ. About half of those responded on the last night, and it was the largest response I'd seen in my ministry up to that point.

I was interviewed by a sports journalist, of all people, who was so fascinated by the crusade that he ran a lengthy feature on me in a sports magazine. He told me that he had never been allowed to know about God and certainly not to write about Him, and so he asked if I could get him a Bible so he could understand some of the terminology. We provided all the journalists with Bibles, and the next night we were covered by newspapers, radio and TV stations, and other magazines—a further answer to the prayers of the church in Oradea from years before. We may never know the full impact of the Scripture on those writers.

From there we went to Kishinev for the second time (the first was my cloak-and-dagger experience in the blizzard with Fred Gough and Jerry Cadenhead). Titus; Bill Northfield; my son, Dave; and I were on cloud nine when we met with church leaders. We told them of the historic crusade we had just held in Romania. They asked us if we would return to Kishinev in the fall for a citywide crusade. Though I had a full schedule of meetings in various countries between May and September, I could hardly wait to get back to preach in both the Soviet Union and Romania in large, outdoor crusades. Though I was, and am, still willing to go anywhere and talk to just one person about Christ, it was incredible to see how God opened doors and ripped down the Iron Curtain.

CHAPTER TWENTY-NINE

HARVEST TIME

With the public proclamation of the gospel behind the Iron Curtain and invitations to speak all over the world, it's probably just as well that I had little time to step back and think about where I had come from. It just didn't seem that long ago that I tried to muster the courage to share my faith as a baby Christian in the bars in and around Baton Rouge.

Now God granted me the unfathomable privilege of preaching His gospel on every inhabited continent, of addressing vast crowds of indigenous pastors and leaders, of calling the world to prayer and revival through my books, and of spending my life in the only way I have wanted to since I came to faith in Him.

I told the pastors in Kishinev that I did not want to hold a big crusade in Moldavia unless I had an official invitation from government authorities. The government officials told the leaders that this would require their checking me out. I knew there was every possibility they would discover I had been arrested, detained, and deported from Leningrad years before. I left it in God's hands. I'll never forget the day the letter came, officially inviting me. All systems were go.

Our fall 1990 trip to the Soviet Union and Romania was unlike anything I had ever experienced. We started in the Soviet city of Bel'cy in Moldavia. The city council had originally said no to the idea of an outdoor public crusade. The organizers appealed to the

245

Supreme Council of Moldavia in Kishinev, which overruled the city council and forced them to allow the crusade for one night.

From the moment the meeting started, things went wrong. Right in the middle of my message a bottle of carbonated water exploded on the stage and startled me. Water spewed everywhere. Then, right in the middle of my quoting John 3:16, the sound system went out. I stopped, and the people sat patiently and quietly for fifteen minutes until the problem could be rectified. No one left. As soon as the power was back on, I finished the verse and kept preaching. Satan may be the prince of the power of the air, but he was a defeated foe that night.

This is what happened next, the way the story was told a few months later in the pages of *Moody Magazine:*

Evangelist Sammy Tippit is used to all kinds of responses. From the bars in his native Baton Rouge, Louisiana, in the '60s to the streets of Chicago in the '70s, and in almost every imaginable venue since, he has seen between one person and several thousand come to Christ.

He has ministered at U.S. political conventions and the Communist Youth World Festival. He has been arrested for his bold witness in countries as diverse as the United States, the Soviet Union, and Romania.

He has preached on every inhabited continent, sometimes to huge crowds, sometimes in churches so small and remote that no other evangelist has ever visited. His team consists of a wife, a two-person office staff in San Antonio, a Romanian evangelist and interpreter, and a half-dozen personal evangelists who pay their own way on trips abroad.

His message is simple, clear, old-fashioned, and direct. Jesus is coming again. Be ready. Repent. Get saved.

. . . He's one of the most widely read evangelicals anywhere. He is a man of history, theology, and prayer. He has pastored several churches and written several books.

And now he stands on a makeshift platform at a soccer stadium, preaching the first public gospel message in the modern history of this Soviet republic. Opposition, particularly from the Orthodox Church, has been intense.

"The evangelicals are not Christians," church leaders say in local newspapers. "They do not revere the Holy Mother."

Yet 12,000 have gathered. The majority of those in the stands are unbelievers; the evangelicals stand at the edges of the crowd. Tippit pauses for the staccato interpretation into Russian after every phrase. While he senses the leading of the Spirit and is confident he is preaching God's own message, he can't help but wonder how the people will respond.

He pleads with them to turn from sin, to come to Jesus, to be assured of heaven. As is his custom, he asks them to show their decision. "If you're willing to make that choice tonight, raise your hand right where you stand."

With arms outstretched, he scans the crowd. How bizarre that they have never heard this message, never worshiped in public. They must wonder about the consequences if they respond—from their friends, from the authorities, from the church. No one raises a hand. "Oh, God," Tippit prays silently, "save souls!"

Nearly a minute passes. Though still no one has raised a hand, Tippit feels led to ask decision-makers to come forward, to take a step of confession before men that they are choosing heaven over hell, life over death, Jesus over self.

From deep in the crowd he sees movement. A peasant woman of perhaps 60 marches down the stadium steps and onto the soccer field, a bouquet of flowers held aloft; she looked like some spiritual statue of liberty. She strides to the end of the platform where she solemnly presents the gift to the evangelist. She crosses herself in the Orthodox fashion and sinks to her knees, crying out to God.

Immediately, from all over the arena, individuals, couples, dozens, hundreds pour from the stands toward the platform. After several minutes, 2,000 stand there smiling, faces wet with tears, praying aloud. At least half are past middle age.

"I want to be there," Tippit says, "when that brave woman is rewarded in heaven."

Dick Eastman of Every Home for Christ offered to help us get Christian literature into the homes of the people of Kishinev in advance of the crusade in that city—which followed the one in Bel'cy. Our ministry would have to share the cost, and that meant we might not be able to meet our salaries and the expense budgets for other areas of the world. I told our board I was willing to forego my salary, though I was unwilling to ask others to do the same. Bill Smyth volunteered his as well. The expense required a financial step of faith unlike any our organization had taken before, but I felt the risk was well worth the window of ministry opportunity. I was willing to shut down the ministry and get another job if the expense broke us; it simply seemed that this was something we shouldn't pass up.

The board encouraged us to go ahead, God met our financial needs, and the response was so overwhelming that the Kishinev post office informed us we would have to come and pick up the responses. Of the 120,000 pieces that went out offering a Bible correspondence course, 60,000 had already come back in huge sacks. We knew then that God planned a mighty work in that city.

> I wasn't sure I wanted to see him. The last time I was summoned to speak to Soviet authorities, I was banished from the country.

The Kishinev crusade began in the stadium on Sunday evening. The next morning I received word by phone that Mayor Nicolae Kostin wanted to see me in person immediately. I wasn't sure I wanted to see him. The last time I was summoned to speak to Soviet authorities, I was banished from the country.

My team and I were escorted to the city council chamber, and within minutes the mayor and his entourage arrived. After we exchanged pleasantries across the table, Mayor Kostin flashed a huge smile. He walked around the table, threw his arms around me, and shocked me by saying, "We are so happy that you have come to Kishinev."

I don't know what I expected to hear, but his next words were even more stunning. After he returned to his seat and we all took our places at the table, he said, "For many years we have persecuted the Christians. We have treated them as the dirt on the floor, the scum of the earth. And we were wrong. The very morality needed to make society function correctly is the morality of the Christians. Prior to the Communists, our forefathers were people of deep faith. Would you help return our people to the faith of their forefathers?"

I was nearly speechless. Swallowing the big lump in my throat, I said, "Mayor Kostin, that is exactly why we have come! We love the Moldavian people and want them to know Christ."

With his approval and endorsement of the crusade, we presented Bibles to the leaders and enjoyed a fruitful ministry with many hundreds coming to Christ. We had a subsequent meeting with the mayor's staff and discussed what *perestroika* and *glasnost* might mean for cooperation between the United States and Moldavia. They were most interested in our coming back to their city and in visiting the United States.

From there we went to the Romanian city of Iasi (Yahsh), where the Orthodox opposition held attendance down for the first few days of the crusade in a huge stadium. The last day, however, the crowd was immense, and it wasn't until later that we realized why. We were videotaped in Kishinev, but the program wasn't aired in Moldavia until two hours before the last meeting in Iasi. They showed our entire service, from music through the invitation, and when people heard we were coming to Iasi, they showed up. It was an amazing turnaround.

We finished with ministry in Galati, revisiting the spot where Titus expressed his willingness to be martyred for the sake of his countrymen, and then to Arad, where we saw our largest crowds ever. We held the crusade in a stadium that held 16,000 people. The first night 14,000 attended, and by the third night, the place was overflowing a half hour before we began. We estimated the crowd to be 22,000.

Before the revolution I preached in churches in Romania where there was not room for the people. Yet I never dreamed I would preach in stadiums that would not contain the people who wanted to hear the gospel. We left knowing that not only were political boundaries being rewritten, but also that God was intervening in the affairs of human history.

Later, we returned to the Ukraine where our first crusade was held in Odessa. The day the crusade was supposed to begin we were informed that we had lost permission to use the gigantic stadium. The authorities meant it for evil, but God made it good.

When we pleaded for consideration, we were directed to a military authority who covertly showed us a cross he carried in his pocket and informed us he was a believer.

He said he felt bad about what the officials above him had done to us, so to try to make it right, we were given use of a smaller stadium. The Soviet military was assigned to direct people to the new location, and afterward they offered to feed the choir and the staff. Imagine that! The Soviets directing traffic so people could get to the right place to hear the gospel, and then giving us that kind of hospitality! Even better, the crowd of about eight thousand jammed the new facility, and they would have looked sparse in the original stadium.

Then there was the weather. Every day the city was full of rain, right up to the time of the meeting. The rain stopped during the meeting and resumed when we finished. One night it appeared to be raining everywhere but at the stadium. I'm still not planning a career as a weatherman, but it sure was interesting to see the Lord work!

We also solved an interpreting problem in a unique way. Our key contact, Vasile Binzar (who now directs God's Love in Action in Moldavia) knew Russian and Romanian, but not English. Titus knew English and Romanian, but not Russian. So, we used Titus as a sort of human language adapter. I preached in English, and Titus stood directly behind Vasile and whispered a Romanian translation into his ear. Vasile translated that into Russian, and without a hitch I was able to communicate to the people!

In city after city in the Ukraine and in Romania, thousands came to Christ. I was overwhelmed. There were times when I worried and wondered how many would last, how they would be followed up, whether they were sincere, and whether they would hang on. When I preached in Alba Iulia, Romania, a friend reminded me that we now had follow-up material and that 90 percent of the counselors at these meetings were people who had come to Christ under my ministry before.

I realized that the real work of follow-up was wrought by the Holy Spirit. He had sealed the decisions before the revolution and would do the same in these historic days.

As we left Romania I was overwhelmed with all that had happened. God had surprised us! Thirty thousand people had publicly prayed to receive Christ in the Ukraine and Romania in just three weeks. Many of those had come to Christ in cities in the Ukraine where no one from the West had ever traveled before.

I wept as I expressed my thanks to the Lord. I never dreamed this would happen in my lifetime. I told Him, "I know it had nothing to do with me and that everything accomplished was in Your divine plan and time. If I never witness this again, I just want to thank You for allowing me to see Your mighty deeds in these days." After returning to the States, full of the joy of the Lord, for a while I had a bit of a problem because I ran into skeptics who could hardly believe what we were telling them. Preaching in the open air in the Soviet Union? Full stadiums? People coming to Christ by the thousands?

At first I took it personally, believing that since they had hardly heard of me, they couldn't imagine that I would have been involved in something so blessed of the Lord. Finally, God granted me peace about it. I realized that it didn't matter whether people knew or believed. We'd been there. We'd seen it. We knew. "Your kingdom has come," I told the Lord, "and we're going to go on with You whether anybody believes it or not."

While ministering in South America and then Great Britain over the next several months, I came to realize what a privilege God had given me. He had put me in the right places at the right times. I was allowed to be involved in both the planting and the harvesting in certain areas, and there is no greater favor from God than that. Someone said that mass evangelism is merely personal evangelism done on a large scale, and that really struck a chord and stayed with me. Any hesitation I had had about seeing a change in emphasis in my ministry disappeared when I was able to see mass evangelism in that context.

The director of Billy Graham's Mission Scotland told of a previous crusade experience. He had invited to some meetings a group of farmers who said they couldn't come because it was harvest time. He said he considered a crusade harvest time. How true.

What was happening to me was that I had been walking into these places during the harvest season. Decades of fervent, faithful prayer and Bible study, often led by humble pastors in hard places, resulted in these great outpourings of God's Spirit. I believe that the wave of the Spirit sweeping through Romania and infecting the hearts of the people made it impossible for the communists to hold down the church any longer. With that many people coming to Christ, the system couldn't stand up anymore either.

I knew it wasn't Sammy Tippit that was doing all this. I had no real organization, no money, no anything. I was merely in the field for the harvest. Months and months later, when we got reports of how the Soviet and Romanian churches had grown, it warmed my heart. At one church in Bel'cy alone, some fifteen hundred said they had received Christ at our crusade. In Kishinev the churches had special Sunday services for new believers only; there were so many that that was the only way there was room. The government also granted permission to build sixty-eight new churches throughout Moldavia! In one Ukrainian city, a pastor reported receiving five thousand new people into his church following our crusade.

Sometimes when I think about having been deported from the Soviet Union as a young independent missionary and then being invited to preach in a soccer stadium, I can hardly make it compute. My goal is to spend my life for God, and He has blessed me beyond measure.

When the Soviet Union went through the turmoil of Gorbachev being temporarily ousted from power and republics seceding despite government intervention, I knew that Kishinev's Mayor Kostin was avidly anti-communist. I immediately wired him that I was willing to come and stand with him and his people, even if it meant standing before tanks and guns. Though he did not take me up on that offer, he knew I meant it, and I believe it sealed a bond between us that will never be broken.

In the fall of 1991 I had the rare privilege of hosting Mayor Kostin, who is also a high ranking parliament leader for all of Moldavia. He visited San Antonio, and then I set up several meetings for him with senators and congressmen in Washington. It was great to help him make important contacts and to even coach him on how to better communicate with Americans.

He was in the States for a month, and he left with a promise that the door would always be wide open to our ministry in his nation. I look forward to the day when we take him up on that. I still shake my head when I think that I helped pull together those meetings of high ranking officials in Washington when not that many years ago I was accosted by White House guards for pasting stickers to their fence!

Looking back on all those years, with all their struggles, difficulties, and trials, I've come to one conclusion: To see men and women who've never before heard the gospel give their hearts to Christ and live for Him has been worth it all, no matter what the cost.

The World for Christ

I don't know whether it's fair to say that a burden can itself become a burden. At times it seems that the burden God has given me for lost souls is so great that I can't begin to do a thing about it. I can preach everywhere I have the time and resources to go, and there will still be millions who haven't heard the gospel.

After having preached in Mongolia, I have a new passion for the lost of Asia. Will there be time to follow that burden? I know I am only one person and that God has called many others. I pray only that they discover the need not only to be called, but also to be broken. I didn't see my need until God broke me, and that's the hard way. Only when He has broken you can He truly use you.

An elderly woman once said to me, "Sammy, you can't expect to win the whole world to Jesus."

I thought to myself, *Why not? Jesus died for the whole world, and our commission is to go into the whole world.* Ever since, I have dreamed of reaching the whole world. I knew there would be danger, difficulty, and defeat along the way. I knew I would never be able to reach every person. But I also knew that I had to spend my life to bring His message of love and forgiveness to as many as I could.

Today as I stand at the threshold of world evangelism I want to give myself to prayer, study, writing, and preaching. There is no nation too difficult, no tribe too obscure, no situation too desperate for the love of Christ.

We can overcome the evil One by the blood of the Lamb and by the word of our testimonies, if we love not our lives, "even unto death" (Rev. 12:11).

If God should bring me to mind when you're praying, would you pray that:

I will be like Christ in character and deed.
I will be a Christlike husband and father.
I will be courageous in calling the church to revival.
I will completely depend on God and never on myself.
That I will walk humbly before the Lord and die to self daily.
And that Jesus Christ will be glorified.

ABOUT THE AUTHORS

For nearly thirty years, Sammy Tippit has traveled and preached on every continent, in countless churches and universities, drawing thousands of people to Christ. He also served as pastor at Hahn Baptist Church in Hahn, Germany, which became one of the fastest-growing evangelical churches in Western Europe under his leadership.

Tippit is founder and president of God's Love in Action/Sammy Tippit Ministries and is the author of eight previous books, including: *Sammy Tippit: God's Love in Action*, *Fire in Your Heart*, *The Prayer Factor*, and *Revolution in Romania*.

Sammy, his wife, and their two children make their home in San Antonio, Texas.

Jerry B. Jenkins' writing has appeared in *Reader's Digest*, *The Saturday Evening Post*, the *Chicago Tribune*, and dozens of Christian periodicals.

His biographies have included books with Hank Aaron, Walter Payton, Meadowlark Lemon, Orel Hershiser, Joe Gibbs, Mike Singletary, and Nolan Ryan. *Out of the Blue* (with Orel Hershiser) was fifth on the *New York Times* bestseller list. His fiction includes *Rookie*, *The Operative*, several series, and book of short stories (*The Deacon's Woman and Other Portraits*). *No Matter What the Cost* is Jenkins' 100th book and his second collaboration with Sammy Tippit.

Jenkins is Writer-in-Residence for the Moody Bible Institute of Chicago and lives with his wife and sons at Three Son Acres, west of Zion, Illinois.